VENTURER COURAGEOUS

Also by James Sanders
HISTORICAL
Dateline — NZPA
New Zealand VC Winners
Our Explorers
Desert Patrols

ART
The Colourful Colony

NOVELS
The Green Paradise
The Shores of Wrath
Kindred of the Winds
High Hills of Gold
Fire in the Forest
The Lamps of Main
Where Lies the Land?
Chase the Dragon
Frontiers of Fear

AUTOBIOGRAPHY
The Time of My Life

VENTURER COURAGEOUS

GROUP CAPTAIN LEONARD TRENT V.C., D.F.C.

A Biography
by
JAMES SANDERS

HUTCHINSON OF NEW ZEALAND

Hutchinson Group (N.Z.) Ltd.
An imprint of the Hutchinson Publishing Group.

32-34 View Road, P.O. Box 40-086, Glenfield, Auckland, 10.

Hutchinson & Co. (Publishers) Ltd.
17-21 Conway Street, London W1P 5HL.

Hutchinson Group (Australia) Pty. Ltd.,
30-32 Cremorne Street, Richmond South, Victoria 3121.
P.O. Box 151, Broadway, New South Wales, 2007.

Hutchinson Group (S.A.) Pty. Ltd.,
P.O. Box 337, Bergvlei 2012, South Africa.

First published 1983
© James Sanders 1983

Design and production by Paper Dart, Auckland.
Typesetting by Saba Graphics, Christchurch.
Printed and bound by Whitcoulls, Christchurch.

ISBN 0 09 154600 1

Heed how the haunted sky lures seekers
to its mysteries.
And though fire may cross their pathways
to the stars,
They who sever the natal cord from
Mother Earth
Shall roam in the realms of Bellerophon
and Icarus and Mars.

So, knight of the wind and the nimbus,
don your mail;
Guide forth your steed to pause at
Heaven's gate;
And your mount becomes a fiery Pegasus
in flight.
Go, venturer courageous, to your goal —
or fate.

CONTENTS

ACKNOWLEDGEMENTS

In setting down the chronicle of an active man's life much background detail needs to be sought and assistance must be begged of some of the people who knew and worked with the subject.

Group Captain Len Trent, himself, has supplied most of the evidence. He returned to his flying log book; and as memory opened old doors he recorded on electronic tape a past so filled with action that his story might well be a composite biography of several lives.

He, too, has supplied most of the photographs that illustrate the book.

To Mrs Ursula Trent I am indebted for her lending me the diary notes her husband pencilled while on the terrible march across Germany as a prisoner of war.

I should like to thank Air Commodore H.A. Probert, MBE MA RAF (Retd) of the Ministry of Defence, London, for his help and advice. And to my fine friend in London, Wing Commander P.B. ('Laddie') Lucas CBE DSO DFC RAF (Retd) I owe gratitude for his guidance, assistance and encouragement.

Mr Arthur Cox, of London, who was an armourer with 487 Squadron at the time of the 'Ramrod 17' operation, has provided me with information from a ground-crew point of view.

Brian ('Tich') Hanafin, now living in Stirling, South Australia, was Len Trent's deputy flight commander on 487 Squadron. He has helped towards the picture of events leading up to the ill-starred sortie of 3 May 1943.

Closer to home, I have had much assistance from Merv Darrall of Howick, Auckland, who was also a pilot on the squadron at the time of the Amsterdam raid. He, like 'Tich' Hanafin, has his own niche in the halls of fame as one of the (later) successful 487 Squadron Mosquito-bomber attackers in the Amiens Prison sortie.

He has supplied photographs and helped fill in many blanks in the captions.

I should like to express to him and his charming wife, Gay, my appreciation of the warm hospitality that always awaits me in their home.

Tom Penn of Pukekohe, South Auckland, was a 487 Squadron

navigator and a survivor of the fateful Ramrod 17 operation. He has given me some graphic glimpses of the raid. And to him and his gracious wife, Elizabeth, I extend my sincere thanks for their generous hospitality.

And to my dear wife — ever helpful and, I'm afraid, too much neglected during my preparation of this book — I am tenderly indebted.

J. Sanders,
Matakana,
North Auckland,
New Zealand
1983

ILLUSTRATIONS

The front cover illustration is of a portrait of Group Captain Leonard Trent by Mr Archibald Frank Nicoll OBE, painted in oils on canvas which hangs in Nelson College and is reproduced by kind permission of the headmaster and the Board of Governors.

The remaining photographs are from the personal collections of Group Captain Trent and Mr Merv. Darrall of Howick, Auckland.

FOREWORD

In the explicit language of the boxing ring they would call it 'a natural' . . . .

If the story of Group Captain Leonard Henry Trent, VC, New Zealander extraordinary, was going to be written then it was plain that one author, among all others, should write it. There were special reasons for matching James Sanders with Len Trent — biographer in one corner, subject in the other. Let us take Trent first.

In an outstanding generation of New Zealand flyers he was himself a stand-out. Like others among his compatriots — indeed, like so many of his fine Commonwealth contemporaries — he came to Britain a year or so before the Second World War to join the Royal Air Force and pursue a military career. Hitler was on the move. War clouds were gathering over Europe. It was quite a decision for a twenty-three-year-old to take to break clean away from his homeland. But Trent knew, just as his Commonwealth partners knew, that here in the Old Country, he would get the finest flying training in the world; this, beyond all else, was what he was after. He was resolved to master the art of flying aeroplanes and all the intricacies of powered flight.

There was, of course, another thought in his mind. If action was coming the place to be was at the centre.

What no one could then foretell was the distance that this whipcord-tight young adventurer from Nelson, son of a dentist, would be likely to travel in the Service. Certainly he possessed many of the attributes that the Royal Air Force sought in an embryo leader — spirit, wiriness, discipline, an instinct for accepting responsibility, flair for a game, and, rather important, an abundance of grit. But a long, rough road stretched ahead.

It was a famous old headmaster of Eton who once said: 'In life, as in footer, it's the last twenty minutes that count.' Trent took the adage and pared it down to the last ten minutes of the game — those final, gasping, unendurable moments when, with everything spent, some unknown, untapped reserves are found and defeat becomes a hairline victory.

I have long thought that a hidden Hand deliberately picked out some people from my generation and earmarked them for survival from the second great holocaust of the twentieth century. Providence seemed to have decided to 'keep them safe' for some special work later on. The cynics will cry 'rubbish'. But how else could Trent have come through his kind of war? How could he have weathered those appalling days of the German break-through in the Low Countries in May, 1940, which ended with the cataclysmic collapse of France?

He was flying Blenheims in 2 Group of Bomber Command at the time, mostly at low level, in what is now accepted as the most lethal rôle of the air war. 2 Group's Blenheim losses then, and for a year or so after, were so horrific that a young pilot officer would rise to squadron leader in a month as squadrons were turned round totally and scant reserves fed into the line.

The story comes through frighteningly, in all its hideous reality, in Sanders' brilliant account of events.

And what of the Amsterdam power house raid by No 487 (New Zealand) Squadron's Ventura bombers on 3 May, 1943, of which Trent, by his own insistence, was the leader? The Squadron was left to the mercy of the Luftwaffe's Messerschmitts and Focke-Wulfs through a dreadful operational blunder by Fighter Command's 11 Group staff and the leader of the Hornchurch wing of Spitfire IXs, and obliterated. Why, but for the tap of the invisible Hand on the shoulder, should he have survived this disaster? Within weeks he had taken his place under Roger Bushell in Stalag Luft III and, with the rest of the courageous team, was soon preparing to excavate the tunnel, 'Harry', and so create the means of the tragic escape of March, 1944.

And why, again, just after Len Trent, fugitive No. 79, had emerged from the tunnel in his own bid for freedom should the exodus have been rumbled by the Germans and thwarted? Had his turn come minutes earlier Trent could well have been one of the ill-fated number of Allied prisoners who, after recapture, fell victims to the cruelty of the Gestapo and Hitler's SS firing squad in a wicked act of calculated, cold-blooded murder.

Read this and, with it, Trent's own diary entries of the subsequent and terrible forced march of prisoners from Sagan to Trenthorst, near Hamburg, and ask yourself why he should have been delivered from this living hell.

Maybe the answers to all these questions will be found in his important, post-war flying activities before he left the Service — work for which, I incline to think, he was purposely being 'kept'.

The fact is that the sum of all his extensive experience, which had taken him, in nearly thirty years, from primitive, light aeroplane flying (what Bader used to call *real* flying) into the age of jet propulsion, thermonuclear weapons and, eventually, to personal command of one of Britain's V-bomber squadrons, was matched by few of his contemporaries.

No serving officer had exceeded the spread of Trent's operational span or the magnitude of his rugged endeavour which had earlier found its expression in the supreme award of the Victoria Cross. As the story unfolds one is left wondering how the human frame could have withstood the pounding of so persistent and relentless an onslaught.

What, then, of the author? What of New Zealand's James Sanders? Why was he the obvious choice as Len Trent's biographer, and why should the two of them make this natural, complementary match?

The answers are twofold. To tell such a story — to be able really to *feel* and transmit such a tale — it is necessary to have lived at sometime through not dissimilar traumas. By the war's end Sanders had himself been through the fire of offensive, operational flying as pilot and crew captain in the Royal Air Force's Coastal Command. There were few types of operations, few forms of attack (or enemy defence) that he hadn't experienced, at one time or another either in his low-flying Blenheim or, later, in his four-engined Halifax.

To understand what the other man is feeling there is no substitute for having experienced at first hand comparable sensations. To know what it is like to see, for the first time, a deep-penetration target unveiled on the briefing map. To sense the gut feeling when, after briefing, pockets have to be emptied of all personal belongings in exchange for aircrew survival kit. To share the forced laughter and bravado of comrades as the flight truck takes the crew to the aircraft waiting out at dispersal in the black and cold of a wet February night. To comprehend the tenseness of the moment when, after hours of searching over water and listening for any suspicious, tell-tale sounds from the motors, an elated voice reflects the radar screen's message: 'Target five miles, Skipper, dead ahead. Steer zero-two-zero' — and how the stomach muscles grip at the news.

Sanders was well aware of all this just as Trent, in his very special way, had known it. But there is something else that sets the author apart. Here is a writer who, through an exceptional pen and with all this background, can recreate the picture which, in wartime, came to torment the mind. One of New Zealand's most accomplished journalists, feature writer for the *New Zealand Herald* in his time, author of upwards of fifteen titles, Sanders has taken Trent's extraordinary life story and made it live.

A 'natural' indeed. I would expect the reader to go the distance with it.

Laddie Lucas,
London,
England
1983

1

THE INVESTITURE

ON 12 APRIL 1946 Squadron Leader Leonard Henry Trent, VC, DFC, of the Royal New Zealand Air Force, was summoned to Buckingham Palace to be invested by King George VI with Britain's highest award for valour in the field of battle, the Victoria Cross. He had earned it almost three years earlier, but had been detained in Germany for many dreary months as a prisoner of war.

The citation, which Squadron Leader Trent was soon to hear so solemnly intoned by the King's herald, had been printed in the London *Gazette* a month earlier. It told the story simply and briefly. Only those who survived — so pitifully few — could know the real horror of the mission.

On 3 May, 1943, Squadron Leader Trent of 487 (NZ) Squadron, RAF, was detailed to lead a formation of Ventura aircraft on a daylight raid on the power station at Amsterdam.

This operation was intended to encourage the Dutch workmen in their resistance to enemy pressure and the target was known to be heavily defended. The importance of the bombing of it, regardless of enemy fighters or anti-aircraft fire, was strongly impressed on the aircrews taking part in the operation.

Before taking off Squadron Leader Trent told the deputy leader that he was going over the target whatever happened.

All went well with the formation until the 11 Venturas and their fighter escort were nearing the Dutch coast. Then one of the bombers was hit and had to turn back.

Suddenly, large numbers of enemy fighters appeared. Our escorting fighters were hotly engaged and lost touch with the bombing force. The Venturas closed up for mutual protection and commenced their run up on the target. Unfortunately, the fighters detailed to support them over the target had reached the area too early and had to be recalled.

Soon the bombers were attacked. They were at the mercy of ten to twenty Messerschmitts which dived on them incessantly. Within four minutes six Venturas were destroyed.

Squadron Leader Trent continued on his course with his three remaining aircraft and in a short time two more Venturas were shot down in flames.

Heedless of the murderous attacks and of the heavy anti-aircraft fire which was now encountered, Squadron Leader Trent completed an accurate bombing run and even shot down a Messerschmitt at point blank range. Dropping his bombs on the target area, he turned away. The aircraft following him was shot down on reaching the target.

Immediately afterwards his own aircraft was hit and went into a spin and broke up. Squadron Leader Trent and his navigator were thrown clear and became prisoners of war. The other two members of the crew perished.

On this, his twenty-fourth sortie, Squadron Leader Trent showed outstanding leadership. Such was the trust placed in this gallant officer that the other pilots followed him unwaveringly.

His cool, unflinching courage and devotion to duty in the face of overwhelming odds rank with the finest of these virtues.

So in the thin sunshine of a London spring day, Squadron Leader Trent drove with his small, proud party through the gates of Buckingham Palace. His English-born wife Ursula was by his side and behind them in the car were Mrs Trent's mother, Mrs K. Woolhouse, and a family friend, Mrs Dorothy Lightband.

Squadron Leader Trent had been notified of his appointment at Buckingham Palace on 27 March — only 16 days before the actual ceremony — and today, at his retirement home on a headland at Mathesons Bay, North Auckland, he recalls with regret his not having the time or the opportunity to have had his parents travel from Nelson to be with him and share some of the pomp and circumstance of that day.

'Overriding a lot of the excitement of the occasion,' he says, 'I felt a sadness. I was thinking, all the time, that *they* really deserved that reward and, as parents, they had suffered the strains and day-to-day worries of any mother and father who were only too aware that their boy was somewhere in the front line.'

War is a waiting game; and the agony and uncertainty is acute for close and loving relatives who are far removed from the chessboard of the battlefield.

Within the palace grounds servants in bright livery and guests in grand uniform were close at every turn. Onwards up the steps to the vast entrance hall went the visitors, trying politely not to gape at the grandeur of the furniture, the carpets, the wall decorations and the ornaments.

Squadron Leader Trent was taken in hand by a palace official, separated from his ladies and ushered into a big reception room where, seemingly, he was well outranked by a magnificence of admirals, generals and air marshals. All appeared comfortably in rapport on a common meeting ground — they had been responsible for the preservation of the Western Approaches' sea lanes, the Mediterranean thrust into the soft underbelly of the Axis, and the mass-bomber raids over Germany. None, for the moment, wanted to rescue a lowly squadron leader from a mild attack of stage fright.

'For a few minutes I felt more abandoned and more lonely than ever before in my life,' he recalls. 'But at last I was rescued when a lone wing commander appeared and we were drawn to each other by strong invisible forces.

'And so it was that I met the notable Yeo Thomas, who had worked so heroically with the French Resistance underground movement and whose exploits had been told in the book, *The White Rabbit*. He was at the palace to be invested with the George Cross and when we were directed into line prior to receiving our decorations, he was right behind me.'

The presentees were carefully briefed on protocol and Squadron Leader Trent had a small hook attached below the flying badge on his brand new uniform so that the King could make fast the coveted bronze cross without any undue fumbling or pin-stabbing.

Instructions were given in detail: 'When your name is called, you will proceed up the ramp, turn left to where King George will be three paces from you. You will bow, proceed two paces forward, when a herald will read your citation. The King may exchange a word or two with you before attaching the medal to your chest. You will then back off two paces, turn right, descend the ramp and then leave the Throne Room.'

What could be easier? A piece of cake, to put it in Air Force idiom.

Len Trent remembers it all so well today:

'We filed in like nervous, first-night actors waiting in the wings for curtainrise. After a delay of five minutes — during which I was able to look over the assembly and find my wife and party very near by — there came an electric change in the atmosphere as the King appeared.

'My name was called and I persuaded my stubborn legs to function. As in most dreams, legs refuse to obey the usual commands. But somehow I managed to make the top of the ramp without stumbling and I turned left. I instantly took two steps forward.

'Oh, my God! I had forgotten to bow! And as the horror of my "black" struck home it is a wonder I didn't faint. The silly scene of Stanley Holloway's monologue flashed through my mind — impudent Sam standing before his King at an investiture, and the Queen interjecting and saying: "Don't give Sam ruddy medal."

'Perhaps my good King George would whip *my* medal away from me and tell me to bone up on palace protocol? Now I was one pace from the King — and he was not looking amused. What shall I do? Bow now? No! Too late, and not enough room. How will I ever live this down?

'But the citation was already being read. And then the King, in a very kind and quiet voice, began asking questions. I was a New Zealander. Was I going to return to New Zealand? And when?

'My reply, from a dust-dry mouth, was almost incoherent. And then he asked how many of the Venturas' aircrew had survived the operation of May 3. Not many, I told him. One of the 11 aircraft had got back to England; but of the ill-fated 10 aircraft carrying a total of 40 men, only 13 men escaped death.

'The little chat ended. And his kindly tones and gentle expression had relaxed me so that, after he had turned and taken the medal off a flat, velvet cushion and attached it to my chest, I was able, with some composure, to shake hands, back off two paces and get down the ramp without stumbling.

'I walked as one in a dream and I still didn't believe it was really happening to Len Trent. I had been to Buckingham Palace in 1940 to receive my Distinguished Flying Cross — one of the early investitures that had been mounted shortly after the Battle of France and before the great air battles we were later to call the Battle of Britain — and of course that had been a great occasion for me, too. But as there had been several of us receiving the same award, it had been more a follow-your-leader ceremony without any of the built-up publicity surrounding this senior decoration.

'I joined my new-found friend, Wing Commander Yeo Thomas, in a small reception room and we were each offered a most welcome glass of Buckingham Palace beer. And we drank, literally, a royal toast. Later, I was reunited with my wife and we drove to a small reception at New Zealand House in the Strand, where we were handsomely entertained and duly photographed and interviewed by the press.'

But, constantly recurring to Len Trent during the formal ceremony and throughout the lighter, relaxed atmosphere after the investiture, were his thoughts on the circumstances that had brought him to this special day — this signal honour.

He cast back in time to the nightmare ordeal of the bomber raid on the Amsterdam target; the blasting of his and nine others of the formation's aircraft; and of the deaths of his two crew members, Flying Officer Roy Thomas and Flight-sergeant 'Tren' Trenery along with 25 other British and Dominion aircrew who perished on that operation. He thought of his navigator and himself desperately struggling to free themselves from the crippled and wildly spinning Ventura, of their parachuting safely into occupied Holland, and of their early capture and subsequent imprisonment by the Germans.

And he thought of his involvement in the big bid for freedom from Stalag Luft III — that later became known as the Great Escape; and of the unfortunate 50 Allied escapers, from a total of 80, who were apprehended and shot by the Germans in barbaric executions, intended as a deterrent to possible future escapers.

He thought of these, the bitterness of battle lingering still, blighting some of the pride that bloomed on that London spring day of 12 April 1946. And he was looking towards the future. The war had ended.

Are our destinies ordained in high celestial places, our tracks and pathways already blazed for us from the cradle to the grave? Or does a man see a star and set a course, allowing no chance or fate to circumvent, hinder, or control his firm resolve?

From his earliest schooldays Len Trent had set his heart on a flying career. Now, nearing the half-way stage of man's traditional three-score-years-and-ten — and the recipient of a decoration to fulfill the most extravagant boyhood ambition — he had no doubts of his tomorrows. He would continue in the service to which he had aspired ever since he was first buffeted by a Gipsy Moth's slipstream and caught the unforgettable whiff of castor oil and petrol fumes mingling with the grassy fragrances of a Takaka paddock.

And after that?

The years would unfold and eventually his Air Force days would come to an end. Len Trent would then sort out the situation when it arose and, customarily, come up with his plan.

2
PIN FEATHERS

LEN TRENT WAS BORN AT HIS parents' home in Tasman St, Nelson, New Zealand on Wednesday, 14 April 1915. And on his fourth birthday the Trents moved to Takaka in the Golden Bay area and about 66 kilometres north-west of Nelson.

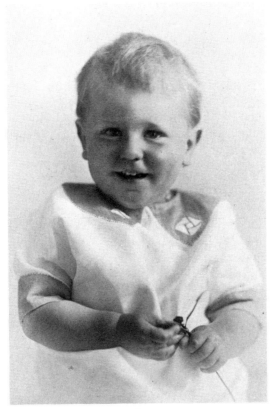

Facing the future with a grin: Len Trent in 1917 — eighteen months old.

In the summer of 1922 an exciting and, at that time, unusual sound disturbed the midmorning air of the Takaka Valley as a Gipsy Moth light aircraft hummed out of the skyline above the marble hills that divided the district from Nelson. It was a working day, with scholars dutifully engaged in their studies. But the aerial buzz, growing louder as it approached the school, drew pupils and teachers alike, in bug-eyed wonder, into the playground.

When the machine's landing ground had been pinpointed — a field about two miles away — scores of little bare feet set out along the dusty road to Wonderland at a fast clip.

'I remember I was overtaken at about the half-way point by my father riding his push-bike,' says Len Trent. His father was the only dentist for miles around, practising as far afield as Collingwood and Farewell Spit. So any aggravating molars, at that time of the day and on such an auspicious occasion, would have to continue their aching.

The pilot of that magnetic flying machine was the late and notable Captain (later Squadron Leader) M. C. McGregor whose outrageous deeds of derring-do had earned him the nickname of 'Mad Mac'. He was to earn a bar to that whimsical title when, at a later date, he dived his aircraft under the traffic bridge at Hamilton and, climbing upwards and over, completed his loop by flying under the bridge again.

But such demonstrations of *élan* and *joie de vivre* were not to be the order of the exercise at Takaka on that summer day in 1922. Mac McGregor was on a 'barnstorming' tour — one of the occupations undertaken by some of the ex-Royal Flying Corps pilots who had put their scant savings into buying light aircraft so that they might continue to enjoy their flying fever. Their enterprise would probably keep the wolf from the door but it would hardly make them tycoons of industry.

Mac McGregor would be only too happy to take passengers on joy-rides at 'ten bob a pop' — a 'pop' being about fifteen minutes of airborne ecstacy.

For a while young Trent was content to watch the little aeroplane take off and land and to listen as, successively, the excited passengers stepped down from the forward open cockpit to gasp out their wonderment of flight to all within earshot. Then, heady with a fine intoxication born of pumped adrenalin and further inflamed by oil and petrol fumes, he persuaded his father to let him, too, experience the magic of the sky.

Mac McGregor, long and lean and nonchalant, with his battered leather helmet, his flying goggles raised above his brows, and his little military moustache clipped in authentic War Birds style, was the very epitome of the daring aviators depicted in *Chums*, that thick, red-covered tome which was every husky lad's guidebook to adventure.

'Two boys at a time,' was Mac's offer. And a lad, bigger than Len, thrust forward and was into the cockpit first. Young Trent perched himself on the fellow's knees. The safety harness was strapped around them, making them as one. And Len was airborne, never to be quite the same when he returned to earth.

His elevated perch was fortunate for, he was sure, the eager lad on whose knobbly knees he sat could not see much beyond Len's shirtback — meanwhile, Master Trent scanned the wide panorama of Golden Bay and all the countryside from the Anatoki Range to the highlands of the Wakamarama.

He vowed, there and then, that some day he would pilot an aeroplane. And, like Mac McGregor, he, too, would fly up the Takaka Valley, stirring the natives from their daily routines and raising envy in the hearts of the young.

He was to realize that declaration many years later.

From that day onwards he avidly read anything and everything, fact or fiction, that told of aeroplanes and flight. He recalls that, some time before his eighth birthday, he was sitting in the garden with his mother, who was darning socks. The term 'million-air' was beginning to be used to describe a pilot who had flown an estimated 1,000,000 air miles — although, at that comparatively early stage of aviation there could not have been many such travel-weary venturers around.

'Mum,' he said, stabbing a small finger at a picture of a leather-jacketed, begoggled pilot standing beside his air-mail machine, 'when I grow up *I'm* going to be one of them.'

His mother gently reminded him that he would have to work very hard indeed. And that puzzled the boy for some time. Why on earth, he wondered, should an ace pilot have to *work?*

Time would tell him the answer — emphatically and often painfully.

By 1923 the Trents were living in a new house they had built in the centre of Takaka and near the banks of the beautiful Takaka River. Len remembers that they were good days. They owned two cars and a Harley-Davison motorcycle. His mother used all three vehicles — which was quite an accomplishment for a lady in the early 1920s.

'She must have been highly coordinated, for she never had an accident or an unpleasant driving incident,' he recalls. 'She started to teach me to drive when I was only thirteen and it may have been those early beginnings — and my probably inheriting some of her inborn mechanical sense — that were to help me in aviation, years later.'

In 1928 Len Trent was enrolled as a boarder at Nelson College — then, as now, one of the premier schools in New Zealand. His first year within the hallowed halls was uneventful; but midway through 1929 he was to receive the first really frightening experience of his young life. At 10.20 a.m. on 17 June the first shock of the Murchison Earthquake set the classroom shuddering as desks rocked and the floor began to move.

'I had experienced small earthquakes before,' Len Trent said, recounting the scene and the terrifying shaking. 'But within seconds I recognized this was something out of the ordinary.

'I was sitting in the front row of desks reserved for inattentive boys. The master was, to me, an old man who had reportedly been gassed in the First World War. I looked to him for guidance, but he was gripping both sides of his table in obvious alarm.

'Whether I was demonstrating my latent qualities of leadership, my powers of self-preservation or my speed in fright, I'm not prepared to claim — but at zero 15 seconds an extra jolt made me think of the huge brick and concrete tower immediately above the classroom. I sprang for the door with the master a very close second.

'Other classroom doors began to burst open. I was among the first outside and in time to see the tall flagpole on top of the tower swaying crazily, to finally snap off and crash to the ground five storeys below.

'Then the four pinnacles, each weighing several tons, cracked from each corner of the tower and I was horrified to see one actually hit the terraces above the sports field and bounce over the heads of some boys running in that direction.

'By a miracle no one was killed; but many were injured that day.

And I look on that experience as my first baptism by fire and perhaps an early demonstration of an ability to think clearly and act smartly in a terrifying situation.'

School athletics: Len Trent winning the 220-yards event at Nelson College, 1931.

He claims that he did not distinguish himself academically while at Nelson College. He failed matriculation at his first attempt — understandably, perhaps, because his parents had by this time moved back to Nelson and had permitted the boy, in leisure moments of increasing frequency, to take up golf, the Trents' family game.

He confesses: 'I had spent more time studying Bobby Jones on "How to Play Golf" than I had applied myself to academic studies. And so, at the behest of my mentors and on the instructions of my parents, my golf clubs were consigned to the attic the following year. I was to realize, if I was ever to play golf again (and Heaven help me if I couldn't) I had better settle down to work.

'So, work I did; and with my matriculation passed at last, I entered the sixth form, waiting to go to university to study for a career in dentistry. I had ample time to practise my beloved golf and that year, 1934, I won the Nelson Golf Club Senior Championship.

'In the finals, played over 36 holes, I was four down after the morning round and all seemed lost. It was probably a case of schoolboy nerves, but I went out after lunch with a do-or-die attitude and played the best game of my career. I promptly got back the four holes I had earlier lost and beat my opponent six and five.'

Although the headmaster of Nelson College was himself a golfer, the game was frowned upon as a sport for pupils. It did not foster the 'team spirit' and so young Trent's achievement did not rate a mention in the assembly hall or a mention in the college magazine. In fact, because he refused to play rugby and cricket once he had become a senior boy, he left Nelson College, in his belief, somewhat under a cloud — a most undistinguished Old Boy academically and athletically.

'Of course, with maturity, I can see the headmaster's point of view,' he says. 'Many schools today recognize that some boys are more independent than others and are more individually assertive than those who follow the herd instinct.

'Perhaps, too, in the world of sport and business it is recognized that the ability to play a good game of golf has its advantages. For instance, I am sure that when I faced the Royal Air Force selection board in 1937 my golf championship win was a strong point in my favour. Thank goodness golf helped to get me into a sports minded service and, no doubt, assisted me in my promotions along the way, as I played in station, group and command teams over many years.'

Len Trent left Nelson College in 1934 in the depths of the Great Depression. The family fortunes were at an all-time low and the cars and the motorcycle had been sold. Although his father was unable to send the boy to university, an uncle was able to pull strings in high places and Len got a job in the clerical office of Tomoana Freezing Works in Hastings where, for 17/6 per week he worked ridiculously long hours calculating farmers' cheques on the 'killing sheets' which came up from the firm's slaughterhouse tally clerks.

After about a year of this soul-destroying drudgery he was told that he was doing a good job and that, God being still in his Heaven, the stipend would be increased to a total of 27/6 the following year. Trent promptly resigned and went back to Nelson to learn dental mechanics under his father's tutilage.

'After about 6 months I was able to repair broken false teeth to my father's satisfaction,' he said. 'And I was sent off solo.'

But there was still no hope of attending university; so when the old firm offered him a much better position in its head office in Wellington he accepted. He could see that, at least, he would be able to support himself.

He found accommodation in Tinakouri St under the care of a kindly old German landlady, Fraulein von Meyer. They were happy days and he shared a room with an office friend, Des Dacre. The two young men had much in common. They both played golf on a three handicap and they assiduously plotted every round they played on a large sheet of graph paper pinned to the bedroom wall. And they both fought out the club championship — which Des Dacre won.

'Poor Des,' Trent later remarked. 'I talked him into joining the Air Force; and he was killed in the second year of the war. He played the piano like an angel. And whenever we boarders fell from grace with our landlady he would simply go to the piano and charm her with her favourite tunes — and all would be forgiven.'

The Labour Party had won office in New Zealand in 1935 and when the following year it decreed that the minimum weekly wage for a worker over the age of 21 would be £3-16s, the instant affluence of an extra £1-18s-6d in his pay-packet — more than doubling his previous wage — almost sent Trent over the moon. It allowed him to think of saving money so that he might take flying lessons and achieve his burning ambition to become a pilot — and a 'million-air' pilot, no less.

About that time, too, he began to take nightclass lessons in aero engineering and aircraft maintenance, purely as a hobby, as the subjects could prove handy and interesting adjuncts to the all-important role of guiding an aircraft through the skies.

It was some time in early 1937 that he read an advertisement in the Wellington *Dominion* morning newspaper inviting applicants for short service commissions in the Royal Air Force. All thoughts of a professional career in dentistry were forgotten. Here was an opportunity — not just knocking but really battering at his door. He promptly excused himself from his office desk and almost ran to the recruiting office at Air Department. He completed filling in his application form and sat back, impatiently awaiting the call to attend the promised interview.

In the meantime his cousin, Ian Richmond, who was a year younger than Len, had persuaded his father to pay his passage to England where he made direct application for entry into the RAF at Air Ministry, London. He had had a provisional medical examination before his departure for England and had briefed Len on the thoroughness of the several medical departments.

In most of the fitness tests, the applicant would have to take his chances on the fundamental workings of his body. But there was one test that any reasonably fit candidate could pass, given fair warning and a bit of time for training. The medical board's requirement was an applicant's ability to hold his breath for a full minute.

Len Trent practised for the several weeks before he might be called for his medical examination and timed himself as a reasonably consistent, if rather purple faced, one-and-a-half minute performer.

His interview before the New Zealand selection board was successful, because, some weeks later, he was instructed to report for his medical examination. Joy of joys! Surely, by now, he must be all but *in* the Air Force! He was almost certain he could really feel pin feathers sprouting from his shoulder blades.

At the appointed hour he presented himself, clean and bright and bushy-tailed, at the medical chambers and was subjected to the minor indignities that aspiring warriors, pledged to perish for monarch and country, must suffer. Inquisitive fingers pressed and probed, curious eyes and ears peered and listened; body fluids were drawn and bottled for closer investigation.

Eyesight tests found the candidate qualified to prescribed standards; and then on he went to the test that had, by now, loomed to extravagant proportions in his mind. Another victim, also, was in the room.

'Can you hold your breath for a full minute?' the doctor asked with the diabolical hiss of a Frankenstein.

The two young men nodded and said they believed they could.

'Well, we shall see. I'll put these clips on your nostrils. And then you should try to hold on for at least a minute the first time — because it's harder the second time you try.'

The doctor had a watch on his desk, but the victims couldn't see its face. 'Okay? When you're ready, take a deep breath — and away you go!'

They both inhaled deeply; and Trent felt that his whole future in aviation depended on this one fiendishly conceived test that was more like an examination for Navy frogmen operating without air bottles. He heard his unfortunate companion's gusty blowout and the doctor's quiet: '*That* wasn't very good, was it! Have a bit of a rest and try again.' The seconds dragged by; Trent could hear his heart booming, and feel the veins on his forehead pulsing. He found it difficult to focus his eyes. Then he heard the doctor say: 'That'll do, that'll do!' And he exploded and gasped.

'Good God,' said the doctor. 'Can you always do that?'

'How long was it?'

'Two minutes and twenty seconds.'

Practice, thought Trent with a rather smug inner glow, makes perfect. And suddenly that crafty doctor had become a very friendly and likeable fellow.

That night, to a small audience at the boarding house, he boasted of his effort. But, try as he might, he could not repeat the performance.

A trivial incident in a life that was to become one of high excitement and bloody action? Not really — for it gives us an early clue to the man's preparation and determination to win when a real challenge, on which so much may depend, is presented.

One day in August 1937 the mail brought him the call he had awaited so long. He was able to quit his desk job in the office of W. & R. Fletcher (NZ) Ltd and report to the Taieri Aero Club, near Dunedin, to begin flying training under the instruction of Alf Burbidge.

This was to be 50 hours of introductory flying to make sure the candidates were sufficiently coordinated to take on the demands of service flying at Royal New Zealand Air Force Station Wigram, Christchurch.

He set out on his train journey to Taieri from his parents' home in Nelson, where he had been spending a couple of weeks' holiday. An overnight stopover at Christchurch found him with an afternoon of leisure, so he took a stroll through the city's picturesque Hagley Park. An elderly gentleman he met asked Trent if he had seen a rare and revered visitor to the park's bird life — a white heron — that was mingling with the ducks and other wildfowl.

'In Maori folklore, the bird is a good omen,' the old man said solemnly. 'For if you behold the white heron, good fortune will follow you through the future.'

He followed the man's directions and tracked down the lovely bird. It was his first glimpse of the graceful white creature and he was to wonder, many times over the years, on the prophetic words of that old man. For surely fortune had favoured him, arduous though some of the struggles may have been, and had given him a double measure of nine lives.

Flying student Trent's log book shows he had his first dual instruction in a De Havilland Gipsy I on 1 September 1937. It was a 10 minute flight of familiarization with the aircraft, straight and level cruising and a feeling of the controls.

'What bliss! It was more than 45 years ago, but I can still remember every detail of that flight today,' he recalls.

Then, after 9 hours and 10 minutes of dual circuits and bumps, rate one and steep turns, recoveries from spins, emergency and precautionary landings, re-starting a dead engine in flight, inverted flying and still more circuits and bumps, he was deemed sufficiently capable of getting an aeroplane airborne and landing it safely in solo flight. The instructor got out of the front cockpit, removed the pin and took out his control column and told the pupil to fly one circuit of the field on his own.

Oh, the magic of those moments of mastery! They live forever in every pilot's memory. Trent trembled with expectancy as he taxied downwind for take-off, weaving the characteristic path the aircraft must follow because it is impossible to see anything dead ahead of the machine when it is on the ground — and precious little, either, when it is airborne.

He turned cross-wind, looking carefully along his take-off path and peering skywards for traffic. A check of the tail trim; and then a move into wind.

Pushing the throttle slowly and deliberately forward, he concentrated on keeping the machine straight with the rudder as it gathered speed and bounded over the grass. And then the tail came up and he was airborne. As the little Gipsy hummed and wallowed its way upwards through the mild turbulences he poked his head out from behind the shelter of the small windscreen to peer past the bulk of the aeroplane's fore-structure and the cross-hatching of struts and flying wires. The slipstream pressed against his face, cramming his song of exultation back into his throat and pouching his weather-side cheek. But it was the wind of fortune he felt.

Whatever happens from now on can never change the fact that I can at last fly, he thought. By my own hands and feet and still stumbling skills I have coaxed an aeroplane into the air without another's guiding hand on the control stick. Yes, I can fly, he realized with a mixture of pride and wonder. Now — can I *land* the machine? A fellow who jumps off a ten-storey building can fly — in a manner of speaking — but it is his landing that counts, if he expects to live and try the trick again.

Down, down on the final approach glided the little machine, its cut-back motor making gentle pop-pop-pop noises and the wooden propeller turning almost lazily. The rigging wires whistled softly in the wind, telling the measure of descent by sibilation. If the sound increased too much, it would indicate too fast an approach. If the music should stop, the pilot had better prepare for a stall.

But student pilot Trent had judged his glide path well enough. The airfield boundary slipped comfortably beneath him, his wings were level and he began to ease the stick back ... back ... back into his stomach. Wheels and tail-skid hit the ground together and, bump-bump-bump, he was down.

By observing a pattern of tribal rites and calling on spiritual and physical reserves, he had achieved something akin to the passing of a pagan warrior's initiation test — an emergence into a select brotherhood. There was now but little more than 999,000 air miles to travel before he would become a 'million-air' and a God, brother of Icarus.

Instructor Burbidge gave his pupil the required 50 hours at Taieri, flying Gipsy and Miles Magister aircraft. Len Trent remembers the 2½ months at that airfield as among the happiest days of his life. The big, beautiful cumulus clouds that he had admired from the window of his office in Wellington had now become near neighbours, standing high in the heavens like gigantic monuments carved from solid marble. Later he was to know the terror and the perils that lurked within their seemingly serene caverns.

In the company of James Vernon and Pat Fisher he travelled to Wigram to don the blue-grey Air Force uniform in the rank of Acting Pilot Officer and to meet the other members of a course of

Three New Zealand fledgling flyers at Taieri Aero Club, Dunedin, in September, 1937. All graduated into the RAF. *From left:* Jim Vernon (killed in Battle of France, 1940); Pat Fisher (survived the war, but badly burnt); Len Trent (survived — miraculously). Trent flew solo, after 9 hours 10 minutes, on 9 September 1937. His aircraft was Gipsy Moth ZK-ACE and his instructor was Alf Burbidge.

twelve now ready to apply themselves to a more disciplined routine of air training.

Their early service flying saw them learning the subtleties of the Hawker Tomtit and the Avro 626 aircraft and there was much accent on instrument flying. Len Trent is amused today to look through his early log book and see the constant references to 'flat turns' — the Wigram method of turning on to a compass course in those hazy pre-war days.

'I am sure I never did a "flat turn" after I left Wigram,' he says today and jokingly ascribes his strong leg muscles to the exercise they got pushing on the rudder bars to try and achieve the almost impossible.

He rapidly realized there was more to an Air Force career than just leaping into an aeroplane and tooling off into the wild blue. Instructors had to be called 'Sir' and there was to be none of the old 'Okay, Alf' if told to start up the engine and taxi out. And so Pilot Officer Trent got off to an inauspicious beginning and soon he and one of his mentors found themselves quite incompatible.

But, after some correspondence and a heartening boost in morale from his old instructor and cobber, Alf Burbidge, he was soon over the hump and gliding down the sunny side, most of his rancour forgotten.

The trainees progressed through their early flying training on Tomtits and Avros to clamber the heights to the cockpits of Wigram's rangy Vickers Vildebeest biplanes. To the young pilot officers the machines loomed huge and seemed incongruously incapable of flight, inviting the satirical pseudo-American drawl in warning: 'Wilbur, she'll never git off th' grarnd!'

But they did get airborne in the Vildebeests and after No. 1 Course — which had included Pilot Officer Sid (later Air Marshal Sir Rochford) Hughes — had left Wigram to sail for England, Trent and his fellow trainees of No. 2 Course became heady as they affected aeronautical prowess — far beyond their knowledge — to the 'sprogs' of No. 3 Course.

Len Trent flew most of his training flights in Vildebeests with Roy Max, who had been a school mate at Nelson College. Max was to survive the war, winning, in the process, the Distinguished Service Order and the Distinguished Flying Cross.

The system required the pairing of trainee officers in carrying out aerial exercises such as cross-country navigation flights, bombing runs and gunnery attacks — the latter being practised with a Lewis gun, mounted in the rear cockpit, firing at ground targets. The training syllabus demanded that the young pilots be able to take the gun apart and reassemble it blindfolded — a skill so methodically indoctrinated in Trent that he was to benefit materially from it later when things got a bit sticky in one period of the 'phoney' war.

Towards the end of his term at Wigram, Trent was sent on a

Vickers Vildebeest aircraft formation flying over Wigram, prior to a Wellington air display, 1938.

cross-country flight with Max as his passenger. It was a lovely day, with here and there some majestic cumulus clouds castling high into the blue sky. Roy Max had calculated the compass course and Len Trent, piloting the Vildebeest, was sticking steadfastly to the heading he had been given by his student navigator. Dead ahead loomed a big, snowy mass. And why should the innocent captain of the aircraft foul up Max's dead reckonings by dog-legging around the mountain of cloud?

No one had warned him of the possible danger that lurked within such an innocent looking pile of cotton wool. So, without a care in the world — and with only a scant few hours of instrument flying on such elementary cockpit aids as the Vildebeest could offer — he approached the fascinating mass.

As every pilot knows, there is no indication of turbulence as the cloud is approached. But, at the instant of penetration, Len Trent knew he was deep in all-enveloping trouble. Bang! Thump! The big gangling biplane was tossed up and thrown down by forces far more incredible than the young pilot had ever imagined. Wings, wires and struts flapped and warped alarmingly and the control column had no more effect on the stability of the machine than would reins and snaffle bit control an iron-jawed buckjumper.

Trent looked to his instrument panel that was dancing in front of him. What succour could he beg of them? Precious little. There was not much more than the primitive turn-and-bank indicator, the dials that showed his height and his airspeed — and the wildly-spinning compass needle that told him nothing more than he already knew. He was in deep, white trouble.

'One wonders how the human frame can stand the stresses, let alone fabric and wood and metal,' he recalls in retrospect. 'I was shocked beyond words and certainly had no idea of the correct procedure to follow in such a predicament.

'I think providence must have come to my aid in that, my first real test of a serious emergency in the air — for that is what it was. If I had tried to turn back by wrestling with the stick and the rudder I would almost certainly have ended up upside down with probably a wing torn off.

'As it was — and as soon as there was an opportunity to control the aircraft — I concentrated on trying to keep the wings level, ignoring all else. When, after what seemed an age of considerable alarm, we emerged on the other side of the cloud, I was shocked to see the whole aircraft heavily coated with ice.

'All this happened in about seven or eight minutes, but it taught me a lesson which was to last a lifetime in aviation. And, incredible as it may seem, no instructor up to that point in my training had thought to warn a fledgling pilot of such a hazard.'

Much later, during the war, he was again almost killed through an oversight in flight briefing by a flight commander who sent him off solo on his first night-flying circuit in a Bristol Blenheim, under British blackout conditions. He had not been told that, immediately on becoming airborne after leaving the comparative brightness of the flarepath, he should fix his concentration on the phosphorescent symbols on his instrument panel. Lifting his aeroplane from the flare-lit runway, he had looked through the perspex for the usual visual horizon of town or city lights. There was nothing but blackness. And, after about ten seconds of peering, his eyes went to the instrument panel. Strangely, the artificial horizon on the Sperry panel was indicating an ominous 45 degree turn to the left — although every instinct and the good old 'seat of his pants' were telling him his wings were level. Could he have really got into such an attitude in so short a time? Impossible! But closer investigation showed him that he was no longer climbing and that his airspeed was rapidly increasing. Furthermore, his direction indicator, spinning its numerals alarmingly across its dial, told him he was now turning left.

Everything seemed to be happening contrary to his natural senses. But fortunately those golden words of wisdom flashed in his mind — 'Believe your instruments' — and he fought against false instinct and climbed to safety.

He had unwittingly executed a turning dive soon after leaving the runway and had missed death by seconds in that phenomenon that killed so many night-flying Blenheim crews — the 'phantom dive'.

He continued to have the odd brush with authority at Wigram. A rather touchy instructor ordered him out of the cockpit for not being able to find a light switch quickly enough in the dark. But in the end, right prevailed and diligence reaped its just reward. On 12 May 1938 in accordance with Paragraph 811, Clause 5 of King's Regulations and Air Council Instructions, he received his 'Badge, flying — pilots, for the use of' — or, in more generally accepted terms, he got his wings.

Volunteers had been called from graduates of No. 2 Course to join the staff of the burgeoning Government airline system; and both Len Trent and Les Ransome elected to put their names forward. But the Officer Commanding RNZAF Station Wigram, Squadron Leader Hodson, talked with Trent and persuaded him to go to England 'for the experience'. This, of course, he was to get in large and unexpected measure.

Back home on final leave in Nelson, he took his sister for a flight which was to have been a 'joy-ride' in one of the Nelson Aero Club's Tiger Moth light aeroplanes. But, not having flown such a machine for some time, and trying not to impose too much gravity stress on his passenger, he stalled at the top of a loop and saw the girl hanging tall, suspended in her safety harness, from the front cockpit. She was not impressed.

Early in June 1938 Len Trent sailed for England by way of Pitcairn Island and Panama. And, from all the signs and portents in that year of grace, he was heading for all the adventure a young pilot could want.

3

INTO BATTLE

SOON AFTER THEIR ARRIVAL in England the New Zealand RAF entrants were instructed to proceed to Uxbridge to be measured and fitted for new uniforms of fine barathea weave and of approved RAF pattern. And the New Zealand tailor-made tunics and trousers, of which they had been so proud, were discarded.

To the men from Britain's far-flung and favoured agricultural dominion, London was a bright and bustling city of a magnitude beyond their earlier imaginings. They travelled to and from Uxbridge and central-city points by underground rail, quickly learning the systems of inner- and outer-circle lines and change-over stations, breathing the heavy and unforgettably-odoured air the trains pumped ahead of them as they raced past the platforms, and delighting in the fragrance of autumn days in Kensington Gardens.

There were many pubs to be frequented and good pre-war English ales to be quaffed. There were plays, featuring notable performers, to be seen and venerable towers to be visited. And, soon enough, they were on their various ways that were to take them, not really unexpectedly, towards battle.

Len Trent's first move towards battle was, quite literally, in a Fairey Battle aircraft. He was posted to 15 Squadron, based at RAF Station Abingdon in Berkshire.

The Battle, a low-wing monoplane powered by a single Rolls Royce Merlin engine, carried a crew of two and was one of Britain's front-line light bombers destined to serve a dual role in both strike and reconnaissance work. In tune with the times, it boasted a three-bladed variable-pitch propeller — an innovation that had left the old Vickers Vildebeest somewhat behind modernity in the arms race.

So there were some sophisticated flying techniques to be

mastered — although Trent, after two short sessions of dual instruction totalling one hour and twenty minutes, got away solo without much trouble on 15 September 1938. One memorable flight during his otherwise happy tyro days at Abingdon was a routine test exercise under the supervision of his flight commander, Flying Officer Lawrence.

Lawrence elected to take the controls for take-off and he climbed the machine and headed westwards. Over Swindon the Battle rolled upside-down, the nose went down and the aircraft stormed earthwards, the puzzled apprentice growing increasingly alarmed and bewildered by his master's reckless disregard of life, limb, machinery and flying disciplines.

At a perilously low height the aeroplane was quickly checked and urgently directed upwards by Lawrence. It was discovered that the flight commander's inter-communication plug had pulled free of its socket and Len Trent had not been getting the instructions. The aircraft had, for too many minutes, been soldiering on with no-one at the controls.

They were happy days at Abingdon, Trent recalls, with boating excursions on the Thames and plenty of golf leavening the Air Force duties on station. The pleasant old agricultural town of Abingdon, barely six good English miles from Oxford as the Battle flew had a population of less than 10,000 in the years immediately before the war. History, hoary and proud, slept peacefully in its ancient stones, disturbed only by the occasional metallic rumblings of a modern knight practising tilting in the aerial lists.

Snugly encased in a Sidcot suit, Trent looked down with pleasure and pride on the countryside that spread like a patchwork counterpane below him. Height tests, to familiarize him with high altitude flying, opened for him a tremendous panorama. A line or two of a poem, of an author either forgotten or never known, came to him:

> *Heavens! What a goodly prospect spreads around*
> *Of hills, and dales, and woods, and lawns and spires ...*

To the north, the clustered spires of Oxford needled up out of the filmiest of ground mists, catching the sun and holding it white on their powdered stones and weathered slates. Here and there a window, at lower level, threw a solar-ray beam straight at him.

Away to the west the Cotswolds rose on their escarpment. At first glance the land appeared devoid of villages — but only because they sheltered, country-shy, in deep-cleft valleys. They lay in sequestered places beneath the hills — such settlements as Alkerton, Chipping Campden, Horley and Upwell.

To the south lay Didcot, standing on the crossroads. And, further yet, and downstream on the Thames, was Henley, drifting into the southeast haze. Eastwards was High Wycombe.

Len Trent looked down from his aerial perch. It was good to be alive. The sun beamed in through the perspex hatch above his head and the Merlin engine in front of him throbbed smoothly. He studied his map, tracking his progress, and felt very contented. He had climbed into this capsule of aluminium alloy and steel and, by his own hands, had caused it to rise high above the mundane and petty world of earthly beings. Within the compass of an hour of his young life, born in a far-flung dominion, he had seen more of England than had many a veteran Berkshire yokel, village-bound below him, seen in a lifetime.

He was very much aware of his gathered skills and conscious of his powers. He now dealt in the spells of modern magic and held in his hands the levers and the switches of devices awful to behold, to be heard and to be felt.

Early in February 1939 Len Trent went on his first skiing holiday to Wengen in the company of his Air Force mates, Roy Max, Jack Edwards and Wally Tuckwell. The alpine resort of Wengen, close by the romantic Jungfrau in Switzerland, proved a wonderful playground for the healthy, exuberant young men — although their fun was not without its hazards. Trent, mounting his little one-man *luge* for a speedy descent of the toboggan run, took aboard Wally Tuckwell. Tuckwell crowded himself on to the nose of the sled, intending to get some bright photographs of both Trent and the passing scenery en route. But the *luge* was designed as a one-seater. The added weight of Tuckwell on its nose fouled up Trent's control and the abused toboggan left the track at a great speed and shot its two passengers into a windrow of compacted snow.

More shaken and bruised than really injured, the little band of adventurers returned, soon after, to Abingdon. And Len Trent found he had been assigned to a navigation course at Hamble, on the outskirts of Southampton, Hampshire. He left Abingdon on 22 February 1939 and was to spend the next 3 months in concentrated study — a sample, perhaps, of the kind of hard work his mother had forecast for him when he had announced his boyhood ambitions of becoming a 'million-air' aviator.

Pilot Officer Trent airborne on a navigation exercise during his course at Hamble, March 1939.

But all was not scholastics. There was still time to play the occasional round of his beloved golf; and it was at the Hook Park club that he met Miss Ursula Woolhouse, the young lady destined to become his wife.

Back to Abingdon again the tempo of training was increasing. Len Trent continued with his practical flying exercises and his theoretical assignments in the lecture rooms. By this time the international news was getting blacker as the newspaper headlines grew bolder and more ominous in tone. While on leave in July he and a fellow New Zealander, Bill Lightband, saw headlines posing the question that all Britons, in their sombre hearts, had been asking over the past months: 'Does it mean war?'

Pilot Officer Trent has a picnic lunch while he reads the *Daily Mirror* in
March, 1939. The headlines suggested he might be recalled to his station
at any minute.

At RAF Abingdon, 1939: Pilots of 15 Squadron 'shoot a line'.
From left: Douglas, Oakley, Webster, Lawrence, Oakshott and Eames.

Three 15 Squadron companions, 1939. *From left*: Paul Chapman, killed at
Sedan in May 1940; 'Red' Eames, who survived the war; Bert Oakley,
RAAF, killed on the Maastricht Bridge operation, 1940.

Prime Minister Chamberlain's talks with Hitler had not been going well. On the blustering day of 15 March the German armoured divisions had entered Prague — and forthwith the British reservists of the three armed services had hastened to their posts. The Auxiliary Air Force had been put on a war footing, volunteers of the Observer Corps were manning their posts and the Air Raid Precaution wardens were ready.

About 10 minutes before 11 o'clock on the morning of Sunday 3 September 1939, a number of high officers and civil servants had gathered in a room in Richmond Terrace, Whitehall, London. Before them on a table and ready to be consulted was a copy of a highly secret tome that set out in chapter, paragraph and clause every necessary action to be taken, in the event of hostilities, by the Royal Navy, the Army and the Royal Air Force, along with all the Departments of State. It was the Government War Book.

But it was hardly necessary for the men to study the directions in that book. Many of those present had, themselves, helped to revise some of its passages during the months between March when Hitler had invaded Prague and the solemnity of that Whitehall meeting on that warm September morning.

There was not much talk. The men were awaiting a message from Berlin — and few doubted the outcome. But when the news did come from the British Ambassador to the German Reich it said, in effect, that there was really *no* news — Hitler had not replied to the ultimatum of the British Government.

The Secretary of the Cabinet entered the room. 'Gentlemen,' he said, 'we are at war with Germany. The Prime Minister directs that the "War Telegram" be dispatched immediately.'

But, by that time, Pilot Officer Trent and his observer, Sergeant Avent, had already landed in France. On Saturday 2 September, they were airborne from Abingdon in the Fairey Battle K9233, destined for a foreign airfield in Operation 'Movement to Betheneville' — and the war front. The personnel and equipment of 15 Squadron had become part of the Advanced Air Striking Force.

The squadron machines landed on Betheneville's grass airstrip, close to a lot of French military activity in the Rheims area. A pub in the village was to be their mess and certain private dwellings had been requisitioned as billets for the officers and airmen. The French bus driver who met the British arrivals had obviously been briefed on the addresses of the families who were to host the foreign visitors; and so, in the best traditions of British fair play, the squadron officers left the bus in strict order of seniority as the vehicle drew up outside each billet.

Trent's luck was not standing by him. He found himself directed to a scruffy attic in a house that might have seen recent days as a brothel. Cobwebs and strings of onions hung from the ceiling and walls and the mattress on the ancient bed was filthy. On comparing notes with his companions, he found that Robbie Robinson had landed in clover and was lodging with a family whose patriarch owned a local factory. Generously, Robinson suggested that he should arrange for Trent, also, to move in. And they could share Robbie's wide, soft — and clean — double bed. The plan found favour with the hosts; and it became a happy Anglo-French association with both nationalities stumbling good-naturedly with foreign phrases and helping each other with linguistics.

The memories of so many of those little inconsequential incidents keep coming back to Len Trent, smiling out of the blacker moments of war. There was Dawson — 'Tit' they called him — who took off for his first solo on a motorbike. He went full-bore across the road into a wheelbarrow full of vegetables and thereby put up the local price of table greens and fresh fruit. And champagne, at something like two shillings a bottle, ensured the men of 15 Squadron had many a merry evening and a hung-over morning after.

Soon the call came for the squadron to move to Vraux, close to Chalons-sur-Marne. In a building soon to be colloquially known as the 'Red House' the commanding officer established his squadron headquarters and made available the top storey as a dormitory for the officers — who, by this time, had received their folding camp beds from England and could now slumber — or at least seek slumber — as a cohesive body. The building, which owed its name to its red tiled roof (and not from any associations with carnal excesses) was the property of the French Air Force and had been a photographic laboratory.

Of vital importance to Britain's Bomber Command in the months — and years — to come was information on the whereabouts of Germany's airfields, factories, power stations, roads and railways. Already the Air Force was gathering such evidence. While home-based bombers were carrying out their seemingly monotonous leaflet raids they were getting photographs of potential targets; while the Battles of the Advanced Air Striking Force were also flying over Germany with sharp-eyed cameras.

On 24 September Len Trent flew his first high level photo-reconnaissance sortie over the enemy's homeland — a flight at 20,000 feet. 'No oxygen' he cryptically noted in his log book.

It was an historic occasion for 15 Squadron, too, for the six Battles that flew the mission gave not only Trent but the squadron its first operational sortie of the Second World War. Proud hearts would beat a little faster in the City of Spires and its surrounding villages when the news eventually got past the wartime censors — for the unit had been unofficially adopted by the burghers and acclaimed 'Oxford's own' squadron.

In the best traditions of the First World War founder-members, the aircrews and ground staff of 15 Squadron were acquitting themselves well in air space and on soil that had known so much of the unit's past glory. Formed at South Farnborough in March 1915, it had crossed to France in the following December equipped for an army cooperation role. It was to serve on the Western Front until the Armistice in 1918.

The excellent photographic and artillery cooperation work rendered by the squadron in assisting the Fifth Army during the attacks on the Ancre Salient in January 1917, earned the special recognition of Sir Douglas Haig. The unit was disbanded in December 1919, and reformed as a bomber squadron at Martlesham Heath in March 1924. In 1934 its headquarters were transferred to Abingdon, which was where the squadron was based at the outbreak of the Second World War.

The device within the squadron's badge — 'a hind's head, affrontee, erased at neck, between wings elevated and conjoined in base', to give the correct heraldic description — is evocative of the time in May 1934, when the unit was equipped with Hawker Hind aircraft. The squadron received its official badge two years later.

The squadron's motto, 'Aim Sure', was to be pledged faithfully and in gallant blood in the months that were to follow that first sortie on 24 September 1939.

Len Trent's adventures on the ground continued to entertain

and, in some cases, startle both himself and his audiences of the moment — both British and foreign. Taking one of the two big BSA motorcycles that the squadron possessed, he set off one day when he was off-duty to visit his cousin, Ian Richmond, who was also a Battle pilot and attached to another squadron of the Advanced Air Striking Force.

Passing a group of French soldiers, Trent gave his machine's powerful engine a swift gunning to make it bellow impressively. But he was passing beneath a spreading chestnut tree and its accumulation of fallen leaves had made a slippery layer of decayed foliage on the roadway. The motorcycle pranged noisily and dramatically; and its pilot joined it in ground loops while the French soldiers trumpeted their laughter.

When he did meet up with Ian Richmond they went walking to explore the French countryside. In a sheltered byway they discovered, to their wonder, a large dump of First World War artillery shells in a stack about a metre high and fifteen metres long. Len Trent took one as a souvenir to add to the squadron's trophy board in the mess at the Red House, lashing it on to the carrier of the motorcycle.

Back at base, he found two huge nails that would serve as supporting pegs for the curio and began to hammer them into the trophy board with the base of the live shell. In his innocence of the vagaries of temperamental, time-weary explosives, he cleared the mess of inhabitants in double-quick time.

A week or two later, when a couple of rounds of .303 ammunition were surreptitiously dropped into the maw of the red-hot mess stove — ostensibly to scare a newcomer medical officer standing close by — the only one in the room not alarmed when the stove lid hit the ceiling and hot coals sprayed the walls was the young doctor.

There can be no doubt that France, during those early days of what was called the Phoney War, was proving a great theatre for youthful exuberance. Here they were — little more than striplings — at battle stations and walking the same French earth that some of their fathers had trod and, in some cases, had enriched and ennobled with their British blood. Now the enemy was but a few kilometres away, leering over the top of the ineffectual ramparts of the Maginot Line. Meanwhile, pleasure and hospitality were at hand and life, for the golden moment, was for living.

Pilot Officer Trent, officially appointed stores purchasing officer for the squadron by his commanding officer — and therefore an early connoisseur of the vintners' cellars and their likely bargains — was such a regular frequenter of a particular wine store in Épernay that he was dubbed 'Lieutenant Épernay' by the genial proprietor and his family.

The wine merchant so happened to be the owner of an area of land that included a relief landing ground used in an emergency by the aircraft of 15 Squadron. But the airstrip was the breeding ground for thousands of rabbits whose burrows pock-marked the turf; so the commanding officer soon won the cooperation of the land owner in organising a squadron rabbit shoot, the target creatures being encouraged to leave their warrens by ferrets kept by the wine merchant's wife.

If his keeping of the squadron's mess exchequer was not enough to keep Trent occupied in off-flying duties, he was to unwittingly earn more responsibilities through his own inquisitiveness. In a walk around the airfield he decided to impress one of the anti-aircraft Lewis gunners with his knowledge of that gun. There

Pilot Officer Trent rabbit shooting during off-duty hours in France, 1939.

were six Lewis-gun defence posts — disparagingly called 'shit-pits' by the bored occupants and he discovered that not one of the twelve twin-mounted Lewis guns would fire if a hostile face or form was to present itself. The tension on the return spring of every gun was faulty. Trent had learned all about Lewis guns in New Zealand and he reported the matter to his commanding officer who immediately declared him officer commanding ground defence. A daily programme of target practice was instituted which later bore fruit in the form of five aircraft shot down on 10 May 1940.

Air training, in those expectant days of the Phoney War, was being steadily increased and practice bombing was high on the list of exercises. A popular manoeuvre involved a trio of Battles flying towards the target in echelon, the leader peeling off to dive-bomb with his numbers two and three support aircraft following. Pilots took it in turns to be leader, so that each could experience the responsibilities of that position.

On one such dive bombing exercise Len Trent was in the lead; and the target for the imaginary bombs was the red roof of the squadron's headquarters, the Red House.

Trent bore down from 3000 feet on the imaginary enemy's stronghold, his bomb load precisely selected and fused, and ready for the touch on the bomb release to send the target to oblivion.

But what should appear but his very agitated flight commander, roaring in beside him and gesticulating frantically to desist. Realizing that something was amiss, he ceased his bombing intent; and when the three aircraft had landed it was explained to Pilot Officer Trent that his machine had not been cleared of its live bomb load since its earlier stand-by for active readiness. And so another Allied target had been saved; and Trent missed any chance of a mention in German dispatches.

On 9 December 1939 15 Squadron was ordered to return to England. They were to be stationed at Wyton in Huntingdon, to be re-equipped with Blenheim IV light bombers.

Len Trent, now shed of his accountancy duties and control of the airfield's ground defences, had fresh responsibilities placed on his shoulders. He was detailed to look after the welfare of the rear party in the role of officer commanding troops. He watched over the safe evacuation of his flock from his seat in a civil Ensign aircraft — G-ADSX as his log book shows — under the control of

The 'Red House', Vraux, France, 1939 — the headquarters and officers' dormitory of 15 Squadron.

a Captain Johnson.

One of his last and important duties before he vacated his post as mess supply officer was to purchase large and conveniently freightable quantities of champagne, perfumes, liquors and such French items as might delight the hearts of the squadron-members' ladies in Britain.

But even in the excitement and hurly-burly of war the customs officers were vigilant; so problems of getting the loot into England were resolved in schemes ranging from the sheer clumsy to the ingenious. Some, with small packages, simply stuffed their contraband in their pockets and lied glibly to the interrogators awaiting them as they vacated their aircraft at Wyton. One pilot, with above-average imagination and a sense of the dramatic, carefully disguised his bottles of champagne as bombs and affixed them to his Battle's bomb racks. Alas — before he could get back to the aircraft to retrieve them a diligent armourer had released them 'dead' and they had hit the ground, bursting with their own frothy explosions.

4

BLENHEIMS TO THE FORE

GARLANDS SHOULD BE REVERENTLY LAID and paeans of
gratitude sung to the memory of the gallant Blenheim. That
wonderful little light bomber — ambitiously called a medium
bomber in the early days of the war — was always at the forefront
of the action, dishing out its modest bomb loads and taking far
more punishment than it deserved.

A Blenheim made the first operational sortie of the Second
World War; and its companions flew thereafter in every
wretched theatre of conflict, from mast-high shipping strikes off
the Hook of Holland to multitudinous duties in Malta, Greece,
North Africa, Singapore, Burma and the hinterlands of Hell.

Pilots learning the rather simple mysteries of the multi-engined
Mark IV or 'long-nose' Blenheim were usually first given
instructions in handling and flying solo the Blenheim Mark I.
There was no great difference in handling characteristics. The
Mark IV had a shade more power, was a bit heavier and, because
of its longer snout, its taxying vision was impaired. If you could
fly one (and almost anyone could) you could fly both.

At the time of the Munich furore the short-nosed Blenheim I
equipped sixteen RAF bomber squadrons in Britain; but when war
came in 1939 only two home-based bomber squadrons were using
them, the Mark IV having superseded them. But there were still a
lot available for training purposes.

The Mark I Blenheim made a sturdy and comparatively safe
training aircraft for pilots learning multi-engine skills. Not many
— even those who were poured into the cockpit straight off Tiger
Moths — found any particular difficulties facing them. They all
seemed to be flying solo in next to no time.

The Blenheim had the distinction of being the aircraft for
which the RAF Central Flying School first developed its 'twin

Pilot Officer Trent in front of a Mark I ('Short-nose') Blenheim of 15 Squadron at RAF Station Wyton in January 1940.

technique' — the novice being taught to hold a twin-engined aircraft low down after take-off to gain single-engine safety speed quickly and to disregard initial gain in height.

The Blenheim verbal cockpit drill also came from the teachings of the C.F.S. The trainee was taught to recite the mnemonic 'H.T.M.P.F.F.G.' before take-off. This memory prompt, meaning 'Hydraulics, Trim, Mixture, Pitch, Fuel, Flaps, Gills' was calculated to forestall fatal absent-mindedness — although some unthinking pilots had been known to wind the trim wheel backwards instead of forwards. And all the power of Samson could not push the control column against the inexorable law of aerodynamics. The aircraft rose, climbed and stalled; and the wreckage was frightful to behold.

Being a contortionist would have helped any Blenheim pilot. Some knobs and switches were positioned behind his left shoulder — the pitch controls, for instance. And the hydraulic service controls, not unlike Victorian lavatory handles, were below him and to the right. The spring-loaded safety guards covering these and the flap plunger helped to chip off pieces of skin and soon gave the pilot the scabby trademark of 'Blenheim hands'.

Getting into a Blenheim was always something of an affair and the trainee soon learned not to attempt to do it while weighed down with a parachute. Having climbed, helmeted, gloved and inter-commed, on to the port wing, the panting pilot would lower his 'chute pack — which also served as a rather knobbly cushion — into the bucket seat. He would then let himself down gently so that, even if the direction was poor, he did not damage his pants, his backside or his vital organs on the various protruding gadgets surrounding his throne.

Although the wings and the ailerons were more or less invisible behind the engine cowlings, the pilot of the Blenheim Mark I had a wonderful view forward and it was a fascinating sight to see the countryside, sliding past below, through the transparent floor of the aircraft's nose section.

Len Trent's first dual instructional flight in a Blenheim Mark I at Wyton was on 15 December 1939. His instructor was a Flying Officer Mottram and the exercise, a 'familiarization with the aircraft', had the pupil tingling with apprehension and agog with awe as his mentor ripped the machine through its low level paces.

The Blenheim's rated sea level speed was 240 mph and whereas not all pilots were able to achieve such speeds, Trent firmly believes that Flying Officer Mottram managed to get every bit of that, and probably a little more as their aircraft raced quail-high over the fens

Trees and hedgerows and telephone poles loomed up ahead of them and their propeller-wash churned the ponds and marshes as the two 840 hp Mercury engines roared them onwards. The normal take-off boost pressure in the Blenheim's intake manifold was +5 pounds. An emergency lever, when invoked, gave a +9 pound fuel intake and was usable, in strained circumstances, for only a minute or two of desperate flying. Sustained use of +9 power was more than each engine's nine cylinders could tolerate.

Nevertheless, Mottram called on the extra force of the emergency plug and demonstrated how a Blenheim would run in on a low level shipping strike to drop its 11 second delayed-action bombs into the hull of the target. He selected a large tree as the imaginary masted ship and raced at it, jinking, weaving and skidding the Blenheim at fence-top height as he dodged imaginary flak.

'Feel this!' Mottram yelled. Just as Trent felt sure the aircraft would bury itself and its occupants in a tornado of branches and leaves, the pilot lifted the Blenheim to brush the topmost twigs. Then he suddenly pushed it down the other side with such force that the carburettors, temporarily starved of fuel, caused the engines to cough disconcertingly. Trent felt his heart had been left somewhere up on the tree top.

They returned to base, still hedge-hopping and skimming power lines on the way. That was to be the last flight Trent was to have with Flying Officer Mottram; the enthusiastic exponent of the techniques of low-level flying killed himself and destroyed a Blenheim the following day.

Once more based on English soil and within comfortable road travel to the home of Ursula Woolhouse at Hamble, and the attractions of London. Len Trent bought himself a near new MG sports car for £90. Fuel rationing had come into full force and many motorists, either called to the services or deprived of sufficient petrol — or both — were selling off their cars in a buyers' market.

On 27 December he flew with Flight Lieutenant Lawrence to West Freugh in Scotland; but the return trip on New Year's Day 1940 was not smooth sailing because the weather was winter at its worst. They got lost in the overcast and after stooging around for an interminable age they were forced to land, short of fuel and daylight, in a farmer's paddock.

The squadron continued its conversion training on Blenheims, Trent's first night solo being, as already told, almost his last. His

The Blenheim Mk IV in which F/Lt Lawrence and P/O Trent flew from West Freugh on 1 January 1940. They were forced down by snow in an emergency field.

flying hours were slowly mounting — although he was still a long, long way from being a 'million-air' when Holland, Belgium and France were simultaneously attacked by the Germans and the 'balloon went up' on 10 May 1940. In a letter home he wrote:

Dear People,

Well the war has started in dead earnest for me, the thing which we have been waiting for has come to pass — ... at 3 o'clock on the morning of 10 May things went up with a bang. The Germans landed parachute troops on all the Dutch dromes and on beaches and in fields. Two of our planes set out during the morning to do single aircraft recco [reconnaissance], also two from 40 Squadron. Both ours returned safely with only a few holes, but one of the 40 Squadron was shot down and the other was so shot up it burst into flames upon landing, but no one was hurt much and the fire was put out ...

At that time Pilot Officer Trent, the junior commissioned member of 15 Squadron, had a total of 450 hours in his log book; of that figure, only 85 hours — including 65 minutes of night flying — had been clocked in Blenheims.

On that fateful Friday, Trent was the pilot of one of the three Blenheims from 15 Squadron detailed to bomb German troops and transport equipment on Waalhaven aerodrome near Rotterdam.

The German moves had been decisive, their opening attacks being on Schipol aerodrome in Holland, the barracks at Amsterdam and the anti-aircraft defences close by. Soon after, parachute troops descended on key points in and around The Hague — Delft, Zandvoord, Ymuiden, The Hook, Eindhoven, Dordrecht and Trent's target — Waalhaven; which they succeeding in capturing.

By the afternoon of Friday 10 May the four major airfields in Fortress Holland — Waalhaven, Ypenburg, Ockenburg and Walkenburg — were in German hands, despite strong Dutch resistance.

The enemy's first move after seizing the airfields was to land large numbers of troop-carrying aircraft and although the Dutch re-captured one or two aerodromes, the hordes poured in. German aircraft also landed in strength on the foreshore of Katwijk, Scheveningen and Wassenaar.

As a result of these airborne attacks, one Dutch army corps in Fortress Holland was immobilized and the Dordrecht district in southern Rotterdam fell to German control.

The Royal Air Force immediately gave all aid possible to the beleaguered Dutch.

Trent took off from Wyton in one of a flight of three Blenheims led by Flight Lieutenant Lawrence. His observer/bomb-aimer was Sergeant Prior and his wireless operator/air-gunner was Corporal Sutcliffe. This, his first aggressive mission over enemy-occupied territory, promised to be considerably more exciting than his high level reconnaissance flight over Germany when he was flying Battles in France. In his letter, he remarked:

> ... Although I had been out over the North Sea looking for ships and subs on odd occasions with every chance of encountering enemy fighters, I had never been out with the set intention of bombing something or bust.
>
> I must say it seemed a bit of a bad dream, and I had to pinch myself to make it clear it was ... no practice.

The flight climbed to 3000 feet and, as they approached the target area, they moved into echelon-starboard formation prior to making their dive-bomb attacks. Below them an amazing sight unfolded as they ran up on Waalhaven aerodrome. About one third of the airfield was crammed with German transport aircraft — great high-winged, tri-motored Junkers 52s that had shed their jack-booted cargoes — while the trampled grass, everywhere free of aeroplanes, was strewn with the spent parachutes from the airborne invaders. From the air it looked like a field blooming with daisies.

Lawrence peeled off for his dive, followed by his No. 2. Then it was Trent — and his bombs were sent on their way. The ground ack-ack was intense as he plummeted earthwards; bullet holes were showing their jagged edges along the Blenheim's wings. God, he thought frantically, this is *war*!

The plus-nine boost, like an overdose of adrenalin, was roaring the aircraft along, surely lower on the deck and faster than Flying Officer Mottram could have coaxed out of any Blenheim? Six Messerschmitt 109s ripped overhead. Jesus, thought Trent, now

I'll have to dogfight my way out of this! But they got involved in another tangle and it was then that Nature, conspiring against the harried RAF aircraft and its crew, set a seagull on a collision course. The bird burst through the twin panes of the front bomb-sighting panel, disintegrating all over Sergeant Prior in a mess of blood and guts and feathers, and letting in a frightful draught.

With the squadron experiencing its first blooding in actual combat and the fighting war now beginning in earnest, certain adjustments within the unit's chain of command were being made. Wing Commander 'Boom' Lywood arrived and took over control of the squadron. The previous commanding officer, Squadron Leader Llewelyn, took over one flight and Squadron Leader John Glenn took over the other — the flight in which Len Trent served.

By noon on 10 May while the Germans were landing airborne troops in Holland, French attempts to advance in Southern Luxembourg had been held by the enemy and the invaders were pressing on into Belgium over undestroyed bridges near Maastricht. Fort Eben Emael had been captured by parachute troops and Liege was thus threatened.

On 11 May the Germans attacked the Albert Canal position in flank with mechanized divisions coming from Aix-la-Chapelle and in front with troops which crossed the northern part of Dutch Limburg and moved on Hasselt.

When on 12 May it was learned that two bridges across the Albert Canal, west of Maastricht, had not been destroyed — and that the enemy was pouring across them — 15 Squadron was detailed to bomb the crossings.

On that Sunday in spring, while the good villagers around Wyton were going to their churches, twelve Blenheims took off for Belgium and the bridges over the Albert Canal. Trent piloted one of the six aircraft in Squadron Leader Glenn's flight.

They approached their target at 5000 feet, vigilantly on the alert for enemy fighters but thankful that, so far, none had appeared. Then came the anti-aircraft fire with such intensity that Trent felt none could survive. Shrapnel was making jagged rents in the wings and the fuselage of his Blenheim when Glenn waved his flight into individual dive-bombing attack. It was an awful prospect that presented itself to the crews — a situation from which, all were sure, none could escape alive. The air was thick with flak which was being hosed up at them in terrifying streams.

The bridge at Maastricht, which was Trent's vital target during the Battle of Flanders, 1940.

Trent gave his machine its injection of plus-nine boost and pushed the column forward, keeping a broad aim on his target while he pushed hard on each rudder pedal, skidding the aircraft away from any steady bead the ground ack-ack batteries might hope to fasten on him.

Bombs gone! Now, screaming down towards the deck — and with his engines still roaring with plus-nine power — he hedge-hopped, weaving and jinking, away from the target area. A line of German soldiers, in an open field, crossed the sights of his wing-mounted .303 gun. He thumbed the firing tit on his control column and saw the tracer snaking out, guiding his aim. 'I'll get a few of them,' he promised himself, dropping the nose of the Blenheim still lower.

But, in his concentration on the now wildly scattering infantrymen, he had not seen a line of tall poplars ahead, drawing dangerously closer, as he ripped across the grasstops. In a heart-stopping moment he hauled back on the stick, clipping the tender spring leaves of one of the trees and pushed his aircraft down again to ground level. The engines hiccupped characteristically and, again in rapport with gravity, they took up the healthy roar of full-powered flight.

Everywhere were the red flames of invasion. Trent and his crew flew past a Belgian airfield with hangars and aircraft blazing furiously. The enraged defenders of both an aerodrome and a homeland now doomed, opened fire with rifles and machine guns, believing the Blenheim to be Hitler's hated Luftwaffe. In a letter home, he wrote:

> ... I passed our Belgian flying field with the Hangars burning and a dozen aircraft burnt out on the field, then a short time later I passed another field with the people running for their lives and throwing themselves with great abandon onto their stomachs. There were no hangars and the few aircraft I spotted as I flashed across, were hidden in trees and carried Belgian markings . . .
>
> The most saddening thing to see was all the swarms of refugees. They were crowding the roads all the way from the frontier and as I roared just over their heads they dropped everything and made for the sides of the roads only to find me gone before their bundles had reached the ground ... I felt so sorry for them I could have cried easily. Thank goodness you people are spared all that. It makes me sick and mad at the same time to think of all the misery those poor people are going through. Their men dashing off to war and the women and children left to fend for themselves.

As if the battlefield in Belgium was not shocking enough on that Sunday of 12 May an incident on the circuit at Wyton, as Trent joined the landing pattern, gave the young officer and his crew an unnerving welcome home. Trent tells it as he remembers it:

> I was horrified to see a Blenheim, turning on to its final approach with a dead port motor, overbank and stall. It dropped out of control to crash in flames ahead of us.
>
> Our knowledge and experience of asymmetric (want of balanced power) flight was practically nil; but in those days, I seem to remember, we were told never to turn towards the dead engine. It was very much later that we learned to understand the dynamics of single-engine control, safety heights and critical speeds associated with asymmetric flight.

After Len Trent and his crew-mates had landed they heard that, of the twelve squadron aircraft that had set off on the Maastricht mission, six had been lost — a 50 percent casualty rate that did not make an encouraging start for 15 Squadron in the first phases of the fighting war.

There were vacant seats around both the officers' and the NCOs' dining tables that evening, and no banter was tossed back and forth around the bars of either mess. Len Trent was particularly shaken at losing his Australian chum, Bert Oakley, with whom he had struck up a very close friendship. Other good mates who would not return were Tom Bassett, Bill Frankish and Robbie Robinson. Later, he wrote:

> ... I think I am still partly stunned. Out of the twelve aircraft that went from our squadron, only six returned to England. The ones missing were all my friends. Bert Oakley and Tom Bassett are missing, my two best friends in the squadron. Of course I never say die, no one saw them shot down, they may have landed anywhere with engine trouble. No one saw much at all except the target, then ack-ack fire, then the tree tops ... We haven't heard from Bert or

F/Lt Paul Chapman, who commanded B Flight, 15 Squadron. He was killed in action at Sedan in May 1940 — the day the squadron lost both its flight commanders.

Tom yet, but it is still early and news will be hard to get out of Belgium. I won't give up hope for a month ... Gosh all my old pals are going missing, one by one, still I feel sure some of them will turn up with many a tale to tell ...

In those early days the anguish of losing close companions was raw. Later, as sensitivities began to numb from the constant exposure to danger and death, a phrase became common throughout all ranks in the RAF. Fred or Harry or Charlie had not been killed, died, passed away or gone to his maker — he had 'gone for a burton'. The true origin of the phrase is lost in antiquity, as are so many sooths and sayings. But probably the most likely theory is that it came from a series of cartoon advertisements for a brand of British beer brewed by the firm of Burton. A character in each sketch would be asking of an absent fellow's whereabouts: 'Where's 'arry?' The plug-line would tell him: 'Gone for a Burton!' A little sad whimsy screened a lot of misery. Otherwise the mess lounge would have become as doleful as the waiting room of a morgue.

14 May was a disastrous day for the Allies. The German advance broke through the French Ninth Army defending the River Meuse and crossed that waterway, so making a breach in the line between Sedan and Dinant. The Allied armies in Eastern Belgium were then in immediate peril of being outflanked.

The gallant Fairey Battles — so recently the machines in which Trent had flown — were putting up a tremendous but costly delaying action against the enemy flood that was now pouring into France. Sixty-seven took off to bomb the bridges between Mouzon and Sedan at 3 p.m. Only thirty-two — less than half — returned.

On 15 May amid the very real concern sweeping the Allied forces, 15 Squadron was moved to Alconbury, a grass airfield in Huntingdon not far from Wyton. And the Blenheims were dispersed around the perimeter awaiting the next assignment from Bomber Command Headquarters.

The European situation was fluid — as fluid as the grey, greedy torrents tumbling through a burst dam. Once over the Meuse, the Germans were eager to exploit their success. By 16 May the forward elements of the British Army were in position on the River Dyle, with the Belgians on their left. The Germans were moving south through a wide gap on the right of the First French Army — which lay on the British right — and were attacking Avesnes and Vervins, about 65 kilometres west of the Meuse.

Now in open country, they were racing for new gains in France and the daylight targets they presented to RAF bombers were troop concentrations, armoured vehicles and transport convoys. By night our bombers attacked railway junctions, marshalling yards and oil dumps in Western Germany and — now overrun by the enemy — Belgium.

Meanwhile, at Alconbury, the Blenheims of 15 Squadron were standing by. Trent was awake and dressed, awaiting the order to take off, at 2.30 a.m. on the morning of 16 May. All day he remained in readiness, expecting any minute to hear the tannoy crackle and call him to the operations room. It was the same the next day; and the nerves of the aircrews were stretched and twanging like fiddle strings. And then, on the morning of 18 May they were summoned from their sleep at dawn and twelve Blenheims were airborne for France to land at Abbeville, east of Amiens, and await briefings on targets.

Len Trent had no idea that the Germans could move south so fast after their rout of Holland and Belgium. After lunch the aircraft of 15 Squadron were ordered to attack enemy troop concentrations on the approaches to Landrecies, with Lawrence leading six Blenheims in close formation at 3000 feet.

'We encountered no German fighters as we approached, thank God,' says Trent, 'but when we sighted tanks and motor transport stacked up near the entrance to the town, we ran into very heavy ack-ack fire as we started our dive-bombing attack.'

The Blenheims bombed independently, hurtling down seemingly into the very muzzles of the enemy guns before unloading their missiles and breaking away in hasty low-level retreat.

Trent, hedge-hopping towards his temporary base at Abbeville at a very low level, had his aircraft hit several times — from both an aggressive Me.109 and fire from the ack-ack batteries. The German fighter gave persistent chase but aborted his attack after a while as Trent kept up his ground-level evasive manoeuvres.

As a gaping hole in the starboard wing suggested ominous structural damage to his machine, Len Trent decided to land at Poix, a French airfield now occupied by the RAF. An examination by a precise and officious engineering officer showed the

starboard main spar — the prime lateral support for the wing —
had been pierced by cannon fire. He promptly 'made the aircraft
u/s' — which is to say he endorsed the aircraft's flying log, the
Form 700, to state the Blenheim was unserviceable and not to be
flown until the damage was rectified.

Meanwhile Trent and his crew had begged a lift to the RAF
mess establishments in the local town, two or three miles away;
the NCOs going their way and their pilot finding shelter at the
Officers' Mess — a requisitioned house — where, finally, he was
able to sit down, weary and famished, for a meal at 7.30 p.m.

But hunger and exhaustion were not to be appeased. Hardly
had he taken his first forkful of food when panic, wildly vocal,
struck the mess. 'Everybody out! The Germans are coming!
They're only three miles away just down the road!'

Len Trent tells of events that followed, the incidents almost as
clear in his mind today as they were more than 40 years ago:

Knives and forks clattered on plates and fifteen or twenty chairs
crashed over backwards as everyone made for the door. I could
find no one to direct me to the sergeants' mess, where my two
crew members were resting, because everywhere was panic
and it was everyone for himself.

Our mess seemed to be in the middle of a small town and I
recalled there were crossroads nearby. I went there and found a
French officer directing traffic — and what traffic it was! Old
cars, farm carts, wheelbarrows, perambulators piled high with
household treasures, old people carrying bundles, small
children and a lumbering French tank all added up to a scene
that was sheer, bloody pandemonium.

It was dusk and the urgent thing was to find my crew. But
where to start? I walked rapidly up one road, returned and
walked as rapidly up another, fearful of losing myself in my
search for the sergeants' mess. Then suddenly, amidst the press
of panic, I ran slap into them. They came weaving along,
grinning and swinging a parachute bag full of champagne and
liquor between them. They were both very drunk and very
happy with life, feeling no pain or panic.

Their faces wreathed in smiles, they greeted me gustily:
'Good ol' Len!' It was the first time they had ever used my given
name. Their slap-happy condition gave poor indications of the

help I could expect in getting our aircraft back to England that night. My evident agitation they thought hilarious and they were more concerned in trying to persuade me to continue the party with them in a local pub.

However, the message began to penetrate with my urgent persuasions and they followed me to the crossroads where I got the military policeman to stop a car going towards the airfield and we were on board in a flash. By the time we had arrived it was quite dark. I found the harassed engineering officer who, fortunately as it happened, hadn't touched my aircraft. But, again, he flatly refused to refuel it or clear it for flight. In fact, he threatened me with a court martial if I so much as moved it.

But I was both frightened and angry and well aware of the consequences of just sitting and doing nothing while the enemy was practically breathing down our necks. So immediately after the engineering officer disappeared in the gloom I ordered my crew on board. There was a glassy crash and a dull explosion as the parachute bag was dropped from the roof hatch to the floor of the cockpit; and by the time I had kicked away the wheel chocks and clambered into the cockpit the bouquet of expensive champers, now swirling around my rudder pedals, would have done credit to the Lido in Paris.

Sergeant Prior, my navigator, was obviously in no condition to plot a course to some safe airfield to the south, even if we knew of any, so I decided to head for our home base in England, using courses I had roughly committed to memory. Checking the fuel gauges, I estimated we would have enough; but, as the Duke of Wellington once remarked, it would be 'a near run thing.'

And so, with no help from a preoccupied ground crew and their big mobile starter-battery, I got engine power by using the Blenheim's internal batteries, holding the machine against her brakes as the propellers bit at the air. Without any delay, or testing the engines for magneto-drop, I simply taxied as fast as possible to a clear stretch of grass, turned into wind and gave the throttles full travel. It was an unknown airfield and there was no flarepath to guide me and so it was with considerable relief that I felt the aircraft lift off, free from any obstruction, and climb away.

I kept my eyes fixed in fearful fascination on the engine

revolution counters, expecting any second to see a colossal magneto-drop reading and hear the ominous cough and splutter of a dying engine. But the cylinders kept pushing out their power and I was soon able to breathe again. Perhaps that is why a pilot has to prove he can hold his breath for more than a minute?

At 500 feet I felt safe and throttled back, climbing gently towards the English Channel. And once over the water I turned north, intending to turn in over the home coast at Orfordness, in Norfolk — supposedly a safe entry lane. However, I was just passing Cap Gris Nez, about a mile out to sea, when I was challenged by a French searchlight.

My Very pistol carried the colours of the day up to 10 p.m., so I pooped off a red-and-green signal, not realizing that the time then was a few minutes after deadline, when the authorized colours changed. So there I was, with navigation lights burning as required by the French, when the first few ack-ack tracer shells came lazily up towards me. It was my first experience of being shot at by night — and it was quite pretty and fascinating, if one could forget the danger.

With all hell breaking loose and flak flying, I switched off my navigation lights, gave the Blenheim plus-nine boost and climbed away from the land to 5000 feet — none of these manoeuvres helping my pilot-navigation reckonings or my fuel consumption. But they did tend to sober my bleary navigator, who began to take more of an interest in our futures — and his own in particular.

A natural desire to reach the English coast, coupled with concern for my dwindling fuel, probably made me turn left too soon. The dead-reckoning navigation of a daylight bomber crew under such gloomy and hazardous conditions could not be described as scientifically reliable.

So we flew over the coast — somewhere in England — and within minutes we spotted a dim avenue of goose-necked flares inviting us to land. Heaven sent! I dived for the circuit, throttled back and pulled the poor Blenheim around in a tight turn, clean forgetting the damaged main spar of the starboard wing. I lowered my undercarriage on a steep turn on to my final approach and was down on solid Mother England, breathing heavily and gratefully, in a matter of minutes.

Soon I was to discover that the only reason the flarepath had been lit was because I had flown right through the Harwich balloon barrage (a highly sensitive area) and only an ignorant German aircraft would do *that*. So the Martlesham Heath Blenheim night fighters had been scrambled to shoot me down. Their lack of success had simply been because they had not anticipated I would try to land.

Next day, reflecting on my night-flying performance, I could only suppose it was sharpened by an injection of adrenalin, promoted by the horrible spectacle of my fuel gauges registering empty.

On that grim sortie on Landrecies we lost both our very fine and experienced flight commanders, Lawrence and Chapman. And, along with them went another very good friend, Flying Officer Clark. Three crews lost out of six. Not good arithmetic at all.

5

DUNKIRK — AND AFTER

BY 19 MAY THE ENEMY in France had reached the Oise-Aisne Canal and the notable Chemin des Dames in the south. To the north they were at the line of the Scheldt held by the British Army. Nevertheless, despite a British counter-attack near Arras on 21 May, the Germans pushed on to reach the sea at Le Touquet.

The Blenheims of 15 Squadron were on stand-by through the hours of 19 and 20 May. About noon on 21 May a flight led by Squadron Leader Llewelyn was briefed to locate and bomb enemy concentrations around Montriel. Trent, included in the sortie, followed his leader into the target area. On the signal to attack independently, he dived to bomb the German tanks and transport vehicles, firing his wing gun for moral support as he ploughed through the usual heavy ack-ack fire:

> I thought of poor old Sergeant Prior, my navigator, just sitting — or, more probably, crouching — in his forward navigation compartment with nothing to do but watch the flak bursting around us while he hoped and prayed. And, when the excitement had subsided and we were heading for home, it occurred to me that he, too, should have a forward-firing gun to help keep his mind off the lumps of hot metal that were being thrown up at us.

So Trent asked the friendly armourers at base to rig up a machine gun to poke through the small triangular window below the clear-vision bombing panel in the nose of the aircraft. They obliged with an air-cooled Vickers K machine gun — as used in the Blenheim's dorsal turret — flexibly mounted so that Prior could spray his fire around a bit.

The Blenheim crew took off on an airborne gun test and when

Trent found a suitable deserted field he dived at an imaginary foe and gave the signal for Prior to fire. Instantly the navigation compartment and the cockpit were filled with cordite fumes and ricocheting brass .303 bullet cases, the spent husks clattering against the perspex panels, metal and men with considerable force.

No garbage bin for their disposal!

So back to the drawing board. The armourers then attached a canvas bag to the side of the gun's breach and the empty cases thenceafter rattled in with a merry tintinnabulation.

But there was never a war without its bureaucracy. The station armament officer heard of the strange and unauthorized secret weapon and ordered its immediate removal until all specifications and machine drawings had been submitted to, and approved by, Group Headquarters. Trent righteously annoyed, said he would refuse to fly without the gun even if, as the armament officer had promised, he would be court martialled.

The gun remained — and it proved a great success.

By this time, some of the war-blooded Blenheim aircrews were introducing their own defensive devices into the aircraft. Pieces of steel armour plating were reinforcing seats and backrests, giving added protection to sensitive areas of the human anatomy. A practice with some pilots was to remove the inside headband of a tin helmet so that the metal dome could fit over the leather flying helmet as the aircraft entered the enemy's range of fire. Not only shrapnel and bullets were the hazards. Splintered perspex could — and did — cause some ugly scalp wounds.

One such victim in 15 Squadron was 'Red' Eames. A German 20 millimetre cannon shell had hit the transparent roof of his cockpit and in the resultant explosion Eames had sustained severe head lacerations. He was admitted to Ely Hospital where he became a fellow patient with Squadron Leader Glenn of 15 Squadron, who was under treatment for a leg complaint.

On 22 May Trent and his crew were briefed to locate the road to Hesdin, along which the German troops were advancing, and bomb the transport vehicles at the head of the column. Like all their operations since the war had begun in earnest on 10 May, it was a hazardous mission and the ground and air fire was wicked. A few days later, he wrote:

I could see a column advancing along the road and into Montreuil, in the middle of which was a square packed with transports. I prayed it was German and aimed one 250 pound [bomb] at it from 2000 feet then continued in a shallow dive up the road, where I could see masses of army transport. I lined the road up and dropped the whole cargo of assorted [bombs]. I was about a 1000 feet and could feel the burst under me, and could also see guns mounted on the lorries firing away as hard as they could go. I then pushed off for the coast flying at a low level and on looking back I could see a couple of huge fires on the road where I had bombed ... I certainly hope they were Germans, they *must have* been, as I couldn't see any refugees. It is very difficult to identify friend from foe from the air, unless you are definitely told they are in a certain place.

The following day, with Glenn still in hospital, Flight Lieutenant Lawrence killed and the sorely battered squadron now peopled with a lot of inexperienced aircrews from Bicester Operational Training Unit, Pilot Officer Trent was smartly promoted two steps to become Flight Lieutenant Trent.

He was given command of A Flight and Flight Lieutenant Jess Oakshott was appointed B Flight commander.

Abbeville Aerodrome, now in German hands, was the target for the squadron's attack on 24 May and Trent led a sub-vic of three aircraft detailed to bomb in formation from 5000 feet. The plan had called for a fighter escort for the Blenheims but if any Hurricanes or Spitfires were around, the bomber crews did not see them. It was on that sortie that Squadron Leader Llewelyn was shot down by Me.109 fighters after he had completed his bombing run and was on his way home.

On 27 May Len Trent led a formation of six planes to bomb Calais; and again the escort fighters were absent. But at least the flight escaped the Me.109s.

By 29 May the Germans had penned down the British Army in the area round Dixmude and Armentiéres while Lille, the last French stronghold in the north, was sorely threatened. Trent led a sortie of six machines to Courtrai, again having no escort fighters to shepherd them over the target. Adding insult to injury, they found on their return to England that Wyton was fogbound, so they had to land at Abingdon.

Lille fell to the invaders on 31 May. The evacuation of Dunkirk

— 'Operation Dynamo' — was taxing every Allied effort in removing the 193,568 British officers and men, together with 123,095 French troops, from the beaches. Meanwhile, Flight Lieutenant Trent was leading his aircraft on reconnaissance and bombing sorties around St Omer, Aire, Hazelbrook, Cassel and Watten. 'No escort,' his log-book entry reads. 'Why we were not shot down, God only knows.'

The Dunkirk sky was no place for any aircraft, friend or foe, while the big sea lift of the beleaguered troops was in train. Anything larger than a seagull moving across the Allied gunsights could expect a furious barrage of naval ack-ack and military small-arms fire. Jess Oakshott, newly promoted boss of B Flight, had his Blenheim's rudder shot away by some misguided gunner on a British destroyer and so when Trent led his vic of three aircraft to a Hondschoote target, at the back of the beaches, he was careful not to fly near the evacuation area.

The following day he led a flight of six Blenheims to St Valerie, looking for German troop concentrations, and a few days later saw him taking another six to Miannay to locate and bomb enemy advance armour and transports.

Soon after, there was another raid on St Valerie; on 14 June Trent led six Blenheims to find and bomb the enemy at Vernon, near Paris. 'We wandered about the sky with no fighter escort, looking for targets,' he recalls. 'Again, we were lucky not to encounter enemy fighters.'

But the stresses of battle were beginning to make themselves clearly manifest. With Squadron Leader Glenn still on sick leave, the strain of constantly having to lead all A Flight sorties with no practical back-up or administration assistance — together with the unending dawn-to-dusk standby for instant take-off, plus the tensions of combat — ended for Trent in what must have been a nervous collapse. He describes the chain of events:

After the Vernon sortie we had been talking in the mess. I had half a pint of beer and went to bed early, feeling perfectly OK but just tired. I got up sometime in the night for a pee and woke up on the floor hugging the loo. No recollection of feeling faint. So, really shaken — as I had never fainted in my life, before that — I clambered to my feet and walked down the corridor to my room.

I next came-to half way under the bed. So I got to my feet, really worried, and managed to sleep without incident through the rest of the night. Although I was feeling reasonably well after breakfast, I decided I had better go and discuss my fainting fits with the station medical officer. I was apprehensive that I could pass out cold while flying.

The MO examined me and declared I needed a short holiday. His findings were that my heart had been beating at such a high rate for so long that I was just plain 'worn out'. This was strange, as I felt quite well within myself and, in fact, believed that I had become case-hardened to operational flying.

Perhaps, preying at the back of my mind, there was the statistical fact that, at that time, the life of a Blenheim pilot was reckoned to be about three sorties. And I had survived fourteen. Also, sadly in my memory, were the fates of so many of my old squadron companions, along with all those fledgling lads straight out of OTU training who had failed to return.

Amongst the early squadron members killed, were: Llewelyn, Chapman, Lawrence, Clark, Oakley, Bassett, Robinson, Dawson and Douglas. Of the original eighteen officers, those still surviving, after a month and 4 days of hectic combat since that fateful day of 10 May 1940, were Eames (in hospital), Oakshott, George and Webster.

Webster was fortunate. Although he had been shot down over France, he had eventually made it back to England. Soon after Webster returned to base, Trent had written to his family:

... Gosh it was so good to see him again. He had been flying and suddenly he spotted some tanks, but too late to bomb them, so he turned back to attack and in his own words, 'they sure turned on the taps'. He in turn dropped all he had on board ... However they shot away his aileron controls, poured all the oil out of both engines, so that they were due to seize up any moment, and also shot all the floor out of his aircraft between his observer and himself. He kept on going towards the coast, but had to go down long before he got there ... Down he went, parked it in a field and destroyed what was left ... From what he tells things are sure a shambles in France. As far as I could make out fifth column activists are spreading all sorts of rumours causing great confusion. He [Webster] heard in Boulogne

that the French had given in and [he] quite believed it ... He tells one
funny story of an R E officer he met on the boat, who was all cut to
pieces and looked the very hell of a mess. This officer was standing on
the road and saw some tanks coming along, so thought he would
thumb a lift. When about 50 yards away they suddenly opened fire on
him, but he miraculously escaped serious injury and hurled himself
through a bramble hedge. He then ran ... with the tanks after him.
They had just gone straight through the hedge. He came upon
another road and found a bicycle which he mounted in haste and
began to pedal like blazes with the tanks still after him and still
shooting. He was chased for about 10 miles but didn't stop for about
20 miles ...

Webster was to be killed in a mid-air accident over Boscombe
Down after the war. Oakshott was killed flying a Mosquito on a
bombing run over Fleuisburg in 1942. Eames and George were to
survive the war.

After his 14 days of leave Trent returned to find he had been
posted to 17 Operational Training Unit, Upwood, to recount his
operational experience and try and explain his phenomenal luck
to the embryo aircrews being schooled for battle.

He had indeed emerged — not entirely unscathed — through a
period of fierce and costly warfare. From May 10 to June 20,
Bomber Command lost 40 percent of its first-line strength —
mostly Battles and Blenheims.

And yet the war had barely begun.

When a combat flyer completed his quota of operations against
the enemy — his 'tour of ops' — and was posted to airborne
instructional duties at an Air Force training unit, it was popularly
supposed that he was 'on rest' and could, figuratively speaking,
put his feet up on the Sperry panel, take out a packet of Players and
let his bright-eyed pupil pull and push the knobs and tits and wheel
the wondrous toy around the sky in gentle circles.

Not wholly so. Many erstwhile battle-weary pilots,
disillusioned by the monotony of tutoring, the drudgery and the
downright dangers of shepherding woolly-brained and ham-fisted
students in the arts of aeronautics, pined to get back into more
positive arenas of action.

At 17 OTU, Upwood, Trent found himself teaching trainee

pilots the necessary skills of formation flying. From the ground, the sight of a flight or squadron of aircraft tucked tightly together might suggest, to the layman, a simple disposition of machines running in juxtaposition as easily as so many motorcars across a stretch of open country.

Formation flying is not that easy, and only practice — constant and often hazardous practice — can achieve effective results. For a start, an aircraft does not have brakes like a car; so it is only by carefully and constantly moving the throttles that a pilot can 'keep station' with his leader. Too little power and his aircraft drops back. And if he over-compensates in trying to make up distance lost he finds himself getting ahead of his leader. That is when wing-tips begin to tangle.

Many pupils, and many experienced instructors who had deserved a better fate, were killed in formation-flying exercises during the war years.

So why did the aircraft fly in formation? A tight three-vic or larger box in close formation presented a far more formidable reception committee for any marauding enemy fighters than did a lonely, laggard aeroplane that had dropped behind its fellows. Importantly, fighter escorts were better able to protect compact formations of bombers.

Leavening his formation-flying teachings in Blenheims were instructional flights in Avro Ansons, wherein Canadian-trained pilots grappled with the charms and mysteries of map-reading their ways across the English countryside while a patient Trent invariably and literally put them back on the right track. 'Aw, Jeeze ... the railway tracks in this country jes' look like a bit of ol' knitting. I jes' cain't sort 'em out!' That was the nub of many a moan.

Nor were the dead-reckoning navigation exercises without incident. One stubborn trainee navigator, pondering his turning points while Trent's Anson puttered along at 2000 feet in heavy cloud and rain, handed his instructor-pilot a course-chit and Trent forthwith swung the aircraft on to the new heading. Suddenly, out of the thick murk of fog and rain and smoke, the steel cable of a balloon flashed ahead of the starboard wing. Trent, in the fastest manoeuvre he had ever made, swung the aircraft hard to port, turning through 90 degrees. He expected, any second, to have a wing clipped.

The young navigator, insisting that the meteorological office's wind forecast *must* be right — and that, presumably, winds remain constant — had refused to believe the wireless operator's director-finding bearings and the erroneous dead-reckoning course had sent the aircraft smack into the Sheffield balloon barrage.

Now, in the month of July 1940 and with fears of a German invasion ever present, even the slow and gentle Ansons were always fully armed with .303 machine guns and with bombs at stand-by. Always prepared to keep his trigger thumb supple, Len Trent invariably set off many 5 second bursts from his forward-firing gun. A favoured target range was a lake near Kettering, Northampton, where boys from a nearby village made an excited audience as, from their hilltop perch, they watched the water being thrashed with white weals as the Anson's attacks drove home.

Trent never returned with much ammunition unfired.

Meanwhile, he was making the most of the occasional day and weekend leave passes that he might win; and his little MG car was put to good use. He and Ursula Woolhouse decided to get married on 7 August.

Wartime weddings were, almost always, short on honeymoon time. The RAF allowed Len and Ursula Trent 3 days before they were back at Upwood and setting up home in a two-family house — one upstairs, one downstairs, and the kitchen shared.

Just a mile from the Trent's new home was a Q-site, one of those mysterious wartime establishments that housed some vital components in the broad scheme of Britain's defences. With an active German intelligence, it could be supposed that the enemy had the place listed as a specific target, for shortly after the Trents moved in a night intruder dropped a stick of eight bombs, exploding at 3 second intervals. The last one, as later discovered, had fallen only 400 yards from the house — although Trent had been certain it had hit the back garden.

About 2 months after he had been posted to Upwood, Trent had the news that he had been awarded the Distinguished Flying Cross for his efforts in the stubbornly-fought Battle of Flanders.

Flying-instruction work on a training station was not all sunshine and roses and it is only in retrospect that some of the incidents of daily events, embarrassing and sometimes startling at the time, emerge with a trace or two of humour bequeathed by the years.

Trent was but one of the many pilots who fell into the Anson's pyrotechnical trap for the unwary. It was wartime practice for every aircraft to carry a Very pistol so that, if challenged by a trigger-happy and (alleged) friendly gun emplacement, ship or fellow aeroplane, the pilot could pop off the recognized 'colours of the day' to announce his harmless intent.

In most aircraft the pistol was holstered in a receptacle that had an aperture opening into the air below the fuselage. When the British flak began to fly, all the indignant pilot had to do was pull the trigger to illuminate the minds of his attackers.

But this arrangement was not in vogue in the Anson. The signal pistol was snugged in a stowage with a solid bottom. When he was challenged (and provided he had been told of the procedure), the pilot would draw the pistol, slide open his port-side window, and so make his peace.

Trent, so soon off Blenheims and so used to sudden challenges and prompt replies, had cause to use his Anson's Very pistol one night when he had six passengers aboard. When the first flash of searchlight challenge appeared he instinctively reached for the trigger of the pistol, close by his left knee. Instantly, the cockpit was filled with white smoke and two red balls of fire ricocheted between the plywood sides, the instrument panel and the perspex windows of the Anson's extensive glasshouse.

The six passengers, moving as one in a wild panic, rushed as far from the excitement as they could huddle — hard up against the bulkhead of the tail section. Immediately, the aeroplane's nose rose alarmingly and a stall was imminent. But, with the pilot's demands for order, his urgent twisting on the trim wheel and his prompt use of the fire extinguisher, some measure of comparative calm returned and they returned smokily to base.

If the aircrews liked low-flying exercises (and most pilots, at least, did), some earthbound spectators were not quite so thrilled. On one map-reading navigation flight around the beautiful Vale of Eversham, Worcestershire, Trent flew his aircraft and his sweating pupil so low that an angry farmer flung up a mangel-wurzel which passed over the starboard wing. It can be reasonably expected that, to his dying day, that strong-armed rustic bored many a gathering at the local pub with his tale of how he 'once hit a bloody aeroplane with a bloody beet.'

Len Trent's time at Upwood gave him opportunities of flying some operational aircraft other than Blenheims and Ansons. A few Wellington bombers, as notable in their day as the lighter Blenheims, came to the station for storage; and it was required that the staff pilots fly the machines as occasion demanded.

Trent, with about 8 hours experience at the controls of the canvas-skinned 'Wimpy', flew one to Hatfield to pick up a squadron-leader friend and his WAAF fiancée. He let the more experienced officer take the controls for the return trip, while the girl, no doubt agog with wonder, sat beside her swain in the co-pilot's seat. Trent, in confidence and chivalry, stood below the astro-dome, keeping a casual eye on proceedings for'ard.

They landed at Polebrook — several times, as it turned out. The first ungodly contact with the runway knocked Trent off his perch, and the unique geodetic framework of the Wellington's fuselage flexed so much that the aircraft's aerial broke. The poor old Wimpy eventually ran out of bounces and a rather embarrassed squadron leader taxied in, collected his fiancée from the co-pilot's seat and shambled off into the nearest obscurity.

Since her man was a squadron leader — and therefore above ham-fistedness — the girl probably thought *all* aircraft landings were supposed to be like that.

In August 1941 Len Trent was promoted to the rank of acting squadron leader; with that went a posting to Warboys, a satellite airfield of Upwood and quite near Wyton. He was to be Officer Commanding Operation Training Squadron.

6

BOSTON BOTHER

THE FIRST BOSTON aircraft to arrive in Britain from the United States was W8363. It was delivered to Warboys, where it created quite a stir; and the newly appointed O.C. Operational Training Squadron, Squadron Leader Trent, was soon to have his first (and almost his last) flight in that revolutionary, tricycle-undercarriaged medium bomber. He tells of his experiences:

Wing Commander Nelson, the chief instructor, flew this wonderful aircraft, the first tricycle aircraft we had seen in England to that date. It had been delivered to Warboys airfield by a ferry pilot who had left one copy of the pilots' handling notes before he departed.

Wing Commander Nelson had studied those notes, familiarized himself with all the knobs and switches in the cockpit, and had taken off and flown for an hour without incident, declaring the aircraft 'absolutely wonderful — like a fighter.' Indeed, it had a bank of four .3 machine guns firing forward and under the command of the pilot's thumb, as well as twin-mounted guns firing to the rear.

He gave me the pilots' notes and suggested I flew the aircraft the next day. There was no provision for dual controls in the cockpit.

Up to this point in my flying experience I had never encountered an aircraft engine with direct fuel jet injection instead of the standard carburettor. Also, the provision for feathering a constant-speed propeller was for me a new innovation but I could well understand the advantages of being able to turn the blades (or 'feather' them) knife-edged to the slipstream to minimize drag should an engine fail. That absence of drag on the side of the dead engine would obviously make single-engine flying very much easier.

And so I spent the evening hours carefully studying everything a pilot should know about his aircraft. Then, at 10 a.m. the next morning, in clear weather, I started both engines of the Boston without difficulty and taxied out to the end of the concrete runway, the booklet of pilots' handling notes handily stuffed in my battledress tunic and my mind running through the vital pre-flight checks.

A final run through the mnemonics of cockpit drill, a releasing of brakes and then, under the interested gaze of instructors, students and ground crew, I opened the throttles to thunder down the runway, feeling a surge of power considerably in excess of that of the old Blenheim.

Great stuff! No trouble in keeping the aircraft straight, thanks to the nose wheel, and I was just appreciating the advantages of the tricycle undercarriage when, at the point of lift-off and with only one third of the runway left, there was a terrific explosion on the starboard side. Instantly, the Boston tried to turn hard to the right. A startled glance showed me flames streaming back from the engine pod, losing themselves in the distance behind my right shoulder.

Here was the dread of all pilots — sudden engine failure at the most critical point of flight, just as the aircraft is becoming airborne but with insufficient runway left to cut all power and apply full brakes.

In a split-second decision I decided to continue the take-off. The alternative would clearly be a high-speed skidding departure from the end of the runway and down a fairly steep hill towards a small creek. So, checking the swing to starboard with hard left rudder, I moved the undercarriage lever to its 'UP' position through a complicated safety gate, then punched the feathering button to stop the starboard propeller, which was pumping fuel to the flames.

Instinctively, I turned off the ignition switches and the fuel cocks to the blazing engine and stabbed the fire extinguisher button before turning my attention to a line of trees on a ridge about a mile ahead.

Fearfully, I saw that I wasn't climbing as well as I had hoped. And then I saw the red lights glowing on the panel, indicating the undercarriage, while unlocked, had not retracted into the wells to give the aircraft optimum streamlining. In my haste to get to the feathering button I had not quite managed to get the undercarriage lever fully into the 'UP' position.

That corrected, the Boston climbed away on its one sound engine like a bird and missed the treetops by 200 feet. But the starboard propeller was still 'windmilling' and making its hindering drag; and the flames were still streaming across the wing surfaces to starboard as I turned, still climbing, on to the down-wind leg.

I made 800 feet and was at that point midway between base and my old station, Wyton. I was terrified that the persistent flames might cause a structural failure, burning through the main-spar alloy so that the Boston was in danger of shedding its starboard wing. I considered bailing out, but then doubted if, at such a low height, my parachute would have time to open and develop before I hit the ground.

By this time I had managed to trim the aircraft for asymmetric flight and it was responding well to 'hands off' control. Still conscious of the propeller windmilling in the breeze, I pulled the pilots' notes from my pocket and turned the pages rapidly to the paragraph on feathering to see if I had overlooked some vital action. But no. I had done everything by the book.

Anyhow, by this time I was in position in my landing pattern to turn cross-wind, ready for finals and, I hoped, a safe touchdown. I noticed with considerable relief that the fire seemed to have died somewhat, so my hopes were rising as I lined up on the runway.

Select undercarriage down! Three green lights — good! Partial landing flap — good, that's working too! Then I saw the station fire engine and crew at the landing end of the runway. Good, someone is on the ball! A mile to go ... full flap ... throttle back slowly ... and on to the runway. A good firm braking to a stop. Then up with the canopy and out like a startled rabbit! The fire engine was alongside, ready with foam and chemicals. But by now the flames had subsided.

The engine failure and subsequent fire had been the result of carelessness, or in RAF parlance 'finger trouble', on the part of an over-zealous engineering officer playing with the new toy.

Common with piston-powered radial aero engines was the tendency to 'hydraulic' if left stationary for any length of time. Oil or fuel that had accumulated from when the engine had last run would gradually trickle down to form pools on the lower cylinder-heads, resulting in diminished compression capacity.

Unless this accumulated oil was gently dispersed by hand-turning each propeller before starting the engines, the pistons in the affected cylinders, punching with power against a non-compressible cushion of oil, were likely to fracture big ends, little ends or connecting rods.

This had happened in the case of the Boston. The engineering officer had started the engines without first turning the propellers by hand. A fractured con rod had collapsed under the strain of full take-off power, causing the engine to blow up. This, in turn, had ruptured the oil pipe-line to the propeller feathering mechanism, depriving Trent of that control.

'Of all the narrow squeaks in a fairly exciting flying career, I consider this episode as an outstanding example of how I really had to think and act fast,' says Len Trent. 'There is no doubt that, had I the necessary height, I would have baled out. But, for staying at the controls and saving this very valuable aircraft, I received a special commendation from the Air Officer Commanding the Group in the form of a "green" endorsement in my log book.'

On 2 March 1942 Trent was posted to Headquarters No. 2 Group as Squadron Leader Operations. The Air Officer Commanding was Air Vice-Marshal 'Nunky' Lees and the Senior Air Staff Officer was Group Captain Bill Hesket, who was, as Trent puts it, 'a marvellous fellow with a great sense of humour.'

The job entailed short bouts of feverish activity sandwiched between lots of time sitting in the operations room waiting. Much of that waiting time was spent playing 'battleships' with a very young Wing Commander Derek Rowe, whom the sage and sear bosses of the bunker had dubbed, with considerable affection, 'The Boy'. Rowe had distinguished himself as a squadron commander flying Blenheims on a series of successful shipping strikes, earning the Distinguished Service Order and the Distinguished Flying Cross. He was terribly frustrated in such a backwater job, but was soon to return to operational flying and to further distinguish himself.

Squadron Leader Trent's tour of duty at Headquarters No. 2 Group was a relatively dull period in his Air Force career, but two incidents are well remembered by him as typical of the humour and the tempo of the time.

One day he flew to an airfield near Peterborough where a New Zealand Spitfire squadron was stationed. It was commanded by Reg Grant; and one of the New Zealand pilots was Len Trent's old Nelson College mate, Mick Shand.

The two Nelsonians had a good lunch together, after which the visitor was invited to view the week's combat films — the camera

Cousins: S/Ldr Ian Richmond (left) and S/Ldr Len Trent in 1942. Richmond, a Stirling bomber pilot, was shot down later that year. Both men attended Nelson College together and were to share the same room as prisoners-of-war in Stalag Luft III.

footage which was automatically recorded when the pilot fired his wing guns. It proved to be a thrilling half hour for the bomber pilot, for the fighter squadron was, at the time, primarily engaged on what were called 'Rhubarbs' — the code name for shallow penetration sorties at low level to pick off railway locomotives. But there were also a few shots of air-to-air scraps.

Trent was impressed enough to ask if he could take the films back to HQ 2 Group to show the AOC and his staff. Shand gave the nod but explained that some footage was of rather poor quality. He would therefore make up a reel of some of their best action footage and send the film to Trent by road.

As good as his word, Shand had the film delivered within the week and the AOC and most of his staff officers assembled in the operations room to see the movies that the fighter boys had produced and edited for the entertainment of lesser and ponderous mortals of Bomber Command.

Mick Shand had spliced into the film some lurid footage from a monstrous blue movie the fighter boys had acquired while passing through Panama. But, because of the probability of WAAF officers being in the audience, the prankster had been advised to let the scenes of lust fall to the clipping-room floor.

C'est la guerre. Or, probably more correctly — *C'est magnifique, mais ce n'est pas la guerre.*

The next episode concerns a visit on 8 June 1942 to the sector operations centre at Biggin Hill, the command centre for all the fighters of No. 11 Group, Fighter Command. This visit was designed to bring Trent up to date on the effectiveness of British Radar, and the fighters in particular, as Trent was soon to return to daylight operations leading bomber formations under fighter escort.

He flew down to Biggin Hill in the nose compartment of a Boston III and the aircraft was piloted by his great friend, Squadron Leader 'Dibs' Griffiths, a flight commander of 88 Squadron, stationed at Attlebridge in Norfolk. Trent hoped to join Griffiths on the squadron in a few weeks' time, aspiring to become commander of the unit's other flight.

It was his first flight in a Boston since his fiery circuit and near disaster a few months earlier; so he was a little apprehensive as he sat, a helpless unemployed pilot, in the perspex nose-cone of the aircraft watching Biggin Hill's short runway becoming shorter and shorter as the Boston gobbled up the yardage on its landing run. But the brakes of the tricycle undercarriage worked well and the Boston landed without difficulty.

Trent was taken down into the underground operations room where everyone was poised for a forthcoming fighter sweep over the Pas de Calais. A huge plotting table occupied the floor space below the balcony on which he stood, and this was surrounded by busy WAAF girls equipped with headphones and long cue-sticks with which they were moving counters denoting the numbers and strengths of each Spitfire and Hurricane squadron, as the Radar plots came directly into their headphones.

So far, as Trent watched, there had been no reaction from the enemy. But as the British fighters gained height and were obviously being plotted electronically by the Germans across the Channel, indicators began to appear, showing the enemy's reactions. Me-109s were swinging away to the south, climbing to try and get the drop on the RAF fighters from out of the sun.

This information was passed to the British wing leader, who acknowledged the message with a short, clipped 'Roger' and then his force changed course to counter the German move. And so the aerial chess game continued with brief exchanges of commands and acknowledgements.

After about 12 minutes the Spitfire leader reported he had sighted about twenty 'bandits' below to the right, and climbing. Then, with a 'Tally ho! Follow me down!' the battle was engaged.

The observers in the operations room could hear, through the amplifiers, every word spoken; and for the first ten seconds every combat commentary was according to the book — 'Watch it, Blue Section. Two bandits closing, half up, port quarter! ... Roger, Red Leader, I have them.' Then, as the dogfight hotted up and a general melee ensued, strange and excited words and phrases came thick and fast: 'Watch it, Charlie! Turn port! Jesus Christ ... that was a close one!' And from out of the wild and frantic cries of warning a plaintive Canadian voice called: 'Bloody hell ... let's get out of here. This is gettin' dangerous!'

The cries of battle went on for another 5 minutes and Trent did not recall any claims of victory. 'But', he says, 'perhaps those aerial successes were recorded in the cine-films, the radio being used only for vital warnings.'

The two bomber pilots returned in their Boston to base where, over a cup of tea, they discussed their observations of the Fighter Command boys in action. They were considerably impressed with what they had seen and, more particularly, heard of the heated dogfights in the haunted sky. The excitement and obvious *esprit de corps* which existed in the fighter squadrons made Trent wish, not for the first time, that he had been posted to a Spitfire squadron.

As they chatted, Dibs Griffiths recalled how, only a week earlier, he had been leading a box of six Bostons in an attack on a target in France. They had just dropped their bombs and were on their way home when they were attacked by a large gaggle of Me-109s and FW-190s. A few FW-190s penetrated the screen of the escorting Spitfires and came zooming up from below. One hung on his propeller immediately in front of Dibs, firing at the wing commander's aircraft leading the homebound Bostons.

For one animate moment Dibs had the German aircraft in his sights at a range of 100 yards or less. Although he pressed the firing button of his battery of four .3 forward-firing guns, he had left the button switched to the 'safe' position. In the 2 seconds it took to twist the gun-button to 'fire', the intruder had gone. And so, too, went one of those rare opportunities a bomber pilot had of emulating a fighter pilot.

Trent remembered the lesson that Griffiths recounted. It was to stand him in good stead on the afternoon of 3 May the following year.

There followed several days in June and July of 1942 when Squadron Leader Trent was able to excuse himself from the operations room of HQ 2 Group and go to Attlebridge to fly a Boston. And every flight confirmed his first impression of that wonderful machine. Every breed of aircraft has its own particular cockpit smell — an odoriferous amalgam of plastic, acetate, leather, oil, petrol and enamel. That fragrance, as seductive or repellant as a woman's perfume, can be as influential as the suitor's earlier conquests or rebuffs.

Trent, despite his first and fiery altercation with the Boston, loved the sights, the scents and the brave, bold feel of the machine. It was almost as manoeuvrable as a fighter — and, with its four front guns, anything could happen.

But the promises and plans for Trent to take over the other flight of 88 Squadron were suddenly dashed. He was called to Air

Vice-Marshal Lee's office one morning in early August 1942 and told quite firmly but sympathetically that he would have to go to Feltwell to command a flight in a new New Zealand-designated light-bomber squadron which the AOC had been instructed to form and be stationed alongside 464 (Australian) Squadron, RAF. The new unit — 487 (New Zealand) Squadron, RAF — would, like the Australians, be flying twin-engined Ventura aircraft.

'Len,' the Air Vice-Marshal said, 'I'm sorry, but with your experience, and as you are a New Zealander, I have no choice.'

7

THE BIRTH OF
487 (NZ) SQUADRON

UNDER THE COMMAND OF Wing Commander F. C. (Frankie) Seavill, 487 (NZ) Squadron was the sixth RAF unit to be designated a New Zealand squadron during the Second World War. Frankie Seavill came from a sheep-farming family at Waingaro. He left New Zealand in 1930 for a career in the RAF, spending a couple of years in Aden before returning to Central Flying School and a spell in Training Command headquarters. With the outbreak of war he was posted on loan to the Royal Canadian Air Force as part of the British Commonwealth Air Training Scheme. On his return to England he carried out a refresher course with Wellington bombers before his appointment to the command of 487 Squadron.

The squadron itself was officially formed at Feltwell, Norfolk, on 15 August 1942, occupying the place on the station recently vacated by 75 (NZ) Squadron. Similarly, the Wellington bombers in which the aircrews of 75 Squadron had made their mark — and in which Sergeant Jimmy Ward had won his Victoria Cross — had also departed. 487 Squadron and its partner on the station, 464 (Australian) Squadron, would now be flying Ventura light bombers on daylight raids.

The station commander was Group Captain R. L. Kippenberger of Waimate, a brother of that notable New Zealand Army leader, Brigadier H. K. Kippenberger, DSO.

The squadron's two flights were also under the command of New Zealanders. Squadron Leader Brian ('Digger') Wheeler, DFC, was appointed to lead A Flight — and Squadron Leader Len Trent, DFC, had B Flight.

Digger Wheeler had left Marton, New Zealand, to take up ranching in the Argentine in 1937, but with the outbreak of war he

New Zealanders at RAF Station Feltwell, Norfolk, shortly after the formation of 487 (NZ) Squadron in 1942. *From left:* Wing Commander F.C. Seavill, Commanding Officer, 487 Squadron; Group Captain R.L. Kippenberger, Commanding Officer, RAF Station Feltwell; Hon. 'Bill' (later Sir William) Jordan, NZ High Commissioner in London; Squadron Leader L.H. Trent, DFC, Officer Commanding B Flight, 487 Squadron; Squadron Leader B. ('Digger') Wheeler, DFC, Officer Commanding A Flight, 487 Squadron.

had sailed to Canada and joined the RCAF in 1940. On his posting to a Blenheim squadron, he carried out a number of daylight raids, sinking two enemy ships before being transferred to Bostons, in which he carried out twenty daylight raids — including a mission pursuing the German battleships Scharnhorst and Gneisenau.

The new squadron's third DFC holder was Pilot Officer G. W. Brewer of Papatoetoe, who won the award on his first operation when he successfully attacked enemy shipping at Dunkirk, despite being badly wounded in the thigh by flak.

Other New Zealand foundation aircrew members of 487 Squadron were: Flight Lieutenant R. A. Reece, Christchurch — the navigation officer; G. A. Park, Dunedin; W. Gellatly, Nelson; T. J. Bayton, R. A. Ferri, T. Whyte, R. F. Edmonds, W. D. L. Goodfellow, Auckland; C. Baker, J. F. Greenstreet, J. D. Sharpe, T. L. B. Taylor, C. J. Baker, Wellington; G. W. Lee, R. W. Second, Christchurch; E. C. Armitage, Dunedin; A. Coutts, Whakatane; B. M. Weeds, J. D. Hamill, Invercargill; G. F.

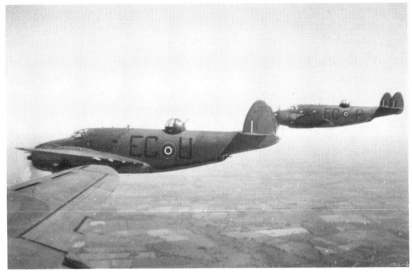

Ventura bombers of 487 (NZ) Squadron in formation over Norfolk.

Whitwell, Tirau; B. S. McCallum, Opunake; R. J. Street, New Plymouth.

Members of the ground crew included: Corporals R. E. Travers, Wanganui; C. E. Bush, Auckland; D. Macara, Gore; Aircraftman H. H. Armstrong, Whakatane.

When all ranks of the new squadron were at last mustered, it was found that about 50 percent of the aircrew members were New Zealanders. The others included Britons, Canadians and South Africans. Wing Commander Seavill's three crew members, for instance, were all Canadians.

When it came to operational experience, comparatively few of the aircrew of 487 Squadron had flown many sorties. Brewer and Gellatly were probably the most seasoned of the junior officers, while Frankie Seavill, himself, had not yet flown in combat. Therefore, it was left to the two battle-hardened flight commanders to school their fledglings — not only in grappling with the vagaries of a new aircraft, but also in converting that machine into a highly mobile and effective bombing platform.

Len Trent remembers those early days on the squadron well:

The new crews arrived straight from their operational training units, very inexperienced and with a minimum of formation-flying hours on Blenheims. The Ventura was a much bigger and heavier aircraft with an added complication — nearly everything in the cockpit was reversed from the Blenheim. For instance, the throttles of the Ventura were held in the right hand and the half-wheel of the control column in the left. And this change, added to the cumbersome, weighty controls, made formation flying, even for an experienced pilot, a most tiring performance.

But even before we got to that stage we flight commanders had a most nerve-racking duty to perform. We had no dual-control version of the Ventura for schooling new pilots; so we had to demonstrate how to fly a circuit, make quite sure that the new boy could recite his cockpit drill of vital actions, then stand beside the obviously nervous fledgling and 'talk' him around — powerless to physically correct him — until we were both safely down.

Under-shoots, over-shoots and stalls — all had to be anticipated and corrected by word-of-mouth. And if the daytime 'dual' wasn't exciting enough, the first night-flying tutorial was invariably a shocker. I am sure my rapid instructions saved at least five sprog pilots — as well as five of my own lives.

After the new pilots had learned the skills to get a Ventura off the ground and back again without breaking it, they were coached in formation flying — a necessary aerial drill for combat pilots, but a hazardous exercise in its schooling for pupils and tutors alike.

The flight commanders began their teachings by allowing only one pupil's aircraft to 'formate' on either port or starboard, so keeping an escape route open should the tyro show erratic and dangerous tendencies. From there they progressed to vics of three aircraft — although the standard of flying thus achieved could hardly have been described as polished, nor even safe. It left the battle-tried flight commanders wondering just how the new boys would perform over hostile territory with the added distraction of ack-ack fire and enemy fighters.

Because of the inherent difficulties encountered in this aircraft (which was after all a modified military version of the commercial Lockheed Electra), progress in operational training was slow and both the New Zealanders of 487 Squadron and the Australians of 464 Squadron felt they had been allocated an inferior aeroplane when such wonderful machines as the Boston and the Mosquito were seemingly available.

There was much grumbling in the crew room at Feltwell as, one after another, the pilots sat down exhausted after formation-flying training sessions, their left wrists aching with the strain of trying to keep close station. Added to that, their eardrums were still ringing with the admonishments from the exasperated flight commanders calling for greater concentration.

The mutterings of discontent grew louder and more frequent — so much so that Digger Wheeler and Len Trent spoke to Frankie Seavill. He, in turn, took the matter of squadron morale to to the station commander, Group Captain Kippenberger.

With commendable tact, the New Zealand boss of Feltwell got in touch with Mr 'Bill' (later Sir William) Jordan, the down-to-earth and tremendously popular New Zealand High Commissioner in London. One day seemingly 'out of the blue', the genial gentleman paid a visit to 'his' boys flying in this, the latest New Zealand squadron to be formed in the United Kingdom.

Bill Jordan's speech to all ranks in the crew room was (as befitted his erstwhile calling of police constable) in the idiom of the serviceman. So the boys didn't like flying Venturas — these 'Flying Pigs' — eh? Well, he was here to tell them that there was already a British squadron of Venturas, certainly 3 months senior to 487 Squadron, and what's more the English lads were coping with the machines. So, Bill said, whatever an Englishman could do, a New Zealander could equal.

Perhaps, the sagacious diplomat challenged, the boys of 487 Squadron could go forth and prove they were *better* at flying Venturas than any other unit? Pigs might fly, eh? Well — go and show the world that pigs *can* fly!

The message got home; and the pilots returned to their tasks with a better will that soon grew to enthusiasm. Their handling of controls became more coordinated. And soon they were wondering why they ever had any problems. Gradually, the nickname 'Flying Pig' was dropped.

Throughout November 1942 the squadron concentrated on low-level formation flying interspersed with exercises in high-level practice bombing.

The low-level practice targets were the Corby Steel Works factories and the St Neots Power Station; the squadron's series of dummy runs just over chimney height no doubt causing alarm and despondency in the hearts of the good burghers — and probably some twittering among the pilots' crew mates.

And then, with no idea as to the planning for the squadron's first operational sortie, the crews carried out a low-level formation dummy attack, carefully calculated as to 'time on target', on Headquarters 2 Group in the town of Huntingdon — an exercise, need it be said, that had the approval of the Air Officer Commanding.

That successful flexing of airborne muscle took place on 28 November 1942, and a day or two later Trent flew and air-tested his machine on a convenient trip to Kings Cliffe airfield, where he had lunch with Mick Shand and showed the fighter pilot around the penetralia of the Ventura. Shand sat at the controls, pushing and pulling the half-wheel through the motions of dive and climb, twisting it to port and starboard and wincing at the weight of aileron heft necessary. He ran his eyes over the array of knobs, tits and dials which, to a single-engine man, must have been confusion compounded. Sixty-three assorted pieces were set around the cockpit within reach and vision of the pilot; each lever, switch and luminous finger waiting to move at the command of authority.

Shand sniffed the Ventura's perfume of plastic and dope with disdain. 'Jesus,' he grumbled, kicking hard on the pedals that moved the twin rudders, 'I'm not impressed.' He looked through the side lights and studied the bulging nacelles that housed the two Double-Wasp radial engines and, no doubt, thought lovingly of the sleek in-line Rolls-Royce power plant that moved his Spitfire twice as fast for only half as much concentration on the part of the pilot. 'I'll stick to what I've got,' he said, 'and be bloody grateful for it.'

He continued to stick to Spitfires for a few more weeks. Then he was shot down over occupied Europe, but survived uninjured. Trent was to again drop in on him — minus his Ventura — at Stalag Luft III in the middle of the following year.

In the early days of December the squadron was told to prepare all its aircraft for its first operational sortie. On 6 December the crews were briefed for a low-level formation attack on the Philips radio factories in Eindhoven, Holland. The squadron was to be part of a large formation involving all the Venturas, Bostons and

Mosquitoes of 2 Group, the whole stream of bombers operating under an umbrella of escort Spitfires.

Low-level flying is always exciting. But over enemy territory it is also very dangerous, particularly if aircraft are flying in formation and so are unable to take evasive action. For any alert ground gunner they offer easy targets.

A single aircraft, flying really low, depends on the element of surprise. The noise of its approach is masked by speed and ground effects, so it has virtually come and gone before the ack-ack gunner is aware of its presence. However, the experienced pilots of 487 Squadron conceded that a gaggle of Venturas, forced to fly at something like fifty feet, could expect little protection from surprise and they realized they were to be prepared for an unusually brisk operation.

Briefed to formate off the port side of 464 Squadron, who were leading the Ventura force and were responsible for the overall navigation of the mission, the pilots of 487 Squadron were further concerned to learn that they were at the end of the bomber stream and therefore open to the full fury of an enemy which, by then, would be wide awake. Trent recalls:

I thought of the unfortunate troopers in the Charge of the Light Brigade as we prepared our maps and our aircraft were bombed up with heavy incendiary missiles capable of crashing through the factory walls before erupting into flames.

We studied photographs of the target, a complex of huge buildings on the edge of the town of Eindhoven. And the biggest building, which was to be my victim, was five storeys high — a bull's-eye impossible to miss.

About lunch time we were all seated in our aircraft, ready to start. The 464 Squadron machines were the first to get moving and then we followed them out on to the wide grass airfield of Feltwell and got airborne. The Australian squadron was to fly a wide circuit to allow us to cut inside, formate on their port side and then head off on a track over Norfolk towards the Dutch coast, following in the wake of the Bostons, Mosquitoes and the other Venturas, flown by 21 Squadron, which were to cross the enemy coast just south of our track.

All went well across the North Sea and we hoped the Spitfire umbrella would arrive over Holland on time to protect us during the run in to the target. We made a brave and exciting sight as our two-squadron force of Venturas, spread out over the water, pressed eastwards at about 50 feet above the waves. Flying so low, a moment of carelessness could prove fatal, for suddenly hitting the turbulence of another aircraft's slipstream invariably caused momentary loss of control.

Fortunately, I had no such problem as I was in the front rank and in formation just to the port of Frankie Seavill and leading my vic of three. Behind, with another vic, was my deputy flight commander Tich Hanafin.

Soon the sand dunes of Holland came into view, concurrent with a frightening burst of black ack-ack explosions and geysers of water erupting to Trent's right and in the middle of 464 Squadron's track. The shell bursts continued every 10 or 15 seconds all the way as the aerial force moved in to the beaches.

Miraculously, no aircraft was hit; although Trent heard later that some of 464 Squadron's crews had some frightening experiences flying through the fountains of salt water thrown up by the exploding shells.

But within seconds the bombers were flashing over the dunes and coursing over the flat lands behind. Trent's navigator, Flight Lieutenant Vivian Phillips, managed to pinpoint their position and reported that the two-squadron formation was about 3 miles north of the planned landfall. At the time this did not seem too serious. Trent believed that the 464 Squadron master navigator would accordingly take gentle corrective action.

It was about then, too, that Len Trent found himself flying directly down a road. And there, right ahead of him, were two cyclists; blithely unaware of the veritable armada of 190 mph-bombers about to over-fly them. Suddenly, at a range of about 400 yards, Trent realized they were German soldiers with rifles slung over their shoulders.

Flying at such a low height he could not dip his aircraft's nose to bring his forward-firing guns to bear on the cyclists — and besides, Trent had bigger targets in mind. But the waggish Viv Phillips seemed to have had the solution: 'You should have lowered your wheels and run over the bastards, Len,' he suggested.

By now the seemingly slight error in the track of the bombing force was sending them right into danger. Trent saw, with shock, that they were flying directly towards the heavily defended aerodrome of Bergen-op-zoom and the flack towers, liberally spiking every vantage point of the airfield, were hosing their deadly streams of fire at the closely-packed Venturas. The pilots, desperately holding tight formation, were unable to take evasive action.

Trent, dedicated to the use of his forward-firing guns since the days of his first tour of operations, pressed the button on his control column and brought his small battery of fire to bear on the crew of a flak tower dead ahead. The ground fury from that source ceased as the cone of fire from the Ventura's two .5s and two .3s found the target.

Suddenly, to Trent's dismay, Frankie Seavill's aircraft disappeared. The CO had been leading 487 Squadron, standing at about 2 o'clock from Trent's vic. Now, the two other aircraft of his vic were soldiering on without their boss. The murderous ack-ack fire had brought the popular New Zealand squadron commander down in the middle of that German-held Dutch airfield.

Pressing on over the flat, open country the bomber crews could see their target clearly defined by the columns of smoke rising

The raid on the Philips factory at Eindhoven on 6 December 1942. Despite the explosion of one of Squadron Leader Trent's bombs only a few yards away, a German ack-ack gunner in the flak post (circled) kept up a constant fire at his Ventura attacker.

Venturer Courageous

What a holocaust! Squadron Leader Trent's camera catches a departing shot of
the bombing of the Philips factory at Eindhoven on 6 December 1942 as the
Venturas of 487 Squadron head for base.

from the attacks of the Bostons and Mosquitoes. A gentle turn to starboard brought the Venturas in line for their run up and Trent had already pinpointed his high target building. Climbing to clear the parapets, he let loose his stick of bombs so that they plummeted into the structure, holing it from basement to roof-top.

As his aircraft cleared the top of the flaming and smoking target, Len Trent glimpsed, on the left hand corner of the building, a German machine-gunner stubbornly sticking to his post and pouring a steady stream of fire at his attacker — albeit none of his bullets damaging the Ventura. 'There,' says Trent, 'was, in my book, a damn good soldier.'

Down to about 50 feet again, the aircraft of the strike force made their ways home to Feltwell in loose formation. And when they had landed and gathered in their debriefing sessions, it was found that Frankie Seavill and his three Canadian crew members were the only casualties of the mission.

It had been 487 Squadron's blooding in combat — and Len Trent's first sortie of his second tour of operations. The survivors had suffered no ghastly wounds and, in the relief of finding themselves alive to fly another day, exuberance reigned around the station. But when the heady *élan* subsided there was to remain, for a long time, a gap hard to fill. Frankie Seavill had been a successful and extremely popular commanding officer and it was a foul whim of fate that he, having been in the RAF since 1930, should have to perish on his first operational sortie against the Germans.

He had taken his responsibilities seriously and democratically. Realizing his lack of combat experience, he had studiously taken part in all the lowly and tiring training exercises — grappling, along with the 'sprog' sergeant-pilots, the confusions of formation flying, the thrills and chills of low-level simulated bombing runs, the apprehensions of night circuits, along with all the bumps in a strangely-new aircraft.

He went to his end, in the manner of his living, as a gentleman of courage.

The rest of December and most of January 1943 saw the squadron involved in a heavy training programme which included high and low-level bombing, fighter-affiliation exercises and, particularly

A Trent's-eye view of the enemy-occupied railway marshalling yards at Dunkirk, France — 487 Squadron's target on 26 February 1943. The bombing height was 10,000 feet. Trent's number-four Ventura in the formation is just coming into the picture.

for Trent, the opportunities for target practice with the use of the forward-firing, pilot-operated guns. That arsenal nest was housed immediately above the navigator's position in the Ventura and, should that crew member not be forewarned, the sudden din of the four guns exploding in unison a few inches from his eardrums was likely to raise both his blood pressure and his ire. When the navigator, Flight Lieutenant Phillips was so effronted he easily forgot rank and cursed his squadron-leader pilot roundly.

Len Trent's log book shows that the squadron's first sortie of 1943 took place on 26 January when he led a box of six Venturas to bomb a target at Bruges. Although they experienced heavy ack-ack fire, they did not drop their bombs because of thick cloud.

On 2 February he led a force of twelve aircraft to bomb the marshalling yards at Abbeville, scoring direct hits. There was some light flak and Trent's evasive action was to outguess the batteries by changing height or direction every 8 or 10 seconds —

somewhat like an aerial game of Russian roulette.

The following day he took a box of six Venturas to bomb a steel works target at Ymuiden on the Dutch coast. But again, cloud obscured the target and no bombs were dropped. Nor did they experience any flak.

On 26 February Trent led twelve aircraft to bomb an enemy searaider in the docks at Dunkirk. They encountered very heavy and accurate flak, all aircraft being extensively perforated although there were no serious injuries. Unfortunately, they missed hitting the ship — a fact that must have caused concern at 2 Group Headquarters.

On 22 March Trent again led twelve aircraft to bomb the oil refinery at Maasluis, near Rotterdam. The results were not startling and the flak was moderate. Visibility was marred by extensive haze. 29 March was a very busy day for Trent. In the morning he led a formation and followed an attack by 21 Squadron Venturas on the Dordrecht warehouses in Holland. And in the afternoon he led a large formation — four boxes each of six aircraft, including Venturas of 464 Squadron — to bomb the docks at Rotterdam. Their aiming was successful.

Bombing up the Venturas at Methwold, April 1943.

On 3 April 1943 487 Squadron moved to Methwold, a satellite station of Feltwell, a mile or two distant from the squadron's birthplace. This, like the parent aerodrome, had a grass field.

The month that it took to shake down and settle in to new

surroundings was spent in both theoretical and practical training. On 27 April Trent took six Venturas to Exeter for a combined operation with aircraft of 10 Group, Fighter Command. After an extensive briefing the bombers and fighters took off on a raid — euphemistically known as a 'Circus' — on a target in Normandy.

On Sunday 2 May Group Captain 'Kip' Kippenberger came over from Feltwell to visit Len Trent. He had something on his mind and he invited the young squadron leader to stroll with him in the spring sunshine. The burden of his concern was that Trent, in the interests of furthering his career, should attend RAF Staff College. He appreciated that Len was still actively flying in his second tour of operations; but Kip needed a quota of suitable officers to put forward for the college — and, of course, automatic promotion on the completion of the course would be assured.

He knew, too, that Wing Commander Grindell, CO of 487 Squadron since the loss of Frankie Seavill, was shortly due to depart to take up an appointment in the Western Desert — thereby leaving the command of the squadron vacant. Len Trent was officially favoured as the incoming CO.

The choice lay with Squadron Leader Trent. Either way, he was practically certain of promotion to wing commander. The leisurely routine of Staff College pointed the way to a safe future. But if he left the squadron half way through his tour, would he not be running away? He talked with the group captain for a few more minutes, tossing the issues back and forth. And then he told his CO that he would remain with 487 Squadron.

'Okay, Len — it's over to you. That's all I wanted to know,' said Kippenberger.

But the following day, Monday 3 May, 1943, everything changed.

8

THE AMSTERDAM RAMROD

THE SUN'S BRIGHT EYE LIT the spring day and all at Methwold that lay before its gaze was golden. When the station came astir and the tasks of the day were being made manifest, Wing Commander Grindell, CO of 487 Squadron, popped his head around the door of B Flight's office and said to Squadron Leader Trent: 'It's Flushing Docks today, Len. And I'll be leading your flight — and the squadron.'

'Hold hard, sir,' replied the flight commander. 'As you remember, I didn't cross the egg-line yesterday; and I've still got my bomb load hanging in my aircraft.' The egg-line, a whimsical datum point fixed by the squadron's aircrews, was an imaginary line a few miles out from the enemy coast. If this line was not crossed, the fliers were not entitled to the rare and prized bacon and egg meal on return.

A light-hearted argument took place. And it was won — or lost, according to one's point of view — by Trent. Later, as the crews gathered in the briefing room, they had the usual flutterings in their stomachs and the nervous visits to the latrines before they donned their flying gear.

Trent, whose battledress had gone to be dry-cleaned of battle sweat, was wearing his 'blues'. Within one hour before take-off for the sortie over the southernmost corner of the Dutch coast, he cleared the patch pockets of his tunic of any give-away memos, tickets or items which could provide clues to enemy intelligence should he be shot down; and, as was customary, he wrote to his wife.

He and his three crew members — Flight Lieutenant V. Phillips, Flying Officer R. D. C. Thomas and Sergeant W. Trenery — went to where their Ventura, V-Victor, stood at its dispersal point. All made their usual pre-flight checks of their

A group of New Zealand non-commissioned aircrew members of 487 (NZ) Squadron in front of Ventura bomber A-Apple at RAF Methwold in early 1943.

Standing, from left: Max Sparks, 'Smithy' Smith, Bob Frizzle, (unknown), Merv Darrall, Ivan Urlich, Bob Fowler, (unknown), Johnny Sharp, 'Steve' Stevenson, White, Tim Warner, (unknown).

Front row: Bob Edmonds, Keith Dudding, Len Muir, Jack Lloyd, Andy Coutts, Ian Baynton, Ron Secord, Bob Pye, 'Curly' Baird, Tommy Sheehan.

Some of the commissioned aircrew members of 487 Squadron at Methwold, early 1943. *From left*: S. McGowan, 'Rusty' Peryman, O.E. Foster, G.W. Brewer, Sqn/Ldr L.H. Trent, Sqn/Ldr Turnbull, Wing Commander Grindell, Terry Taylor, Don Church, Tom Penn, (unknown), Gabbites, Gordon Park. All, with the exception of Sqn/Ldr Turnbull, were New Zealanders.

respective departments.

But as the men of the attacking force were preparing to enter their machines there came a hail from an operations room messenger: 'Everybody back to the briefing room!'

When all the crews were seated Wing Commander Grindell announced there would be a new target. An early lunch would be prepared.

Fluttering butterflies took the fine edge off most appetites. And when the men returned to the briefing room they heard from Grindell that they were to bomb the electrical power house on the north-western edge of Amsterdam — a target and city which had never before been attacked by the RAF.

It was considered an important target; British Intelligence having reported that the Dutch workers in power houses throughout Holland were awaiting a lead from their Amsterdam colleagues to stage mass strikes because of British bombing. Intelligence placed much — probably too much — stock in what the Dutch underground had to say.

In the Methwold briefing room, on that bright morning of Monday 3 May 1943, the aircrews of the impending mission learned the facts of life (and death) concerning the operation which was to become known as 'Ramrod 17' — a Ramrod being the code name for a 'press on regardless' foray.

On the previous day, both Bostons of 107 Squadron and Venturas of 464 Squadron had unsuccessfully attacked the Royal Dutch Steel Works at Ijmuiden. The Bostons' bombs had overshot the target although the Australians' Venturas had damaged the coke factory, sulphate plant, benzole unit, the compressor and various store houses.

Now the plan was for six Bostons to make low-level attack on the steel works. In conjunction — and as a diversionary move — twelve Venturas of 487 Squadron would fly to Amsterdam and bomb the power house. Fourteen Ventura crews were to attend the briefing, thereby allowing for two aircraft on stand-by in case of last minute emergencies.

The Ventura force was to rendezvous with escort Spitfires from 118, 167 and 504 Squadrons over Coltishall airfield at 1700 hours, flying in two boxes each of six aircraft below 100 feet, the distance between each box not to exceed 500 yards. After crossing the English coast, bombers and escort Spitfires were to descend to sea level until 33 minutes out from Coltishall, flying at 190 mph indicated air speed. Then all aircraft were to climb rapidly at 165 mph to 10,000 feet, which was to be the bombing height.

For the second time that day, Squadron Leader Trent and his crew went to their aircraft. And at thirteen other dispersal points around the airfield at Methwold there was the same urgent pre-flight activity. Seated in V-Victor, Trent went through his cockpit checks, keeping a constant eye on time to ensure his force would be airborne to keep the appointment over Coltishall.

The lid of the auxiliary control box was open and he noted that his parking brake was on, the master switch was on and the undercart selector was down and locked; and its emergency by-pass valve was wired open. Hydraulics, generator, gyropilot and cabin door were also checked.

He set his fuel selectors to the rear main tank, adjusted throttle, mixture, pitch, supercharger, air, gills and oil knobs and levers and signalled the waiting ground-crew airmen to turn each propeller by hand for a couple of revolutions before applying power.

Again, he looked at his watch. Good. Everything seemed to be on time. His engines were now running. As he waited for the oil to warm and course through the arteries of the Double-Wasps, he looked around the field as, one by one other machines of the force burst into life. Two of the Venturas had, however, developed faults which meant that the reserve aircraft would be brought into the breach.

At 1643 hours Squadron Leader Trent eased V-Victor off the grass runway. By 1647 hours all twelve of the aircraft were airborne and off on their first leg towards Amsterdam. Trent takes up the story in his own words:

Three miles from the Coltishall aerodrome we could see the Spitfires taking off and skimming the trees in a left-hand turn, to station themselves 100 yards on both sides of our formations. Right on time and all well, we set course for the Dutch coast.

We continued flying at 100 feet to avoid detection by the enemy radar. We hoped to get within 10 minutes of the Dutch coast before being plotted; at which point we'd do a full-power climb to bombing height. In this way we were usually able to complete the bombing run and be homeward bound before the

German fighters could get into position to attack.

The enemy were not usually 'scrambled' until the bomber formations appeared on the radar screens. Then they had to take off and climb to get us within range of their forward-firing guns, keeping in mind our high and medium protective fighter cover. But only rarely did we catch a glimpse of this support. It was, however, a great comfort to feel that it was there, for the Ventura was cold meat for any aggressive German fighter. A dorsal turret with two .3s and the two .3s firing aft under the tail, was hardly a deterrent for a determined enemy in a cannon-firing fighter.

Admittedly, the Ventura pilot had two .5s and two .3s firing forward under the command of his thumb, but flying in formation and unable to manoeuvre quickly, he was not likely to have an opportunity to bring down any but the most naive German flyer — although, of course, such characters did exist (even if briefly) in air combats.

However, remembering the hard-luck story of Dibs Griffiths' gun button being in the 'off' position when a FW-190 crossed his track — and my own earlier and satisfactory experiences — my first move after leaving the English coast was to test my guns and leave the safety button on the 'fire' position.

Shortly after the formation had left the home coast and were skimming over the wavetops, Ventura Q-Queenie, piloted by Sergeant A. G. Barker, turned away and headed back to base. A hatch cover had come loose. This left only eleven bombers heading towards the target. As it was, Barker and his crew were to thank their lucky stars as the outcome of the mission unfolded. Already, the stage was being set for black tragedy.

The German Governor of Holland had decided to pay a state visit to the city of Haarlem that particular afternoon and fighter reinforcements of the Luftwaffe had been brought from as far as Norway and France to attend a convention of fighter pilots at Schiphol Aerodrome.

Some of the best of Goering's men in the Western Sector were there, ready and alert, as their lectures and discussions proceeded, to stand watch over their governor's welfare in Haarlem — a matter of 12 or 13 kilometres away to the north-west.

Both these functions — the Governor's visit to Haarlem and the convention of Luftwaffe fighter pilots — were unknown to British Intelligence when the Ventura bomber force was briefed. The track of the Amsterdam-bound aircraft was straight between the two hot spots.

By any other name, it was to prove as deadly a trap as any ill-defended gaggle of bombers could enter. To add to the hazard, there had been a bungle on the part of a wing of Spitfire IX fighters of 11 Group. Five support aircraft of 122 Squadron and eleven of 453 Squadron left Hornchurch at 1520-23 hours and, after refuelling at Martlesham, got airborne about 20 minutes too soon. Furthermore, instead of flying at low level until the Dutch coast was reached, they immediately began a climb to operational height. Obviously, the German radar picked up the Spitfires' movements and the Luftwaffe was on high alert. The seventy enemy fighters assembled at Schiphol had FW-190s to tackle the Spitfires and Me-109s for the bombers.

Realizing that his Spitfire IX squadrons were not only much too early but well north of their correct course — and so would not have enough petrol to complete their task — the Air Officer Commanding 11 Group had ordered their return.

Squadron Leader Trent led his bomber force into a climb at 1735 hours and soon, in clear weather, they reached the Dutch coast at 12,000 feet. But whereas the escorting Spitfires of 118 and 167 Squadrons were keeping close stations, the twelve Spitfires of 504 Squadron, which had come up from 10 Group for the operation, had found the climb to operational height too steep and at too low a speed. Unused to flying in formation in climbs of this type, they had dropped far behind.

Trent takes up the story again:

At 12,000 feet over the Dutch coast, and still not a shot fired, we were as yet unaware of the enemy fighters jockeying for position. Of course our escort knew all about the situation, but I was not informed.

Although my aircraft had recently been fitted with a VHF (Very High Frequency radio) set to be in contact with the escort, the Venturas around me had not had their magnetos and plugs properly screened (against electrical interference) and so my set was virtually useless. However, I was not unduly bothered, for we had an arranged signal that if for any reason the escort couldn't cope, a Spitfire was to fly across my bow, waggling his wings. I had never seen that signal and didn't ever expect to see it.

From a cloudless sky and in good visibility we could see Haarlem and just make out Amsterdam, 10 minutes' flying time from our position over the coast. We levelled off and, using the extra 2000 feet we had gained to increase our speed, I thought it was just a case of 'Look out, power house, here we come!'

My wireless operator had taken up his usual position in the astro dome. He was responsible for reporting the range and bearing of fighters attacking from beam and rear. The formations were reported in good order and I got the 'thumbs up' from my numbers two and three — the only Venturas I could see from my position in the cockpit.

It was at this point that more than twenty enemy fighters bore down on the Spitfires of 118 and 167 Squadrons which formed the close escort, while thirty other fighters attacked the Ventura force. The Spitfires of 504 Squadron, slow in their climb, were about 3 miles behind when the action began. The aggressive FW-190s charged in ahead of the RAF fighters, effectively cutting off assistance to the bombers. And although the close-escort Spitfires tried to stay with the Venturas, they were so occupied with fending off the attackers that they dropped well behind their charges.

Suddenly, things began to happen. Flying Officer Thomas, from the astro dome, shouted: 'Here's a whole shower of fighters coming down on us out of the sun; they may be Spits — twenty, thirty, forty ... Hell's teeth, they're 109s and 190s!' He called to Sergeant Trenery, our gunner: 'Watch 'em, Tren!' Then he began to give me his evasion patter: 'The 190s are engaging the close escort — so get ready to turn starboard, sir. And now the 109s are heading for us at 1000 yards ... 800 ... turn NOW ... 600 yards. They're firing. Give 'em hell, Tren!'

I could hear Tren's guns rattling away and smell the cordite. And as I turned to starboard I could see the enemy fighters coming in, one after another. About a dozen had attached themselves to my box and the same number were attacking

Flight Lieutenant Duffill and his box.

Duffill's aircraft was hit in the first attack and it went down with smoke pouring from its tail. I was to hear, long after, that he managed to regain control of the machine and get it back to base with two of his crew seriously injured — but not before one of the gunners had destroyed an enemy aircraft. Duffill's Ventura was the only one of the eleven to return from the mission.

Next to fall victim was my number five, who was set on fire. And as the last of the attacking wave whipped by just underneath us, I straightened up and turned back on course, searching the sky for signs of the top-cover Spitfires. I had caught a glimpse of a glorious dog fight going on miles back — so obviously the close escort was more than busy.

Our attackers could be seen pulling around underneath, with the obvious intent of attacking from 'the starboard again. By this time we were approaching Haarlem and, as I realized later, they were trying to make me turn away to the south — and to keep turning. This, to a certain extent, they were achieving. But I wasn't going to Haarlem, anyway. But about this time I had a horrible idea where I *was* going, if that top cover didn't arrive bloody soon.

Now there were only four Venturas left from the eleven that had crossed the Dutch coast. And the German attackers must have been exulting in their victories. Again they bored in on the valiant quartet.

As they came at us on our starboard, I turned slightly to the right to'get the wings out of the way, thus giving our gunners a clear field of fire up to the last moment as the fighters ducked under our sadly depleted formation. It also presented a difficult full-deflection shot for the attackers.

As they came in this time I could see, at the ominous range of only 400 yards, the leading edges of the fighters' wings suddenly burst with flames as their wing guns poured shells at us. And this ugly sight continued until it seemed a collision was inevitable. Down, under and to the right again — and still we hadn't knocked one out of the sky.

But now my number four had been hit and had gone the way

of number five. That had all happened in something like 2 minutes, which seemed like 2 years. I suppose the thought processes get speeded up a bit in such situations.

But I now realized that something had gone seriously wrong and that the top cover could not help us. What to do? We were on our own in a hopeless situation, obviously 'in for the chop' in a matter of minutes. We might as well be shot down over the land as come down in that rough sea — even supposing we managed to get back that far.

However, if the idea of turning for home ever occurred to the crew, they certainly didn't voice it. My navigator, Viv Phillips still had his eyes on Amsterdam and was urging me to keep turning left towards it whenever I could.

Again the enemy bored in from starboard bow and beam. From half up and 1500 yards they would wing over in loose pairs and come darting at our flanks like pack wolves ravaging the remnants of a buffalo herd. Once again at 400 yards I saw the twinkling flames from the leading edges of the fighters' wings and I pulled up slightly to put them off their aim and give them room to get underneath.

And then an encouraging thing happened. There was Leutnant von Prune himself! Instead of diving down, this merry goon pulled around level in front of our formation. I am sure he misjudged our speed and obviously he had been studying anything but the armament of the Ventura. There he was, banked towards us — the range about 150 yards. He appeared very close. I scarcely had to move my aircraft. He was flying straight towards the centre of my old ring-and-bead sight.

There was a terrible vibration as I pressed the firing button. One ... two ... three seconds of assorted .5 and .3 ammunition ripped out to meet him. Got him! His wings suddenly rocked and he slowly turned upside-down and he was last seen going down on the starboard side, vertically and very fast.

Since the war a Dutch civilian, who was then a youth of eighteen, has written an account of what it all looked like from the ground. In his account he reports a Me-109 diving into the ground at this point. However, we didn't have time to follow the 109's progress to the ground — another pair of fighters was already shooting at us.

Frankly, I was amazed that we had lasted so long. Eight

Flying Officer S.B. ('Rusty') Peryman, Len
Trent's 'most reliable Number Two' whose
Ventura was shot down seconds before
Trent's aircraft on the Ramrod 17
operation. F/O Peryman was killed.

minutes had gone by and only now were we approaching the
target. From hereon, it was a succession of attacks. Just then,
my number three Terry Taylor pulled out with his port engine
in flames.

And so Rusty Peryman, my number two was our only
companion Ventura as the first of the Amsterdam built-up area
appeared in the bombing sights. Suddenly, about a dozen or
more black puffs appeared just ahead and slightly right. Good, I
thought, at least the fighters will stand back a bit now. The
black puffs started to appear all over the place and sometimes
we could feel the bumps and hear the bangs. But, most
surprising of all, the fighters took no notice of the ack-ack and

appeared to redouble their efforts to get us before their own ack-ack batteries could claim kills.

My navigator now started to direct me onto the target and at the same time my fire controller was shouting the range and bearing of the attacking fighters and imploring me to turn right while my navigator was saying: 'Left, left ... steady ... 10 seconds to go ... steady ...' I had to tell my poor controller, Roy Thomas, to shut up. I never heard him say another word.

My mouth was as dry as a bone, for the ack-ack was everywhere and I wasn't able to take evasive action. 'Left, left ... 5 seconds to go,' Viv Phillips chanted as I concentrated on keeping correct height and air speed. The bombing run was lasting a lifetime. And then there was a jubilant 'Bombs gone!' But when I looked up from my instrument panel I discovered my number two had gone. We were on our own.

As I reached for the lever to close the bomb doors, I thought: 'Down on the deck is our only chance.' But even as my hand came away from the lever there was a frightful bang and, horror of horrors, all the flying controls had been shot away. The engines were running perfectly so I waggled the stick and kicked the rudder pedals again to convince myself it was true. 'We've had it, chaps,' I called. 'No controls. Bale out. Abandon aircraft, quick!' My navigator dashed past me from the nose and disappeared into the main fuselage to collect his parachute and jettison the main door.

I struggled with the controls for perhaps another 5 seconds before the aeroplane suddenly reared right up. Although I throttled back, the nose wouldn't drop; and the Ventura fell off the top of the loop and promptly whipped into a spin. I jettisoned the hatch above my head and ripped off my safety straps and helmet. But in those few seconds the old aeroplane had really got wound up and the forces of the spin kept throwing me back into my seat. I started to fight like a madman to get out of that top hatch.

I remember getting my head in the breeze and my left foot on the throttle quadrant. Then there was a bang and I was outside. The aeroplane had broken up. A glance at the ground was sufficient to show that I was at about 7000 feet. And as I reached for the rip-cord I suddenly thought of the enemy fighters. I had always had a nightmare fear of being shot in my parachute descent and this was still uppermost in my mind, even in my present situation. I had seen a parachutist called Quiller do a delayed drop in New Zealand and it didn't look too bad, so I hung on to the rip-cord handle and kept an eye on the ground.

I fell surprisingly slowly — or so it seemed. 'I'll pull the cord at 3000 feet,' I thought. But just before that approximate height I found myself on my back, falling head first. I couldn't right myself quickly; and as I didn't like this attitude of fall, I gave the rip-cord a good smart jerk. The shroud lines came whipping out and one tangled with my right leg before I managed to kick free. And then I was pulled up with a jerk.

I was suspended in space at about 3000 feet. Then, to my consternation, several large hunks of aeroplane went fluttering by like large autumn leaves. But my luck held and nothing hit my canopy. I found myself still clutching the metal rip-cord handle like grim death. As I dropped it and watched it fall away, I saw myself heading towards a huge area of water. I thought of pulling on one side of the shroud lines, but decided to leave well alone. Then, as I glanced towards the target area I saw a large column of black smoke rising skywards. 'Good,' I thought. 'That'll be the bombs.' But, thinking it over afterwards, it was probably poor old V-Victor burning.

There was something wet on the back of my head and an investigation revealed lots of blood on my exploring hand. Fortunately, it happened to be a small scalp wound probably sustained after I had taken off my tin hat. Wearing the added head protection over the top of my leather flying helmet had become standard battle-station procedure with me, ever since my early sorties in Blenheims.

My left leg was aching and I had an awful feeling that I might have to land with a broken limb. By this time I was less than 100 feet from the ground and I saw with some relief that I was going to miss the large stretch of water by several hundred yards. Then I was over a ploughed field and the ground was suddenly rushing at me. Bang! I went end over end and finally came to rest half stunned and spitting out earth. Then the parachute canopy, caught by the wind, pulled me flat on my back and dragged me at high speed over the furrows before I banged the quick-release disc and came free of the harness. The silk 'chute billowed away with a Dutchman in pursuit.

Several people soon gathered. As I dusted myself down I looked ruefully at the left trouser leg of my 'number-one blue' uniform. It was rent from top to bottom. But, thank God, my leg was not broken — just badly bent. 'Escape is the first thing I do,' I thought. I looked at the dozen or more Dutch people standing near and asked: 'Do any of you people speak English?' No response. Then I heard a shout and, looking over my shoulder, I saw a German soldier with a gun, running towards me and waving frantically. I knew I was finished, so far as freedom was concerned, so I took my escape kit from my pocket and dropped it behind me so that the Dutch people could see. I kicked some earth over it and walked to meet my captor with my hands high.

The German advanced with his gun pointed at me in a business-like way and carefully frisked me. '*Du kommst,*' he commanded; and I limped off in the direction indicated. A quarter of a mile away was an ack-ack post of heavy guns. As we drew near the many gunners gathered to see their *Tommi* prize.

A corporal dressed the wound on my head and, as he finished, an officer drew up in an open car. He promptly started to question me in passable English — but he got nowhere. He seemed intensely interested to know what my target had been.

We were about to drive away when I heard a shout: 'Hi-ya Len!' There was Viv Phillips, tossing his usual deference to rank to the Netherland winds in his relief of reunion. And what a sight he looked! Wet strands of hair and rivulets of blood streaked his face. His entire body was wet with black slime. It appeared that the release-box of his parachute had stopped a bullet and the mangled metal could not be turned. He had been dragged by the billowing canopy through two dykes and across several fields before he could finally get his arms around a post and hang tight until help arrived.

His head wound, too, was dressed. And I was to see, as time went by, that around the scar a peculiar little metamorphosis took place. Above his brow an inch-wide strip of silvery white hair steadily and permanently slashed a track through the thatch of otherwise jet-black locks. In the post-war years it was to stand Phillips many a pint in the local pub.

We were taken together to a German officers' mess in the

middle of Amsterdam and given coffee and cigarettes and a further (and, for the enemy, unsuccessful) interrogation. Later, we were taken to a military hospital for closer attention to our wounds. Then, after the doctors had stitched up our gashes, we were moved to a huge military barracks — where the cell doors of solitary confinement clanged behind us.

I sat on a narrow, hard bed and stared into space for hours, wondering what had gone wrong. Had I, in pressing on with Ramrod 17, made the right decisions? What a shock it was going to be for my poor wife. These disturbing thoughts accompanied me to the interrogation centre of Dulag Luft, about 10 days later.

The fortnight of solitary confinement that followed was a time of soul-destroying purgatory for Trent. He was given no books to read, so, alone with nothing but his anguished thoughts, he spent hour upon hour polishing the brass buttons of his tunic until his handkerchief, the overworked buffer, almost disintegrated. One day, he discovered a matchstick on the floor of his cell, so he split it into minute slivers with his thumb nail and devoted the rest of that day to fashioning intricate patterns with the wood fibres.

After 2 weeks of what the Germans hoped was a 'softening up' period, Trent was taken to the comfortable office of a tall, genial officer who, in excellent and cultured English, asked the prisoner if he had had some good books to read while languishing in the cell.

'What?' the German feigned considerable surprise when Trent shook his head. 'Why, we have an admirable library of English books here.' He said that he would take him there, later. Then he suggested a cup of beef tea. Would Squadron Leader Trent like that? Indeed he would — and soon an orderly came in and presented the New Zealand 'guest' with a steaming hot cup of genuine English 'Oxo' — a beverage that Trent long remembered as a magic potion, its warmth a buffer against the chill of despondency and its sustenance a salvation from the near-starvation rations of the solitary-confinement cell.

The German chatted amicably with his prisoner. Would the captured pilot like to make a broadcast to friends and relations in Britain — to let them know, of course, that all was well? It could be arranged, easily. After all, it was but a German gesture of —

well, common humanity.

No, Trent told him. British service regulations stipulated that no broadcasts be made by anyone taken prisoner by the enemy. Nor, he told his persistent interrogator, would he disclose anything more than his name, rank and service number.

'As you will, Squadron Leader Trent,' smiled the German. 'But it may interest you to know that we have already a fairly comprehensive dossier on you.' He tapped his desk blotter. 'Would you like to see it.'

Trent, his curiosity aroused, said he would. The intelligence officer drew from under the blotter a file and handed it across the desk. 'Go on, have a look at it.'

The dossier, covering about twenty or thirty pages, was labelled: 'Squadron Leader L. H. Trent, DFC (RAF)' and Len Trent grew more amazed as he turned the pages. The history traced back to his schooldays at Nelson College, the date of his matriculation, his Air Force training through Taieri and Wigram, the squadrons in which he served in England, his navigation course at Hamble, his operational flying experience and the various dates of his promotions, the formation of 487 Squadron and the fact that his Ventura, V-Victor, carried the squadron code letters EG.

Trent's past, through German eyes, lay before him in incredible detail. Now, he wondered, what have they got to say in deciding my future?

9

AMSTERDAM AFTERMATH

We meet 'neath the sounding rafter,
And the walls around us are bare;
As they shout to our peals of laughter,
It seems that the dead are there.
So, stand to your glasses, steady!
We drink, in our comrades' eyes,
A cup to the dead already —
Hurrah, for the next who dies!

Those lines, from a poem peculiarly called 'Indian Revelry', are ascribed to W. F. Thompson who was supposed to have composed them while serving in the British Imperial Army in India during the plague.

Some of the Royal Flying Corps men, with a sense of theatre, resurrected the nineteenth-century poem and introduced it to their airfield messes in the First World War. They put the words to music and when they were roisteringly drunk — as they so often were after battle — they would shout their defiance to death in song.

Whereas not all the aircrew members of 487 Squadron in 1943 may have been familiar with the poignant verses, those who were left in the unit after the terrible shambles of Ramrod 17 would have paused in silence and, probably, blinked tearful eyes had some bibulous bard intoned the words. With the crews of ten aircraft missing, and the survivors of Duffill's C-Charlie in hospital after their fortunate return to base, there were forty-four vacant chairs at Methwold on the evening of 3 May.

Merv Darrall of Howick, Auckland, has vivid memories of that tragic day and its sombre night, as all at the station waited and hoped for news that, perhaps, some of the crews might have force-landed at other airfields in England.

'Methwold was like a morgue,' he said. 'It seemed that damn near the whole squadron had been wiped out. "Tich" Hanafin and I were about the only two B Flight members of 487 Squadron in the mess that night.'

Darrall and Hanafin, having recently flown sorties, had not been listed to fly in the Ramrod 17 raid. However, both were destined to gain prominence in the squadron's brief but gallant history when on 18 February 1944 they piloted their 487 Squadron Mosquito bombers in the successful piercing of the Amiens Prison walls.

Merv Darrall had joined 487 Squadron in March 1943. He had come, as a flight-sergeant, from a staff-flying stint in Canada where he had been instructing in such aircraft as Northrop Nomads, Fairey Battles and Avro Ansons. With about 400 hours in his log book he took part in his first 'op' — a raid by twelve of the squadron's Venturas on the oil refinery at Maasluis, near Rotterdam, on 22 March. A week later he again attacked a Rotterdam target when twenty-four aircraft from both 487 and 464 Squadrons successfully bombed the docks.

'The Ventura days were good,' he remembers. 'We young lads were apprehensive of the machines when we joined the squadron and learned that we were to be involved in low-level operations, but Len Trent and Tich Hanafin inspired us with confidence. Len, we knew, had done a fine and "dicey" first tour on Blenheims; and Tich had clocked up about 170 hours of shipping strikes — also flying Blenheims.'

Merv Darrall remembers that Flight Lieutenant A. V. Duffill's aircraft (AE916: C-Charlie) arrived back at Feltwell at 1855 hours. The navigator was Flying Officer F. J. Starkie and the wireless operators/gunners were Sergeants L. Neill and Turnbull. On the findings from their de-briefings, all were recommended for immediate decorations. Distinguished Flying Crosses went to the two officers and the non-commissioned officers received the Distinguished Flying Medal.

One man's view of a battle can differ markedly from another's, so much depending on the occupations and urgencies of the moment. So it is understandable that, even as two or three witnesses to a motoring accident can each come up with his own version of events, so too can the recollections of those actively involved in battle sometimes conflict, one with another. Nor do historians, necessarily, help greatly.

Flight Lieutenant Duffill's aircraft, the leader of the A flight box which followed on the starboard quarter of Squadron Leader Trent's B Flight box, was one of the first hit by the enemy fighters and it fell away with so much smoke streaming behind that the Germans must have decided they had made a 'kill' and so left C-Charlie to its fate.

Duffill's navigator, Flying Officer Starkie, opened the bomb doors and managed to release three bombs. And, as the fires within the aircraft were gradually brought under control, the crippled Ventura staggered home.

Merv Darrall, who saw the battered machine, says the effect of the enemy cannon fire was, as he understates it, 'rather alarming.' Furthermore, grim facts had been brought home — the Ventura's turret Browning .3s were of little use against the armour of an FW-190.

The precise order in which the bombers fell immediately after Duffill's departure has not been established. What is known is that three Venturas were so badly mauled that they were either ditched or fell out of control into the sea as they tried to struggle back to England. Those aircraft and their pilots, navigators and wireless operators/air gunners were:

No AE956: H-Harry. Flight-Sergeant A. E. Coutts, Flying Officer L. E. Richball, Sergeant D. C. Robinson and Sergeant W. D. L. Goodfellow — all killed, lost at sea.

No AE798: D-Dog. Sergeant-Pilot J. Low, Sergeant H. W. Toombes, Sergeant J. C. Lynas, Sergeant A. E. Downs — all killed, lost at sea.

No AJ478: A-Apple. Flying Officer O. E. Foster (POW), Flying Officer T. A. Penn (POW), Sergeant R. W. Mann (POW), Sergeant T. W. J. Warner (killed). Aircraft ditched 20 kilometres off the Dutch coast.

Tom Penn, now living at Pukekohe, has vivid memories of the Ramrod 17 raid. He was the navigator of A-Apple and can bear witness to the relentless starboard attacks by the German FW-190s:

There has been some talk of the FW-190s tackling our Spitfire escort while the Me-109s attacked the Venturas. But, believe me, all I saw were 190s coming at us.

At first, they stood off a bit as though suspecting some sort of trap on the part of our Spitfires. Then they began making solo runs at us until, soon, they were coming in persistently in force.

They seemed to be working to a predetermined pattern based on the vulnerability of our blind spot. They would come diving down from 2 o'clock high and seek to come up underneath us, raking us with cannon fire.

Our crippling attack came when we were hit on the starboard side from below. The cannon shells tore in, ripping through the starboard wing-root in a long, wide seam that began near the aircraft's nose and ended with the dorsal turret being knocked out of action.

A shell hit the bombsight and another passed under my left armpit before exploding. I was temporarily knocked unconscious by the blow and from flying debris; the whole of my left side was to remain black with the bruising for a long time after.

Foster's controls were hit and damaged. He, too, was dazed and semi-conscious before he recovered enough to keep the aircraft airborne.

Petrol was pouring out through the fractures in the starboard tanks and fuel lines, so I immediately switched off the cocks on that side and made frantic signals to Foster — our intercom was, by now, out of action — that I was going aft to assess damage.

As I moved into the body of the aircraft I was drenched with spray. I was soon to discover, to my considerable concern, that it was petrol. In fact, the floor of the Ventura was awash with the stuff. I could see that Tim Warner was trapped in the dorsal turret, so with some difficulty I managed to free him and make him as comfortable as possible against the main spar. At that stage he seemed more dazed than badly injured.

Moving for'ard again, I looked towards the target area and could see only one aircraft ahead of us. We had no maps with us, by this time. They had blown away through the gaps in our fuselage. But I have vivid recollections of our being directly over a big complex of crossroads. We opened our bomb doors and dropped our load as the target area was just coming down the drift wires. Our aircraft had been badly hit again and we turned desperately for home.

Foster decided against abandoning the aircraft over enemy territory as long as there remained a hope of reaching England. Besides, the crew had now only three parachute packs between them — one having been wrecked by enemy fire. But now over the sea, and with the damaged Ventura sinking lower by the minute, ditching seemed to be their only chance of survival.

Although the day had been sunny, there had been a persistent high wind and the sea was decidedly choppy. Nevertheless, Foster managed to pull off a commendable ditching. As Tom Penn was helping the still dazed Tim Warner out of the wallowing aircraft he saw that the inflatable rubber dinghy had not automatically burst free of its compartment in the manner claimed by its manufacturers.

Penn was making his way to unstrap the emergency hatchet so that he could hack the dinghy free when the aircraft suddenly nose-dived to the bottom of the sea. With the tail of A-Apple sticking straight up in the water, Penn was imprisoned within a chamber of compressed air. But not for long. Having struck the sea bed, the Ventura began to settle horizontally and the large bubble, containing Penn, belched out through the escape hatch, bearing him with it.

Tom Penn does not know the exact time of their ditching, but believes it was after 1800 hours. The four crew members emerged alive from the sunken aircraft and floated, supported by their mae-west life jackets, for 2 or 3 hours before being picked up by the enemy.

Tim Warner, however, did not survive to be imprisoned. He died, presumably from internal injuries, after about an hour and a half in the water. His body was recovered on 7 May 1943.

Over occupied Holland, three Venturas of the Ramrod 17 force were brought down about the same time — 1745 hours.

No AJ200: G-George. Flight-Sergeant J.D. Sharp (POW), Sergeant H. Gibson (killed), Sergeant A. Stevens (killed), Sergeant D. R. Rowland (killed). Shot down at Vijthuizen.

No AE684: B-Baker. Flying Officer S. Coshall (killed), Flying Officer R. A. North (POW), Sergeant W. Stannard (POW), Sergeant D. H. Sparkes (POW). Shot down at Bennerbroek.

Two amazing stories of escape emerge from the destruction of B-Baker. Flying Officer Rupert North, the navigator, was in his compartment in the nose of the aircraft when the Ventura was rocked by a series of explosions. He looked back through the bulkhead doorway behind the pilot and saw that the body of the aircraft was in flames.

He scrambled along the narrow passage to the cockpit and saw his pilot, Flying Officer Coshall, reaching up to release the escape hatch above his head. North made his way towards the fire extinguisher on the wall near the bulkhead door and was about to grasp it when he was met by a tremendous burst of flame. With the opening of the pilot's escape hatch, the rush of air had drawn the fire forward into the cockpit.

Seeing that the pilot was ready to leave, North grabbed his parachute pack and, desperately determined to escape the inferno, clambered up through the hatch without first clipping the closely-packed canopy to the lugs on the front of his parachute harness.

To the layman it should be known that crew members in bombers wore parachute harness with detached parachute packs — unlike fighter pilots whose all-in-one safety gear allowed them to sit on the pack, which became a rather knobbly cushion — particularly as it usually contained a tightly-packed inflatable dinghy.

As North plummeted downward he frantically endeavoured to clip the parachute pack on to his harness. In his desperation he found to his dismay, he had clipped the right-hand ring on the left clip. He would have to unclip the thing and start again — in the full flight of free descent — unless he risked being supported by only one catch when the suddenly opening canopy brought him up with a jolt.

He decided to leave things as they stood. He pulled the cord, the 'chute opened — and he drifted downwards to the awaiting arms of the enemy.

Sergeant Stannard, one of the North's crew mates, was trapped in the tail of the burning B-Baker. Suddenly the aircraft disintegrated in an explosion. The tail section containing Stannard broke free and miraculously glided down to hit a tree. The gunner was stunned. When he regained consciousness he was in the hands of the Gestapo.

The third Ventura to be shot down at 1745 hours was No AE731: O-Orange, whose crew were Pilot Officer T. L. B. Taylor (POW), Pilot Officer M. Shapiro (POW), Sergeant L.

Littlewood and Sergeant T. S. Tattam (both missing).

The navigator, Monty Shapiro, has been listed in various documents and reports as killed in the crash but Len Trent reports that his erstwhile squadron companion is still very much alive and well and now living in London. Whereas pilot Terry Taylor eventually found himself imprisoned in Stalag Luft III along with Trent and 7 other survivors of the Ramrod 17 force, there does not seem to be any record of Shapiro reaching the same camp — hence, no doubt, the supposition that he died in battle.

The fates of Sergeants Littlewood and Tattam are unknown.

Pilot Officer Taylor's story of the crippled aircraft's crash in polder country north of Vijthuizen, was told to Len Trent during their frequent walks around the prison ground 'circuit'. It is an amazing tale of desperate action laced with large quantities of luck. Trent tells of Taylor and his adventures in his own words:

Terry Taylor, as I remember, was in the photographic business before the war and lived either in Whangarei or Auckland. He was a very pleasant lad and soon proved to be a particularly good pilot, especially in formation flying. So I invariably picked him to fly as my number three — stationed off my port wingtip — where he would stick, whatever the formation's manoeuvrings, like one of the RAF's famous Red Arrows.

On our 3 May raid we had just passed Haarlem with the air battle at its height, when my controller, Roy Thomas, called from the astro dome that Taylor's aircraft had disappeared — although he had not seen it hit, as he had been busy directing our evasive tactics as we repeatedly banked to starboard to give our turret guns a clear field of fire against the attacking fighters.

That left only our aircraft and Rusty Peryman's T-Tommy, flying number two, in the air — so far as we could see.

Terry Taylor told me that his Ventura had been raked by cannon fire and had burst into flames. Both starboard and port windows of the cockpit had been shattered by the attack and the fierce draught was sucking the fire so that it threatened to envelop the pilot. The windscreen had become covered with dark oil so that his forward view was completely obscured.

In agony with burns, he ordered his crew to bale out and then, finding his own parachute pack was beyond recovery in the fire-filled body of the aircraft and that the flames were increasing in the cockpit, he decided to make a quick end to his suffering. He dived steeply towards the ground at something like 350 mph. However, the speed of his descent began to lessen the extent of the flames and to clear his windscreen of oil. And Taylor began to have hopes of salvation as he saw the open country that now lay below him. He decided to try and crash-land the aircraft.

He levelled his descent somewhat and the Ventura hit the marshy land on its belly at about 250 mph, bounced high several times and eventually came to rest in a sufficiently compact state as to allow the injured pilot to make a hasty exit before the bombs in the still-burning hulk could explode.

Taylor had run about 50 yards before he was amazed to hear cries coming from the wrecked aircraft. Hardly believing that his crewmen had not parachuted to safety, he rushed back and tore at the fuselage door, which had jammed — and so prevented the men's escape — and helped his fellow survivors from the fire.

Together, at a safe distance, they saw the remains of O-Orange disintegrate in a mighty burst of flame, smoke and noise as the bomb load exploded — before they were captured, hospitalized and imprisoned by the Germans.

Len Trent and Terry Taylor were great friends and communicated with each other for some time after the war until, about 15 years after their release from German hands, Taylor died of a brain tumour.

At 1750 hours, Ventura No AE780: S-Sugar was shot down over Bornstrasse, Amsterdam. Its crew were Flying Officer S. ('Steady') McGowan (killed), Flying Officer E. B. Thornber (killed), Sergeant C. R. Smith (killed) and Sergeant I. F. Urlich (POW).

Sergeant Ivan Urlich, now living in Hawera, owes his life to the prompt and courageous actions of his pilot and his navigator, McGowan and Thornber. Seeing their gunner unconscious in his turret, the two officers dragged Urlich out, clipped his parachute pack on to his harness, hooked his right hand into the rip-cord handle and pushed him out of the doomed aircraft. Urlich recovered in time to open his canopy and float down to the comparative safety of a term of imprisonment. His three companions died in the crash of S-Sugar.

At 1753 hours Ventura AE713: T-Tommy was shot down at Hernbrug, south of Zaandam. All crew members were killed. They were Flying Officer S. B. ('Rusty') Peryman, Pilot Officer E. T. Williams, Sergeant G. E. Southam and Sergeant J. E. Allison.

Ventura AE716: U-Uncle crashed in a polder west of Amsterdam at 1800 hours. Its crew were Flying Officer T. L. Baynton, Flight-Sergeant P. B. Davies, Sergeant L. E. Price and Flight-Sergeant H. G. Lammercraft. All were killed.

It was just after this that Squadron Leader Trent's V-Victor, the last of that ill-starred sortie, plummeted into Kometen Polder near the Fokker plant.

Back at Methwold there still remained some hopes — even as late as 6 May — that news might tell of forced-landings or of crewmen who had parachuted to safety into friendly hands. But the roll call, after officialdom had resigned itself to the full losses, showed only six crews and eight aircraft left in 487 Squadron.

Morale had suffered a swiftly-dealt blow; not only within the remnants of the New Zealand squadron but also throughout the flights of the sister Ventura units — 464 (Australian) Squadron at Feltwell and 21 Squadron at Swanton Morley.

Arthur Cox of Clapton, London, joined 487 Squadron early in 1943. He was a general armourer and, being particularly interested in his trade and in aircraft generally, he would often fly as a passenger on air-test flights in the Venturas. He speaks highly of the rapport that prevailed between ground staff and aircrew men of the squadron and he 'always felt that, in the estimation of the flying chaps, the armourers were a well-liked section.'

He remembers when the station learned of the Amsterdam disaster. 'It was a beautiful summer's day and Charlie Bush, who was in charge of B Flight armoury, came cycling round to give us the news. He was crying his eyes out.'

Charlie Bush was himself fated to meet a violent end. One evening he unwittingly drove his utility truck into the arc of a spinning Mosquito propeller.

Arthur Cox also recalls Max Sparks 'really going after his fitter after he (Sparks) had had a mag drop on one engine before take-off on the Amsterdam Ramrod.' Sparks was a pilot of one of the Venturas that was unable to get airborne for the raid. 'The following day Sparks told the fitter that he had probably saved his life.'

Cox says that after the Amsterdam affair it seemed that the atmosphere of the squadron changed overnight. 'A whole lot of new replacement chaps arrived; and when we switched to Mosquito aircraft the armourers became divorced from the aircrews because there were no gunners on Mosquitoes.'

The Allies had gained nothing from Ramrod 17 — which, of course, was one of the gambles of warfare. It could have been a resounding success — if ... And so, the tally of 'ifs' mount up in a doleful litany of might-have-beens. *If* the raid had been planned to miss that reception party of seventy crack Luftwaffe fighter pilots at Schiphol; *if* the Spitfires from Hornchurch had not 'beaten the gun' by 20 minutes and climbed immediately into enemy radar range after refuelling at Martlesham; *if* the escort Spitfires had given adequate protection to the Venturas; *if* the Venturas had been recalled before crossing the Dutch coast — the operation might have succeeded.

A cryptic summary of that abortive attack on the Amsterdam power station can be taken from one sentence made by Flying Officer North, navigator of Ventura B-Baker, following his capture: 'I went ... to hospital in Amsterdam — where the electric power was still operating.'

A report by a high officer of 12 Group, Fighter Command, on Ramrod 17, dated 6 May 1943, gives the following findings:

'This operation was originally designed by No 12 Group to consist of 12 Ventura aircraft going out from base at low level and pulling up on approaching the Dutch coast to be at 10,000 feet over Amsterdam, to be covered by two L.R. (Long Range) Spitfire V squadrons. Normally, an operation of this type proceeds a considerable distance on its way before the Germans get any reaction from their RDF (Radio direction-finding) and the chances are, therefore, that it will get into the target area before any appreciable German reaction takes place. However, in view of the increased reaction in that area recently, I ordered two Spitfire IX squadrons of No 11 Group to provide "cover" for the operation and an additional L.R. Spitfire squadron from No 10

Group to strengthen the escort.

'2. Had the whole of this cover and escort been in position, and had they proceeded to the target area in satisfactory manner, I believe the operation would have pursued a normal course.

'3. I attribute the main cause of the failure of this operation to the fact that the two Spitfire IX squadrons of No 11 Group providing "cover" over the target area, after refuelling at Martlesham, left the ground some 20 minutes before it was necessary for them to do so. Further, instead of proceeding at sea level until approaching the Dutch coast and then climbing to attain their operational height over the target area, the wing commenced climbing straight away from their base at Martlesham. When they were approaching the Dutch coast it was realized by the AOC No 11 Group that they were not only very much too early but well north of their correct course to target. In these circumstances, AOC No 11 Group considered that they would not have sufficient petrol to complete their task and accordingly ordered their withdrawal.

'4. The action of all 11 Group Spitfire IX wing had caused violent reaction on the part of the Germans with the result that, by the time the main party arrived 12 miles off the Dutch coast they were met by a very strong force of German fighters who had a height advantage, and with whom a running fight ensued all the way in to the target and out again.

'5. This state of affairs was further aggravated by the fact that the enemy fighters, flying in four separate formations, commenced their diving attacks on the main party from above, whilst two of the three Spitfire escort squadrons were still behind and climbing, and only the close escort squadron was in position on either flank of the Venturas. The result of this was that instead of having five squadrons to cover the Venturas (two of them being Spitfire IX squadrons) only one of the three Spitfire V squadrons (the close escort squadron) was in its correct tactical position when the attack opened. This squadron closed in on the Venturas which carried straight on to the target, whilst the remaining two Spitfire V squadrons were forced to break to engage succeeding waves of German fighters which dived firing on the main party from above, and continued the dive to come up and attack the Venturas from below. In the general melee some of the bombers, it is believed, turned back whilst others continued on to the target.

In the resultant fighting the three Spitfire squadrons gradually became split up, although the close escort squadron made every endeavour to stay with the Venturas right to the target. This was, however, most difficult as they had continually to turn to ward off attacks which made it increasingly difficult for them to keep up with the Venturas.

'6. That the three Spitfire V squadrons were not in a better tactical position when the attack opened is due to the fact that the climb of this wing was carried out by the leading squadron too steeply and at too low a speed for the squadrons which were following. This resulted in No 504 Squadron, which had come up from No 10 Group for the operation and who were unused to carrying out climbs in formation of the type required for this operation, being left too far behind and below and they took no serious part in the fighting. It is reasonable, however, to assume that these three squadrons, normally, would have each been in their correct tactical station relative to the Venturas well before crossing the Dutch coast. They were not to know that the Hornchurch wing had already "flushed" up the German fighters and that the latter were already preparing to attack them with height advantage well out to sea.

'7. I attribute the blame for the failure of this operation firstly, to the inadequate "briefing" of the Hornchurch (Spitfire IX) wing, and, secondly, to the tactical errors of the Hornchurch wing leader in taking off some 20 minutes too soon and then climbing to operational height from his base to the target, thereby "flushing" up a large force of German fighters who were waiting with height advantage to descend upon the main party.

'8. The blame for this appears to lie between the Operations Staff Officer of No 11 Group who prepared the orders and briefing arrangements for Hornchurch, the Sector Controller, Hornchurch, and the Hornchurch Wing Leader. These serious shortcomings are being investigated more fully and I propose to take appropriate action when the full facts are before me.

'9. The responsibility for withdrawing the high cover rests with the AOC No 11 Group. At the time he made the decision to withdraw the Spitfire IX wing he did not realize that the Hornchurch Wing Leader had climbed straight away from the English coast instead of keeping low, and there were no enemy plots at that time on the "table". In view of the fact that the subsequent plotting of his wing showed them to be well off their course to the target (in addition to being 20 minutes too early) and feeling that they would have insufficient petrol to complete their task, the AOC No 11 Group decided it was better to withdraw them before their intention became known to the Germans. He, therefore, ordered their withdrawal, and the Controller at No 11 Group informed No 12 Group Controller that this action had been taken.

'10. On receipt of this information, SASO No 12 Group (in the absence of the AOC) considered whether to issue a recall signal also to the main party. He decided against a recall: firstly, because R/T touch could not be established until the formations had climbed from sea level to cross the Dutch coast (they had still not reached a height at which they could be picked up by our RDF); secondly, because to try and communicate with the Bomber Leader through and with the concurrence of No 2 Group would take at least 10 minutes, which would be very late; and thirdly, to send such an order as the party were rapidly approaching the Dutch coast would inevitably have caused confusion, and might lead to a premature return of part of the fighter force.

'CONCLUSIONS

11. (i) I consider the failure of this operation was primarily due to the following reasons:

(a) Inadequate "briefing" of the Hornchurch wing;

(b) Hornchurch Wing Leader proceeding with his wing towards the target area approximately 20 minutes too early and climbing to operational height straight from the English coast instead of remaining at low level until approaching the Dutch coast;

(c) The withdrawal of the Hornchurch cover wing (Spitfire IXs) from participation in this operation, made necessary by their too early take-off and considerations of petrol shortage which resulted thereby.

(ii) The serious errors given in paragraph 11(b) above, provided the German RDF system with ample early warning of our intentions and enabled the Germans to put up a numerically greater force of fighters of superior performance in position, and with

tactical advantage in height ready to descend upon the
Venturas and their escort wing (Spitfire Vs) well
before they had reached the Dutch coast.

(iii) A full investigation into the shortcomings outlined
above has been ordered by me and I propose to take
appropriate action when the full facts are before me.'

The full facts of that Amsterdam Ramrod may never be known.
Certainly, there were additional reports from 12 Group; and 2
Group — whose Venturas were the prime sufferers in the raid —
filed a lengthy document outlining events according to the
bombers' point of view. Explanations from high places in both 10
Group and 11 Group kept lines of communication — within and
between Fighter Command and Bomber Command — busy
through the month of May.

But there were squadrons to be rebuilt and re-equipped — new
men to fill blank places, new aircraft to replace lost and redundant
types, new tactics to be developed and new targets to be studied.
There was a war to be won. So, in time, the furore that had
bubbled over the flames of Ramrod 17 settled to a simmer as the
heat was lowered.

But for many long days and lonely nights, that sunny, windy
afternoon of 3 May 1943 would live in the memories of the
relatives and loved ones of forty young men lost somewhere in the
haunted sky above Holland.

10
K R I E G I E

KICKING HIS HEELS for having fallen into this mess, Len Trent gloomily surveyed the scene at Dulag Luft — although not much of a panorama spread out before him. Certainly, he had been released from solitary confinement and had been taken to the Red Cross side of the prison camp. And, true to his word, the suave German major who had interrogated Trent had allowed his prisoner to peruse the selection of books in the camp library.

Fearing this cultural privilege might be one of those 'one-off' occasions, Len Trent selected one of the fattest volumes he could find on the shelves to help fill the interminable hours of waiting. It was a novel of life and struggle for achievement in the mill centres of Yorkshire — *Fame is the Spur*. As more Allied prisoners arrived in the holding camp in their ones and twos, the total of captives grew until there were sufficient to send a trainload to a more permanent home. By the time he was herded, along with about fifty or sixty other RAF officers, to the railway station, he had almost finished the book.

Their destination was Stalag Luft III, a camp that from its beginnings had been an arena where incredible battles of British wit and ingenuity were fought against stolid German disciplines. Later, its name would be linked in history with Nazi atrocities and mass murders.

It was situated close to the town of Sagan, on the Oder River, not far from the Polish border. So, for the prisoners packed tightly in boxcars, the train journey was long and considerably uncomfortable. They arrived late in the afternoon and were marched from the Sagan railway station to the gates of the camp's north compound — which at that time, mid-1943, was the second and comparatively newer part of Stalag Luft III. The east compound had been in existence for about two years before the northern area was opened in the early months of 1943.

When the new 'purge' of RAF officer prisoners arrived at the gate there followed a customary delay while transit guards exchanged manifest lists and receipts with the guardhouse keepers. During this time, considerable curiosity had been evoked within the compound and a gathering of about 300 inhabitants had congregated in a big semi-circle to inspect each arrival as he stepped within the prison grounds.

'I walked into the compound rather sheepishly,' Trent remembers. 'A fellow, under such circumstances, had certain feelings of guilt or, more definitely, embarrassment as he paraded his misfortune before two or three hundred pairs of eyes — quite forgetting, of course, that every man behind the wire shared those feelings.

'Anyhow, I had not stepped a dozen paces before a loud laugh and a shout went up: "Len, you silly old bastard — I bloody well knew you'd turn up, sooner or later!" It was my cousin Ian Richmond, from Takaka.'

Richmond had been shot down while piloting his Sterling bomber over Holland. In one of the peculiar coincidences that crop up from time to time, Len Trent was to receive towards the end of 1982 an inquiry from a Dutch war-historian friend asking if he could trace a New Zealand pilot named Ian Richmond. It appeared that the Dutchman had come across the 40 year old wreck of a Sterling and had established the name of the captain from the aircraft's records. Sadly, Ian Richmond had died but a few months earlier. He would have been delighted with the discovery.

'To complete my reception committee,' continued Trent, 'was my old friend and ally Mick Shand, whose Spitfire had been shot from under him, necessitating a parachute descent into enemy hands. So, with Ian on one arm and Mick on the other, I was led to my new board and lodgings — Room 10, Block 104 — and three Nelson College old boys were together again.'

The prisoners' ritual of examining every new face to enter Stalag Luft III was more significant than mere idle curiosity. The Germans — the 'goons' — had a crafty scheme whereby, every so often, they would infiltrate the camp with a 'plant'; a German dressed like a British flyer and briefed with much RAF information. In perfect English and in practised jargon he would try to pass himself as the genuine article in his endeavours to fossick information' on escape plans, hidden radios and other *verboten* activities.

As may be imagined, the trick did not last for long. Any incoming prisoner who lacked a referee among the older inhabitants was immediately brought before the British screening committee who cross-examined the stranger so assiduously that a phoney would have no chance of standing up to the interrogation. When such an imposter was discovered, the Senior British Officer would request the Camp Commandant that the man be removed forthwith. Great shouts of derision would rise as the embarrassed actor was escorted back to his own kind.

On his way to his quarters Trent's eyes took in his surroundings. North compound was about 300 yards square — a dismal area surrounded by two 9 foot barbed-wire fences spaced about 5 feet apart. Between them were thick coils of barbed wire; and about 30 feet inside the main fence a warning wire had been stretched. The mere placing of a foot on or over that wire, Trent was to learn, was an invitation to a trigger-happy goon to shoot with intent to maim.

Every 150 yards along the fence line a 'goon-box', inhabited by alert sentries, stood high on its piles, while at night — as Len Trent was also to learn, quite dramatically — sentries patrolled outside the wire barricade.

Inside the compound a *hundfuehrer* and his vicious dog kept a watch for any so daring as to break curfew. The *'hund'* was invariably a vicious alsatian. One night Mick Shand was sleeping under the two open windows, when they were all awakened by a terrifying snapping and snarling dog tearing about their room. It had come in over Mick's feet and out over his head in pursuit of Henry Murray's cat 'Bianca' — the only cat in the compound.

In the northern half of the compound were fifteen hut blocks built in three rows of five — plus a kitchen block, a theatre and latrines. In the centre of this complex was the fire pool. The southern end of the compound constituted the *appell* ground and general recreation area.

Inside the northern end of the prison grounds was the *vorlager*, which contained the camp hospital, the prison (which even the goons called 'the cooler') and the coal store. A high barbed wire fence separated the *vorlager* from the main compound and at the eastern end of the enclosure the German guardroom stretched between the two sets of main gates.

Block 104, which was to be Len Trent's address for some time to come, was the central one of the five immediately facing the vorlager. It, like the others, contained a total of eighteen or twenty rooms, each about 15 feet square, with a dividing corridor.

Room 10, Trent discovered, housed several New Zealanders. There, besides Mick Shand and Ian Richmond, were Billy Griffiths, Jeff Salt and Henry ('Piglet') Lamond — who had trained to fly at Wigram with Len.

Lamond owed his incarceration to about 800 feet of meteorological trouble. Flying a Sunderland 'boat', he had been instructed to take his aircraft into a quiet Grecian bay and, in the blackness of night, set the machine down on the water without benefit of landing lights and so rendezvous with remnant escapees of the British Army.

But his briefing instructions had been scanty and the weather forecast either non-existent or just downright false. He had flown into a frontal system and his barometric altimeter untruthfully told him he had something like 800 feet of altitude still in his savings account. Alas. Henry hit the water at a terrible speed. The Sunderland disintegrated and he was dragged 30 feet below the surface with remnants of the flight deck still around him. He was one of the few survivors who managed to swim to shore and join the band of people he had been sent to rescue. Eventually, after being on the run for some time, he was captured and sent to Stalag Luft III.

Trent and Lamond still correspond and share a common interest in golf.

One of the first sights to meet Len Trent's eyes as he entered the inner confines of Block 104 were two prisoners standing on a grey blanket as they made strange adjustments to their trousers. Said Ian Richmond: 'There you are, Len — that's your first introduction to Kriegie life!'

Trent nodded and smiled politely. He had schooled himself against a lot of the surprises that might be in store for him at Sagan. But he was puzzled. It was, also, the first time he had heard the word 'Kriegie' applied to his life. It was, he soon learned, an abbreviation of the German for 'prisoner of war' — *Kriegsgefangene.*

The men adjusting their clothing were 'penguins' — those whose task was the disposal of the bright-yellow tunnel sand that was being excavated from the prisoners' burrowings 30 feet below the compound. They secreted the stuff in two long tubular pouches made from the legs of long-john woollen underwear, supplied in large quantity by the blessed Red Cross. These carrier bags, suspended by a cord around the neck, ran down underneath each trouser leg of the penguin. A pin held the bottom of each tube closed and the sand-disposal expert had but to walk nonchalantly (he certainly couldn't run) to where a friend would be digging a patch of garden in the mean, grey soil of the compound. Pausing with a foot in the trench as though making sowing-and-harvesting conversation, he would pull the cord that released the pin. The gardener would then turn the sods to cover the yellow tell-tale sand that poured from the trouser cuff.

Tunnel 'Harry' was well under construction. But Trent, a new boy, would be left to become acclimatized with his new surroundings — should that ever be really possible — before being invited to contribute his efforts to the prime task of reaching freedom. Tunnelling was paramount in thought and deed.

In the days immediately following his entry into Stalag Luft III his early concerns were meeting up with fellow survivors of the 'Ramrod 17' raid and piecing together their stories. As the camp contained only officers of the Air Force, the full list of non-commissioned aircrew who escaped from the wrecked Venturas could not be verified. But the men who had arrived to accompany their leader behind the prison wires at Sagan were Flying Officer Viv Phillips, Flying Officer O. E. Foster, Flying Officer Tom Penn, Flying Officer R. A. North and Pilot Officer Terry Taylor. This small band were to cover many a mile 'walking the circuit' together. Flying Officer Monty Shapiro, as earlier mentioned, has been misreported in some military documents as having been killed on the operation. Whatever his adventures in enemy-occupied Holland, he does not appear to have reached Stalag Luft III.

When Len Trent was introduced to the master plan of the tunnelling operations he learned that, besides 'Harry' — which had its entry under the tile base of a heating stove in Room 23 of Block 104 — two other tunnels were also being driven. 'Tom' began in a dark corner of a concrete floor by a chimney in Block 123 and was heading, about 30 feet below the compound, towards the western enclosure fence and an estimated breakout hole within the pine forest that bordered the camp. 'Dick' had probably the most craftily-devised entry trap ever attempted by prisoners determined on tunnelling. In the concrete floor of the washroom of 122 block was an iron grating, about 18 inches square, that covered an overflow well about 3 feet deep. About a foot up from the bottom a drain pipe led off the water — which meant that there was always a foot of water lying in the sump below the pipe's opening.

Minskewitz, a wiry little Polish officer in the RAF, had become the acknowledged expert in devising tunnel trapdoors. While some of his stooges kept watch outside, he baled out the water and mopped the sump-well dry with old rags. Then he chipped away one wall of the concrete pit to lay bare the soft earth that awaited the assaults of the tunnellers. He then cast a new slab, from cement and aggregate pilfered from supplies left unattended by German *arbeiters*, and fitted it where the broken wall had been. He sealed the cracks with soap and sand, replaced the grating and poured water down until the sump was again full to the overflow pipe.

It soon became but a matter of a minute or two to remove the iron grating, bale out the well and remove the concrete slab. Later, when the shaft became deeper beneath, the diggers would lower themselves down, the slab and the grating would be put in place and the water poured into the sump; the workers could then tunnel away with comparative peace of mind, knowing that only a ferret with divine powers (and there were none of *those* anywhere near Sagan) would be able to find them.

Trent's first duty as a newly-recruited penguin was to throw himself — literally, flat out — into the languid pleasures of sunbathing. Stripped to the waist he would emerge from Block 104 casually carrying a bundled grey blanket. He would wander to a sunny spot in the compound, spread the woollen cover over the loose soil and become absorbed in one of the many books found in the camp library. To the ever-watching goons this form of relaxation by the prisoners was commonplace. The inmates, being officers, were not required to toil in work parties; so bored bodies abounded around the enclosure. But what the guards could not see was Trent surreptitiously working his kilogram of yellow tunnel sand (which he had carried out in the folds of his blanket) into the dark grey soil of the compound.

Over and over, critics who had never experienced life in Stalag Luft III have expressed incredulity that the tunnels, with their

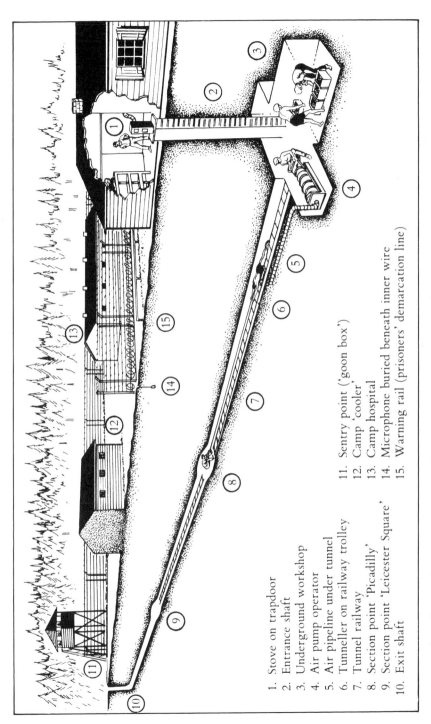

1. Stove on trapdoor
2. Entrance shaft
3. Underground workshop
4. Air pump operator
5. Air pipeline under tunnel
6. Tunneller on railway trolley
7. Tunnel railway
8. Section point 'Picadilly'
9. Section point 'Leicester Square'
10. Exit shaft
11. Sentry point ('goon box')
12. Camp 'cooler'
13. Camp hospital
14. Microphone buried beneath inner wire
15. Warning rail (prisoners' demarcation line)

Diagram of Stalag Luft III escape tunnel 'Harry'. (With acknowledgements to Ley Kenyon's sketch in Paul Brickhill's book *The Great Escape*.)

amazingly ingenious ancillary equipment such as air pumps, workshops, trucks and railway tracks, could have been sunk and driven beneath the feet of the guards without the Germans knowing.

Perhaps the most amazing fact is that when, eventually, the Germans *did* know that at least one tunnel existed, they could not find it despite the ceaseless vigils of the ferrets and the ringing of the compound with sunken sound detectors. Sand was the enemy, the ever-present encumbrance, the traitorous, yellow informer that the sweating diggers and their many-strong band of penguins had to move and hide. 'The meek shall inherit the earth,' one tunneller wryly observed after a tunnel collapsed on him and his mate had to pull him out by the ankles. But he carried on scooping out the spoil, shoring up the walls and ceiling again with slabs sawn from the camp's wooden bed-boards. Nevertheless, the tunnel inched further towards freedom and the penguins waddled away with the stuff sagging down in long-john pouches inside their trouser-legs. The prisoners' gardens became heavily impregnated with yellow sand. It was slyly deposited beneath the scuffling feet of hockey and soccer players. It was stuffed under dormitory blocks and above ceilings, packed into dozens upon dozens of empty Red Cross boxes. Later, it was crammed tightly into one of the abandoned tunnels' when the full emphasis of escape was centred on the one route.

The officer commanding Block 104 was Wing Commander Mindy Blake, DSO, DFC. He, like Trent, was a New Zealander who had joined the RAF before the outbreak of war and the two soon found they had something more in common than merely being kindred-countrymen.

Blake, lithe and compact as he then was, had observed his thirtieth birthday on 10 February — a month or two before Len Trent entered the camp. He had gained his Master of Science degree at Canterbury University and had lectured in physics, concurrent with becoming the New Zealand Universities' gymnast and pole-vault champion, before joining the RAF in 1936. After commanding a fighter squadron in the Battle of Britain he had been shot down over enemy-occupied territory and taken prisoner of war.

In leisure hours between tunnelling activities, Blake taught Len Trent the techniques of gymnastics. They constructed a set of parallel bars and in a short space of time the willing pupil progressed to become a better than average performer. In return he taught Blake the rudiments of the golf swing. By some mysterious means — probably through the thoughtfulness of some golfing addict in the Red Cross organisation — an old No. 5 iron had been sent into the compound and Trent had managed to get his hands onto it. But not one golf ball could be found — not a single, ancient guttie or a wide-smiling Silver King was unearthed from their searchings and beggings.

Disappointed but not dismayed, Trent set about making a test model. First he fossicked for a near-round pebble about the diameter of a finger nail. Around that he wound the rubber-seal strip from a Red Cross coffee can to form a resiliant core. Then hundreds of yards of cotton, bound tightly, increased the diameter to make a sphere of near-standard proportions. Finally, some pliable leather from an old boxing glove was cut, somewhat in the pattern of a tennis-ball case, and sewn tightly and neatly to make the cover.

True, it was not a ball to challenge the flight of a well-struck Dunlop 65, nor yet raise envy in the hearts of Messrs Penfold Inc. — but at least, says Len Trent, it bored its way through the air like a little russet-hued champion. Encouraged, he made a second ball along the same lines and the master and his enthusiastic pupil spent many hours swinging and chipping with the No. 5 iron — undoubtedly the most versatile club that could have been endowed to them.

To say that Mindy Blake became keen on hitting a golf ball would be a classic understatement. He became rapt and enchanted in the mental disciplines and muscular coordinations of the golf swing. When he was free of prison bonds he (like Len Trent) elected to continue his RAF service career. Wherever and whatever his station or department, golf became his consuming sport. A large coir mat, such as are favoured by golf professionals for the purpose of indoor swing instruction, was invariably a prime part of the furnishings in any office inhabited by Mindy Blake.

Len Trent recalls calling on Blake — by then a group captain and the boss of his own RAF station in England — and learning that his erstwhile pupil, by diligence and an enthusiasm bordering on obsession, had managed to whittle his handicap down to 4. Nor was that all. His latest cards showed that he was due to be chopped to 2. The apprentice had surpassed his master.

On his retirement from the RAF Mindy Blake went on to develop and market with tremendous success, a rod-like mechanical device — the 'Swingrite' — which, when set to simulate the appropriate golf club and swung with the correct rhythm would produce a satisfying click. International sales grew and Mindy Blake became a very wealthy man. He wrote a couple of books on golf and introduced what he was pleased to call 'the golf swing of the future' — which simply stated, propounded a decidedly open stance, a braced right leg and the ball teed closer to the right foot than in the conventional address.

In practically all fields of sport and muscular endeavour except golf, claimed Blake, changes of style and techniques had brought surprising advances. Golf, too, was now due for a shake-up he contended.

The last time Len Trent saw Mindy Blake, his old Stalag Luft III cobber had come a long way from hacking at a leather-jacketed ball with a rusty 5 iron. He was captain of the popular Wentworth Golf Club and had grown rather tubby and thin of thatch with the affluent life and the flight of the years.

Sadly, that tremendously enthusiastic and highly successful pupil of Len Trent died quite recently. Unquestionably, he had played his golf and lived his life in the finest traditions of his chosen service — *Per ardua ad astra*. Through adversity to the stars.

It was not long before Len Trent met the dynamic, driving force behind the many escape plans continually plotted and discussed among members of a hard-core committee in the camp. Roger Bushell, a squadron leader whose Spitfire had been shot down by five Me-110s in May 1940, was a big and tempestuous man who, before the war, had been a British ski champion. He had also been a barrister. He was suave, persuasive, dogmatic and coldly determined to escape from any wires or walls the goons put around him. He was 'Big X', the OC of the escape organisation.

Although the tunnels were confidently considered the ultimate means of freedom, 'Big X' and his syndicate would aid and abet any one-off stunt that promised a show of success. Bob Stanford-Tuck, that notable Battle of Britain fighter ace who was an inmate of Stalag Luft III, hit on a plan that was fraught with hazard and doomed, by unwitting interference, to early disaster.

At regular intervals an aged civilian waggoner would drive his horse-drawn, open-topped garbage cart through the gates of the compound, collect the assortments of empty cans and cartons and cinders from the various rubbish receptacles, and presumably trundle his load out to the local refuse tip.

But the goons were not fools. *Mein Gott! Nein!* They had required that the sides of the wagon be pierced with rows of holes, about 4 inches in diameter. Every time the laden vehicle stopped at the gates on its departure from the compound the guards would vigorously thrust long sharp steel poles through the holes on each side.

One afternoon, while the garbage cart was doing the rounds of the camp rubbish bins, Trent saw one of his mates — seemingly casual as he leaned against the corner of a hut — casting his eyes warily for the appearance of any ferret.

'Something on?' Trent queried in a whisper.

'S-s-sh! Don't look! Don't look!' cautioned the stooge from the corner of his mouth as the garbage cart drew alongside them.

Then, whistling blithely, there emerged from the doorway of the theatre block a fellow carrying an ashpan of live coals from the grate of a heating stove. Seeing the garbage cart so conveniently handy, he thereupon emptied the pan on top of the load of rubbish.

Suddenly, there was a violent eruption from the depths of the cart. Empty Red Cross Cans and cartons flew high in the air as Bob Stanford-Tuck leapt up, frantically slapping away at the red-hot embers that had invaded his hiding place and settled on his flesh.

Tuck had taken a mighty gamble — more chancy than a pull of the trigger in Russian roulette — in supposing that he could have dodged the stabbings of the goon gatekeepers' lances. Maybe the stretch in the cooler that he received was a damn sight better than a hole in his belly.

A comparatively simple escape plan was once put to Len Trent. As needs moved it, a horse-drawn cart known to the prisoners as the 'honey cart' would call at the camp to haul away the accumulations from the latrines. Where its freight was ultimately deposited was not precisely known, but information gleaned from some goon sources suggested that local meadowlands profited from its fertilizing properties.

Need it be said that the contents of the cart, which was in fact a tank on wheels, did not receive the same careful scrutiny from the gatekeepers as did, for instance, the loads in the refuse wagon.

It was suggested that Trent, a slim and agile fellow, had but to slip into the tank just as the driver was ready to leave the compound. He could hold his head above the level of the load, his clothes bundled and wrapped tightly and held aloft, and when the cart was safely past the guards and heading for pastures new, the fugitive could emerge and head for the river — where he could wash off the effluence.

Len Trent declined. The idea smelled a bit, he reckoned. Why be so bloody fussy questioned his abettors. Was he not up to his neck in it already?

Many other and more sanitary escape plans were constantly being plotted. During Trent's term in Stalag Luft III several freedom bids succeeded, even if the roamings of the bold venturers were brief and their punishments, on recapture, harsh. The ingenuities and audacities displayed by all the escapers or would-be escapers almost beggared belief.

When the invasions of body lice in the prison camp reached epidemic proportions it was the practice of Obert Von Lindeiner, the camp *Kommandant*, to arrange delousing purges. An armed guard party would enter the compound and the squads of infected prisoners would be marched through the main gates and down the road a kilometre or two to the fumigation block.

The routine parade details had been carefully watched by Bushell's men. Also, most meticulously studied, were the details of the German rifles that were slung over the shoulders of the guards — and some almost-perfect replicas had been carved from wooden bed-boards and stained with Red Cross boot polish. Along with this, Bushell's tailoring department had been making Luftwaffe ground-staff uniforms from blue-grey RAF clothing — the colours being close enough to each other to pass muster. German insignia had been copied in coloured cloth and the white-metal badges cast, in delicately carved soap moulds, from melted tinfoil salvaged from Red Cross food canisters and cartons.

When all plans for the proposed escape were completed, the prisoners' complaints of body lice were voiced and, in due course, the armed party of six Luftwaffe guards marched through the gates and waited outside the infected block. But the men inside were tiresomely slow in gathering all their lousy clothing together. ' *'Raus! 'Raus!'* The leader of the guard was getting impatient. But still the men inside the hut dawdled as they sorted out their clothes. Then some of them began bickering and a scuffle began; and the guards were quite occupied in trying to stem the fracas.

Meanwhile, in the next hut an unusual transformation saw six British prisoners suddenly become armed and uniformed sons of the Fatherland. They hastily marshalled their squad of Kriegies — itching to be free of the compound, more than from the bites of imaginary lice — and impudently marched them through the sets of double gates and past the *postens* in the guardhouse.

Once clear of the immediate surroundings of the camp they made a bolt for the woods. However, as soon as the real guards and their party of prisoners came to the gates the ruse was discovered. Although some of the escapers were at large for several days, not one involved in that plan ever reached England.

Meanwhile, the disposal of tunnel sand was omnipresent in the minds of all involved in the excavations of 'Tom', 'Dick' and 'Harry'. Roger Bushell was fiercely insistent that no-one should ever murmur the word 'tunnel' in case, in an unguarded moment, the mention of it might get to the sensitive ears of a ferret. The code names had to be used by the Kriegies at all times.

But that rule, apparently did not apply to Oberfeldwebel Glemnitz, the chief of the goon ferret squad. Glemnitz did, at least, have a sense of humour — which could not be said for his second-in-command, Unteroffizier (Corporal) Griese, who was commonly known as 'Rubberneck'. He did, indeed, have a long neck and was forever pushing it into every corner of the compound.

So diligent were Glemnitz and Rubberneck in prowling around the blocks that Roger Bushell detailed two men to follow the ferrets like shadows. Rubberneck put up with this baiting for a couple of days until, with some impatience, he called back to the two botherers: 'You know, you are just vasting your time back there. Why do you not kom mit me alongside and talk. Then I can practise my English mit you. Ja?'

The Kriegies shrugged; and obliged. The conversation proceeded idly; and then Rubberneck asked: 'How long do you t'ink the war vill go on?'

Again, the Kriegies shrugged: 'Not long. We're winning.'

'Not long, eh?' Rubberneck smiled craftily. 'Well, tell me *this* — how long is your *tunnel*, eh?'

Silence from the two prisoners. They could almost hear the chuckle of inner gleer that bubbled within the German. The bastard knew bloody well that there was a tunnel *somewhere*.

Glemnitz, in his turn, was being baited. One day, he sagely tapped his head and ventured a bold but tangled piece of English colloquialism: 'You t'ink I know fook nothings.' He grinned sardonically: 'I tell you, I know fook *all!*'

The Kriegies, whose pleasures were simple and few in Stalag Luft III, almost wet themselves with mirth.

11

TUNNEL TROUBLE

WITH THE ONSET OF autumn's chills, the practice of sunbathing and the surreptitious spreading of tunnel sand into the dust of the compound had to be abandoned and other methods of spoil disposal resolved.

Billy Griffiths had become an advanced student of the German language and worked hard on its rhetoric and idiom. In fact, he later became an accredited German interpreter. In his continuing conversations with some of the more approachable and educated guards — particularly one named Rudi — he came to know precisely when any particular block was to be singled out for a snap search by the ferrets.

The habit of the Germans was to descend suddenly on a dormitory block and ransack it from end to end and from floor-blocks to roof-ridge. They sought the workings of forbidden radios, the manufacture of both sharp and blunt instruments for tunnelling, the forging of anything that was the copyright of the Fatherland and, of course, the evidences of any tunnel.

Customarily, the Germans went about their search procedures by rote. An armed guard would arrive outside the prison gates and there would be the usual delay while the *postens* examined documents before admitting the search squad.

During this prolonged pause the prisoners in the hut marked for close inspection — unwittingly forewarned by Rudi — would have time to conceal any evidence of 'verboten' activity. It was known to the Kriegies, from past experience, that any block so searched was likely to be left undisturbed for at least a month or more. So, as soon as the fossicking guards had departed, the penguins would continue depositing cartons of sand above the ceiling and below the floor, the counterfeiters would get out their pens and brushes, inks and papers again and continue their forging of gate passes and German and French identity documents, while 30 feet below, the tunnellers would be inching their ways towards escape.

By this time Len Trent, a senior squadron leader, had been promoted from sand-disposal duties with the penguins to the post of block commander. Along with this office went the administrative duties of supervising security and disciplinary measures within the dormitory building. A carefully placed matchstick here and a yard or two of black cotton stretched there would indicate to him, should there be any disturbance to the devices, the presence of a ferret furtively seeking to secrete himself beyond the trapdoors that led into the ceiling cavities or the narrow space below the floor. Trent would also carefully rake the dust around the hut's foundations to clearly show any footprints of goon prowlers.

At that time the prisoners' theatre was a recent addition to the sparse amenities of Kriegie life at Stalag Luft III. It had been built immediately south of Block 119 and closeby the *appell* (or roll-call) parade ground. It had a reasonably roomy auditorium, a large, elevated stage and — of considerable importance to the tunnel syndicate — a spacious area beneath the stage that would take large quantities of excavated sand.

Penguins working on 'Harry' would move along the corridor of Block 104 carrying their burdens of sand from the entry trap of the tunnel at the northern end of the building towards the door at the southern end, en route to the theatre. Under the guise of amateur thespians on their way to rehearsals, they would lump pillowcases full of the tunnel sand under a pile of colourful costumes and stage props — their progress through the compound carefully watched against ferret interception by strategically placed and vigilant duty pilots.

At least one goon who was often lured away from his post by the blandishments of Billy Griffiths and his brews of Canadian coffee was Rudi. Rudi lived in the Ruhr — whenever Herr Hitler and the Third Reich would allow him leave from Sagan duties — and Billy was able to get a lot of information from the German, especially after he had come back from leave to his home district. The morale of the civilian population, any significant troop movements, the extent of Allied bombings and the gist of proclamations from the Fatherland leaders were sent back to

Britain in a pre-arranged code devised by Air Ministry.

While Rudi chatted and drank Red Cross genuine coffee — that nectar of the gods so long denied the Germans — the penguins would hurry past Griffiths' doorway with their loads of sand. And as soon as the caffeine-sated Rudi showed signs of departing, a signal would send the sand-carriers ducking for cover.

One afternoon, after a particularly entertaining chat in German with Griffiths and with his belly warmed with coffee, Rudi discovered with concern that he was 10 minutes late in reporting to the guardhouse. Flustered, he ran to the door that opened on to the corridor; but a wary stooge, anticipating just such an emergency, was standing just outside the door with an empty pot in his hands, ostensibly on his way to returning the utensil to its owners a few doors along the passageway. As Rudi came bounding out, a laden penguin came shuffling along the corridor. Seeing this, the stooge deliberately collided with the German, pushing him back into the room and sending the pot clattering to the ground — thereby warning the others.

With profuse apologies and a great fuss, the clumsy offender and Billy Griffiths helped Rudi to his feet and brushed him down thoroughly as the alerted penguins ducked into the nearest doorways.

Glemnitz, need it be said, knew that the prisoners had organized their stooges into a highly effective band of duty pilots to watch every movement of the ferrets entering or leaving the compound. That such an organization, spying against the lawful duties of the Fatherland gaolers, could so exist under his very nose was annoying in the extreme. But there was really nothing he could do about it but accept the situation philosophically. Rubberneck wanted all the duty pilots who could be identified cast into the cooler, but Glemnitz maintained that a clandestine bunch would soon be formed and would watch from the windows. He said it would be better to let them remain in the open, where he could see them.

Glemnitz did get his revenge in some measure, however. He sent in a gang of *arbeiters* to cut down the pine trees that had been left standing around the huts in the compound. This meant that from outside the wire the goons could see everything that was moving inside the camp grounds. Then, to the considerable concern of all who were working on 'Tom', the tree fellers set to clearing the edge of the forest outside the wire fences on the western boundary of the prison. Soon, the trees had been cut back about 20 or 30 metres.

It was a low blow. Work on 'Tom' had been going well and at the rate of 8 or 9 feet a day the tunnellers had burrowed under the wire on the western side of the camp. In a couple of days they would have reached the edge of the forest before digging upwards to break ground within the cover of the trees. Now, of course, that shelter had been removed. The tunnel was already just over 200 feet. They would now have to dig at least another 100 feet to emerge within the forest. And, they thought with concern, there would be all that extra sand to be carried away and hidden.

By this time tunnel 'Dick' had been abandoned in the interests of concentrated work on 'Tom' and 'Harry' and the sand from the two remaining projects had been tightly packed into its burrow until it could not hold another penguin-load. More and more Red Cross boxes were brought into use to take the spoil from 'Tom' so that the sand could be stowed under the bunks in Blocks 101 and 103.

Then the wily Glemnitz sprang a surprise. He organized a snap search of Block 103 and the boxes of sand were found. He sent heavy wagons into the compound and they rumbled around and around the huts, crushing the prisoners' gardens and trembling the earth. If there was a tunnel below, the German was determined it would be collapsed.

Glemnitz knew there was a tunnel — the yellow sand was conclusive evidence — and he logically concluded that it must have its beginnings in the shelter of one of the nine blocks that were closer to the wire enclosures. After considering one or two huts for total ransacking, he chose Block 123 — where 'Tom's' trap-door was a well-concealed slab in the concrete floor close to the chimney.

One morning a gang of *arbeiters* marched in, shovels at the ready, singing a German marching tune. They then proceeded to dig a trench 65 yards long and 15 feet deep — the length of Block 123 — certain in their belief that they would uncover any tunnel. However, they had miscalculated and were more than 15 feet too shallow.

Grimly, the tunnel organizers watched, from their window position in Block 122, as the ferrets moved around inside 123. For more than 2 hours the Germans peered and prodded and bashed until one of them, a fellow known to the Kriegies as Herman, flung aside his iron pinch-bar in frustration. It hit the concrete floor alongside the chimney with a hollow 'clunk' and Herman, alert and now exultant, picked away at the seal and lifted the concrete slab.

Glemnitz was almost ecstatic with glee; and even Rubberneck was smiling thinly. Von Lindeiner, the camp *Kommandant*, along with Hauptman Pieber, the officer in charge of the north compound, arrived at the scene and soon nominated a venturesome ferret to explore the tunnel. He was a smiling little man called Charlie Pfelz and it took him about half an hour to worm his way to the end of the burrow and hack his way out again. He emerged grinning to report just how close the Kriegies' plans had been to success.

Von Lindeiner, with some good grace, had to concede the prisoners' feat of subterranean engineering was masterly. In fact, he said, he would like the prime architect of the scheme to step forward to be personally congratulated and to take his place as a guest at the Kommandant's dinner table. No strings attached, vowed the boss of Stalag Luft III. The man, after being entertained in a gentlemanly fashion, would be returned promptly to the comfort of his couch within the compound.

But the Kriegies were not falling for *that* line of blandishment. God—and the Third Reich — knew what would happen to Roger Bushell if he should so put himself in the hands of the Germans.

The captured tunnel of 'Tom' remained an exhibition piece for about a month as parties of German prison experts from every corner of the Fatherland were shown the incredible workings of the *Tommi* prisoners. The underground workroom, the air-pump chamber, the system of shoring, the railway and its trucks, and the ingenious electric-light installations were studied and photographed. And after that, there remained but the destruction of the tunnel and its workings.

The usual method was flooding — and incredible as it may seem, there had been ninety-seven earlier tunnels dug and discovered since 1941. However 'Tom' was too long, too deep and too strongly shored to be caved-in that way. Instead, Von Lindeiner brought in a squad of German Army engineers and their explosive expert tinkered around for a couple of days, laying gelignite charges and trailing wires.

At 3 p.m. on the appointed day, the whole camp stood by to watch the fun at the engineers stolidly moved around the area and the funny little engineer stood by his exploder. But he was not a first-class explosives expert. He had been liberal with gelignite and faulty in his placings of the charges. The blast erupted up the shaft of 'Tom', taking a sizeable portion of the roof of Block 123 high into the air, shattering the concrete floor and knocking the chimney to a crazy angle.

The British audience — about 1500 strong — cheered lustily.

Later, a gang of *arbeiters* came in to clear up the debris and repair the wreckage of block 123.

Billy Griffiths, his ear tuned to any snippet of German conversation, overheard Glemnitz telling another ferret that they need not expect any more tunnel trouble in the north compound as it was obvious that the prisoners had used every stick of available wood to shore the now destroyed 'Tom' tunnel. And if they should be so bold as to try again, Glemnitz would notice the steady disappearance of bed-boards.

Bushell was told and he immediately organized the biggest confiscation of bed-boards yet levied. He collected almost 2000 within two days and stored them down the shaft of 'Dick', reasoning that Glemnitz, believing he had discovered the sole tunnel in the compound, would not be watching bed-boards for a while.

With the completion of the south compound, the Americans were separated from the British prisoners and moved to their new quarters. With them went Glemnitz. Rubberneck, ever keen on promotion, took over as head ferret, under the command of Hauptman Pieber, in the north camp.

Far from slackening of his vigilance after the discovery of 'Tom', the surly Rubberneck seemed to be even more suspicious than ever. Because of the ferrets' increased attentions, Bushell decided to discontinue work on 'Harry' until the heat died down. Instead, he gave his attentions to organizing 'wire jobs' and anyone who believed he had a good plan for getting through the heavily-guarded fence could apply to the escape committee for assistance. One or two managed to get through, but were free for only a couple of nights.

Jack Rae, a New Zealand Spitfire pilot, and his Canadian mate called Probert made a bid one night. So cautious were they that it took them 7 hours to crawl 250 yards while they hugged the ground to dodge the sweep of the searchlights. When they finally got to the wire they had only two strands to cut when they were caught by a guard.

Each was given a month's solitary confinement in the cooler. Probert trying to escape while going to the toilet one day, was shot in the shoulder and hospitalized for a month before being returned to the compound.

In a nauseous television series that had too long a run a few years ago, the Allied prisoners of war of an imaginary camp were depicted as a wise-cracking, well-fed bunch of multi-nationals having the fun of their lives as they wandered, apparently unhindered, through the camp kommandant's office and even came and went, without let or hindrance, through the confines of the camp. Such scant amusements as the real-life prisoners might have enjoyed at Stalag Luft III shone like bright candles in the darkness of monotony and, often, despair. Black tragedy was sometimes present and more than one man was driven to suicide or desperate acts that saw life finished off by the sentries' bullets.

Towards the end of the bitter Silesian winter of 1943-44 the finishing touches had been completed within tunnel 'Harry'. It was a marvellous piece of engineering ingenuity. Below the stove in Room 23, Block 104, the entry shaft descended vertically about 30 feet to a chamber complex that contained the sand-disposal area, the workshop and the nook where the air pump was housed. And from there the tunnel bored northwards for about 250 feet, burrowing under the *vorlager* area, the outside wire barricade and the roadway before its exit shaft rose to the break-through point just inside the edge of the forest. A few inches of soil and matted grass roots had been retained as a shallow cap over the escape shaft.

A wooden railway track, made from beading strips off the hut walls, had been laid most of the length of the tunnel and from two enlarged galleries, whimsically called 'Piccadilly' and 'Leicester Square', the little wooden, flanged-wheel trucks were hauled backwards and forwards. In the days of excavation they had carried the spoil from the tunnel face to the sand-dispersal chamber. They would be carrying escapers in the other direction when the time came.

Earlier in the project, the men working at the face had to rely on the fitful light from slush lamps while, at the same time, tolerate as best they could the choking fumes from the open, fat-fuelled flames. Later, however, born of craft and cunning, masterminds seized on the idea of confiscating some lengths of electric wiring, socket fittings and light bulbs. Then, by re-directing some of the camp's power supply, modernity came to the tunnel and the diggers' toils were well lighted and, accordingly, somewhat lightened.

Lack of adequate ventilation had proved an early problem, until one of the bright minds came forward with the plans for an air pump. Two canvas kit bags sewn end to end made the bellows. They were ribbed with circular wooden frames so that the whole air bag could be compressed and expanded like a huge accordion. Inlet and outlet valves were fitted and to operate the pump one of the tunnelling gang would sit in front of the cradle and, by pulling and pushing on the handle, slide the bellows backwards and forwards along its wooden runners.

Naturally, there had to be a pipeline system to collect fresh air from the surface and send it to the tunnel face. The bottoms of empty powdered-milk cans from the Red Cross parcels were removed to make cylinders about 8 inches long and 4 inches in diameter. These were joined end to end and the resultant air pipe was laid along the bottom of the tunnel. As the burrowing progressed, new cans were added to the link. If the ingenious methods employed by the prisoners seemed excessive, then there were good reasons. The Germans, suspecting the presence of a tunnel, had sunk sound-detectors around the compound, circling the wire fences with subterranean microphones. However, they were not buried deep enough. Somehow, they could not imagine that the prisoners would be tunnelling 30 feet below the surface — until, of course, they discovered 'Tom', by which time their sound-detectors were well installed.

For too long, Rubberneck had been showing far too much interest in Block 104. One cold March day be brought in a squad of ferrets and guards and moved at a fast jog towards the hut. The surly goon ran down the corridor, throwing open doors in the hope of catching some malpractice in the making and, with cries of 'Raus!' clearing out the occupants. For 4 hours he and his men scoured 104 from top to bottom.

Roger Bushell decided that, despite the lingering winter bleakness, it was time to break the tunnel. Quite apart from Rubberneck's increasing suspicions, the escape leader was worried that the thin shell of earth covering the escape shaft might cave in any day, despite the reinforcing shoring the tunnellers had effected from below. So, on the night of 24 March 1944, with snow lying cold and revealing on the ground, the great escape began.

About 600 Kriegies had taken active parts in the tunnel schemes and the ancillary escape organization — the tunnellers, the penguins, the counterfeiters who forged the passes and documents, the disguise experts and the tailors who made bogus clothing. But the escape committee reckoned that, at most, only about 220 would be able to get through the tunnel during the hours of darkness. Therefore, the names would be put into a hat after the committee had chosen about 70 men who had put in most work on the plan — with particular attention to those who could speak German — as deserving candidates.

According to his drawn number, the escaper would take his place to move through the tunnel.

Len Trent drew 79. He was to be disguised as a French workman and he spent his last moments of that night in Block 104 memorizing the details of his supposed background in French — a language in which he was, happily, reasonably proficient — and making last-minute adjustments to his newly-acquired 'civilian' clothing. His meticulously forged identity papers were in his pocket and he carried with him a good stock of Red Cross chocolate bars as emergency rations.

At 7 o'clock precisely, a prisoner called Richards shook hands with his mates. 'Goodbye, you bastards,' he said. 'Sorry I can't stay. See you in London after the war.' Richards was one of the band of 'hardarsers' — those who, not versed in the finer details of linguistics, must try to stolidly bluff their way across a hostile land and past suspicious border guards, while their more sophisticated fellow escapers could brazenly converse, as needs might demand, with inquisitive officials.

Richards made his cautious way to Block 104. At 30 second intervals all over the compound farewells were being exchanged as others gathered their escape gear together and crept forward to be checked in, first at Block 109 and then at the tunnel entry at 104.

There came a moment of panic when a tally clerk standing near the trap of tunnel 'Harry' saw a German *unteroffizier* come striding towards him with jackboots clumping on the floorboards. Three escapers, dressed in their civilian clothes, dived into the nearest doorway, shocked and shivering. And then it was discovered, with glorious relief, that Tobolski, a Polish pilot in the RAF, had elected to disguise himself as a Luftwaffe soldier. The uniform, converted from RAF blue-grey, was a masterly piece of imitation complete with swastikas and eagle badges and the colour of the cloth was but a shade bluer than the German grey.

Tobolski, who spoke excellent German, was to 'escort' Wing Commander Harry Day (travelling in a civilian double-breasted overcoat made from a Fleet Air Arm greatcoat) to Stettin, where they would try to stow away on a Swedish ship.

After what seemed an interminable age while new ropes were being fitted to the underground trolleys, the men clambered down the ladder in strict order until there were seventeen waiting in position in the workshop area. It was about 9.30 p.m. that Bushell finally gave the signal to break the seal at the escape end of the tunnel.

Johnny Bull set about trying to remove the boards that helped stop the earth-covered trap from caving in. But he was running into difficulties as he struggled in the dark. Already, it was 10.30 p.m. and the air was thick and fetid; and the men waiting behind were in agonies of apprehension. And then Bull broke through — and got the shock of his life. The surveyors had miscalculated. The tunnel was too short. Instead of surfacing within the cover of the forest trees it had broken ground about 10 feet short of the timber line. Furthermore, the goon-box, under which the tunnel had burrowed, was only 15 yards away. Bull could see the German guard peering at the compound as he swept the beam of his searchlight across the camp.

'Jesus!' Bull muttered in despair. And when he drew back and told his findings to his incredulous companion, Marshall, he sighed: 'Go and have a look yourself.'

Was the whole plan to be abandoned after all those months and all the toilings of more than 600 men? No. All the forged documents had been date-stamped and all had been keyed up so that nerves were twanging like fiddle strings. 'We've *got* to go tonight,' said Roger Bushell after they had conferred.

And then Bull had an inspiration. He had seen, about 10 feet from the hole and right on the edge of the forest, one of the spy nests that the ferrets had put up when tunnel 'Tom' was being dug. 'Put a controller in that shelter,' Bull said, 'and tie a rope to the top of the ladder. The controller holds the other end, and when he sees the way is clear he gives a couple of tugs and the fellow crawls out. Warning tugs will mean that he has got to freeze and lie doggo until the danger has passed.'

Bushell agreed there and then. And the mass escape was in motion.

Bull crawled out and reached the shelter of the ferret spy-nest. He studied the movements of the sentries in the goon-boxes and timed the wanderings of the guards who patrolled the strip of roadway outside the prison grounds. And when he saw the hole was clear of interference he gave two tugs on the rope and up came Marshall. Together they watched the wire patrollers come into sight again, stop below the goon-box, and wander gloomily back again into the shadows.

Marshall took the end of the rope, patted a farewell to Bull, and signalled Valenta to emerge. Valenta crawled out onto the cold snow, reached Marshall in the shelter of the spy-nest and, in turn, took the signal rope and tugged for Bushell to come forward.

And so the bold venturers crawled out into relative freedom.

12

A   SMELL   OF   FREEDOM

THERE WERE MANY DELAYS in getting the escapers through the tunnel. Some, either because of their body bulk or the fact that they were carrying large bundles — or both — had difficulty in squeezing through the narrow burrow. More than once some of the shoring boards were knocked down and there were some hindering and dangerous falls of sand. So it was about 3.30 a.m. that Len Trent found himself at last at the foot of the ladder and ready to climb up the shaft to open country.

He saw the instructions and warnings that Bushell had had posted near the bottom rung. The message told him that the exit trap was in full view of the goon-box and its trigger-happy machinegunner, that there was a signal line leading to the ferret spy-nest about 10 feet from the hole, and that he had to crawl towards the screen, holding the rope in his hand as soon as he had received the all-clear double tug from his predecessor.

Squadron Leader Trent, escaper number 79, poked his head cautiously into a land of snow beyond the wire. The freezing bite of the morning air, compounded in chill and heightened in purity in contrast to the fetor of the tunnel fug, was sweet with the fragrance of the pine woods and rich with wild promises. Its sharpness stung the membranes of his nose and brought moisture to his eyes.

'My God, my God!' He whispered his exultation — which was also a fervid prayer of thanksgiving. Time telescoped upon itself and in a vivid flash the past and the present and the future merged and tumbled joyously around him. He was already back in England with Ursula and little baby daughter Christine. And now, in the fields around Methwold, daffodils would be peeping through the snow as, blossom by blossom the spring began.

He felt the all-clear signal on the rope as 'Lang' Langlois, doing a stint as exist marshal, beckoned him out of the hole. Mick Shand, number 78, had crawled to the cover of the trees and was waiting behind a pine for the arrival of his long-time cobber.

Trent was inching along the ground, now wet with the melting of the snow by seventy-eight crawling bodies, when he got a series of frantic tugs from Langlois. He froze, bellying close to the cold earth, with his chin chilling in a puddle of ice water. Directly behind him, and approaching steadily, came the plod, plod, plod of jackboots and the snapping of frosted twigs. One of the fence-patrol guards had, for some reason, decided to leave his regular beat along the outside of the wire to cross the road towards the edge of the forest.

Trent soon realized the German's intent. The fellow had stopped almost inches from the tunnel hole and was fumbling with his trousers. He was going to pee; and Bob McBride, waiting in the shaft to emerge after Len Trent, seemed in line for the full flow.

Trent, his heart hammering, heard the guard's sudden intake of breath and his surprised grunt. A shadow had moved and the German had discovered the hole almost under his feet; and the *pfennig* had dropped — the *Tommi* prisoners were escaping. *Mein Gott!*

There was the clack of a breech bolt and a shot shattered the stillness of the cold, dark air. Trent could almost feel the sledge-hammer blow of a bullet as the guard let go another blast. He leapt to his feet and pushed his arms as high in the air as he could stretch. In the urgency of the moment he yelled — or *thought* he yelled: *'Nicht schiessen, Posten. Nicht schiessen!'* ('Don't shoot, sentry. Don't shoot!') But, according to later information from one of his fellow unfortunates who was within earshot, Len Trent actually urged the guard: *'Nicht scheisser.'*

Of the two surprised protagonists, however, Trent would probably have been the more likely, at that time, to take heed: 'Don't shit.'

The guard, with loud Teutonic trumpetings, was calling to the guardhouse as he was hauling McBride out of the hole by his hair and covering Trent and Langlois with his rifle, held pistol-like. Mick Shand, meanwhile, had fled like a startled stag through the pine woods.

Shand made a valiant bid for freedom. He was on the loose for 5 days and managed to get into the mountains of Czechoslovakia before he was captured, waist deep in the snow, and imprisoned again by the Gestapo.

Although the guard was not getting much cooperation from the guardhouse, his fellow custodian in the goon-box had been quick to turn his machine-gun to menace the trio of escapers as they were prodded towards the gates of the compound. He shouted wild warnings every time one of the prisoners attempted to lower his arms.

After about 10 minutes delay, Trent, Langlois and McBride were admitted to the guardroom where a stove was glowing. Dawn was still 2 or 3 hours away and, quite obviously, most of the camp guards were sleeping soundly. The night-watch sentries were getting more and more agitated as they tried to rouse the officers by telephone; and as there were only two guards left to watch over the three prisoners, there was an opportunity for the would-be escapers to sidle up to the stove and, as they sought warmth, discreetly stuff such evidence as maps, forged identity papers and other items into the fire.

In Trent's 'French workman's' overcoat pocket he had stowed nine bars of vitamin chocolate as emergency rations. Knowing that it was a punishable offence for any prison guard to be found in possession of prisoners' food or cigarettes, he cautiously moved around the room, dropping a chocolate D-bar into a pocket of each of the eight German greatcoats hanging on the pegs along the walls. He had one piece of chocolate left over — so he slyly slipped it into a brief case.

He had hardly completed his mischief before Oberst Von Lindeiner burst into the room. He was a tall, imposing officer and he spoke reasonably good English. He snapped questions at the prisoners. Where was the tunnel? How many had escaped? What time did the break start? Who were the leaders? What hut or huts were involved?

Trent, the senior officer of the trio and the prime target of the Kommandant's attempted interrogation, was stubbornly non-committal. In a white fury the German whipped out his pistol and pointed it at a spot between Trent's eyes — where its muzzle trembled like a deep, black well of doom.

'If you do not gif me answers to my questions, Squadron Leader Trent, I vill shoot *you*, first!'

The three apprehended men immediately thought of some inaccurate answers which, if not wholly believed by the Kommandant, at least prevented their annihilation on the spot. They were stripped naked as they were searched and then consigned to 3 weeks solitary confinement on *strafe* rations in the punishment cells of the *vorlager*.

So why leave all his chocolate bars in the guards' pockets? Trent would be in urgent need of such nourishment on the near-starvation diet of the solitary cells. So when the opportunity presented itself he went along the line of German greatcoats and took back his earlier donations.

Soon, a Luftwaffe corporal — a fellow more amicable than his kind in the guardhouse and with a good turn of English phrase — appeared and escorted the three prisoners to the cells.

'You will all strip and be searched,' he commanded.

'But we have already been stripped and searched,' protested Trent.

The corporal shrugged. 'So *again* you will be stripped. Those are my instructions, Major.' He gave Trent the army rank equivalent to squadron leader.

The bars of chocolate were discovered. 'So?' The corporal smiled. 'You were stripped and searched before you came here, eh?'

Len Trent made a philosophic showing. 'Ah, well — we won't be here very long. The Russians are moving on to Germany fast, and they will be here to rescue us before our 3 weeks in the cooler are completed.'

'Major,' the German corporal said very quietly. 'You may mark my words well. The day will soon come when you British will be fighting, alongside we Germans, *against* the Russians.'

At that time and place, Trent thought the corporal's statement was the funniest piece of dogma he had heard in a long while.

In solitary confinement, Len Trent found the days dragged painfully slowly. The cell, a concrete cubicle about 10 feet by 6 feet, had a bare-board frame to serve as a bunk. But there was no paillasse, nor were there any blankets. He was, however, allowed to keep the pseudo-civilian overcoat that he had been wearing in the escape bid. Otherwise, he would surely have perished from the cold.

For exercise he was allowed a daily one-hour walk in the close confines of the cooler's yard. But as his food ration was barely above starvation level he did not have the energy, during the last week of his sentence, to walk for more than a few minutes.

While he was in the cooler he heard another prisoner being locked in the adjoining cell and, communicating through a ventilation grill, he discovered the new arrival was Mick Shand. Seemingly, the two New Zealanders' lives had been tracking parallel since their schooldays at Nelson College. Students together — RAF trainees together — prisoners together — aspiring escapers together — and now, down but not defeated, the two recaptured adventurers were living next door to each other in the solitary cells of Stalag Luft III.

Shand, it transpired, had been taken to a Gestapo prison at Guerlitz after his recapture in the Czech mountains and had been subjected to rigorous questioning. During his 2 weeks' incarceration, along with some of the other Stalag Luft III escapers, he observed that his companions were being steadily taken away from their cells in ones and twos.

'And when am *I* going to be sent back to Sagan?' Shand kept asking his gaolers.

Shand, before long, *was* sent back to Stalag Luft III. At the time, he did not realize how lucky he was. His mates, held by the Gestapo, were being taken out and murdered by the thugs of Hitler's favoured SS corps.

When Trent's term in solitary confinement ended he was taken back to the prison compound and such comfort as Ian Richmond and Billy Griffiths could administer. With the benefits of Red Cross chocolate and the balm of coffee in his belly, he was soon able to face up to life — if, indeed, that really was the name of it — in the day-to-day prison routine.

From Richmond and Griffiths, Len Trent learned how prisoners and gaolers at Stalag Luft III had reacted to the big escape. As soon as the surprised guard's shots were heard by the escape marshals in Block 104 there was an urgent move to withdraw all those waiting their turn in the tunnel and an immediate start on destroying forged papers and all possible incriminating gear.

It so happened that the men near the escape end of the tunnel *had* heard the shots and had believed that each escaper was being killed as he emerged from the hole. They whispered fearfully: 'Let's get t' hell out of here,' and in turn began propelling themselves back on the trolly towards, first, the 'Leicester Square' and then the 'Piccadilly' stage-points until, finally, they were clambering up the ladder to the entrance shaft into Block 104. Soon each man, imagining he was the last of the would-be escapers not nabbed by the Germans, emerged gasping: 'Tunnel's spotted. The ferrets are coming down through the hole!' But each time it was only another of his mates.

When they had established that the last prisoner was out of the tunnel they closed the entrance trapdoor and moved the stove back over it. Meanwhile, fires were burning all through the block as men burned their papers and maps. They stuffed items of civilian clothing under paillasses and ripped away the buttons, so patiently sewn on by the tailors. Some, in their haste to return to their own huts, leapt out of 104's windows and drew fire from the gunners in the goon-boxes.

In room 23, where 'Harry's' entry trap was hidden beneath the stove, Crump, one of the escape marshals, heard a scraping and scratching beneath the floor and knew that the ferrets had crawled in from the escape end and had found their way to the entry shaft. They were groping for the trapdoor.

They could bloody well find their own way out again, Crump reckoned.

Soon after daylight had broken, a seventy-strong column of Germans in full riot-squad gear marched into the compound carrying, as well as their tommy-guns, several mounted machine-guns. They formed a meancing ring around Block 104.

Von Lindeiner strode, very upright and very angry, into the compound and, as the guard clicked their heels to attention, the Kommandant made straight to the hut. Rubberneck's squad of ferrets drew their revolvers while several of the guards stamped inside 104 yelling *'Aus! Aus!'*

The prisoners began to emerge, expecting perhaps to be mowed down by machine-gun fire. As each man cautiously set foot outside the ferrets would seize him and make him strip naked as the snow fell on his bared skin. Every stitch of clothing was minutely examined by the ferrets and every garment that might faintly resemble a piece of civilian attire was suspect and flung on to a pile.

While this undress parade was in progress an agitated German officer came running from Block 104 to say that one of his men, the usually happy Unteroffizier Pfelz, had entered the escape end of the tunnel an hour before and they couldn't find the entrance trap to release him. Surely he must die of suffocation unless he was brought out at once? Could someone come soon and show where the trapdoor was hidden? *Bitte?*

One of the prisoners not involved in the search parade, having no particular squabble with harmless little Charlie Pfelz, lifted the concrete slab and Charlie, blinking up at the daylight with considerable relief, climbed up. He marched straight up to Oberst Von Lindeiner, who was angrily overseeing the examination of the Block 104 people's clothing, and reported his discovery. Rubberneck surveyed the little scene balefully. He, as head ferret in the compound, would have to answer for such a tunnel being carved right under his jackboots.

The Kommandant walked along the rows of British prisoners standing in various stages of dishabille. Those who seemed to be ring leaders of the escape or who merely showed arrogance or cynical amusement were consigned, by a snapped 'Cooler', to solitary confinement. Von Lindeiner would have sent all of the paraded prisoners to the cooler. But there wasn't room in the cells. He barked at the men before the parade was dismissed: 'If there are any more disturbances here, I will, myself, shoot two of you.'

His patience was running thin. The security of his camp had been tested and broken. Already, he knew that he would be marked for arrest and such punishment as only the Third Reich could conceive and deliver. And when, after identity checks had been matched against prison photographs and it was discovered that seventy-seven people had escaped, the men knew that the Kommandant's threat was not just a wordy bluff.

Events were to show — much later to Trent and his fellow prisoners — that, from that total of escapers, only three were still free a fortnight after the break. And of those, two had already arrived in England while the third was well on his way.

As the bitterness of disappointment lessened to a numbing acceptance of routine life in the compound, and as more strength returned to his undernourished sinews, Len Trent settled back into the monotony of prison existence. There were, to be sure, some diversions that brought a little light into the gloom. The Gestapo arrived at Stalag Luft III and six stony-faced thugs, moving around the huts with cloak-and-dagger stealth like over-acting Hollywood villains, turned over every stick of sparse furniture for evidence of *verboten* activity. Their quest not fulfilled in the north compound, they searched the other prison areas of the camp and eventually descended on their own kind in the *kommandantur* complex.

And, lo! What a disgrace! They discovered that the righteous Oberst Von Lindeiner, the boss of the camp himself, was involved in a bit of black-marketing. A Luftwaffe pilot flying a transport 'milk run' between Sagan and Denmark was bringing in some fine wines and foodstuffs and a private larder and cellar had been set up for Von Lindeiner under the *kommandantur* cookhouse.

This transgression of trust, on top of the Kommandant's laxity in allowing a prison break, was the final straw. Von Lindeiner was taken away for court-martial.

The new Kommandant was Oberst Braune. And soon after his arrival came the reprisals. He ordered the prisoners to attend three *appell* parades a day, he had the camp theatre closed and stopped the distribution of Red Cross boxes and food tins.

Tunnel 'Harry', of course, had to be demolished. But after the unfortunate affair of blowing up 'Tom', the Germans didn't want a repetition of such a fiasco. They settled the problem by emptying sewage from the honey wagons down the entry shaft before sealing it off with concrete. The exit end of the tunnel was caved in with cautiously placed charges of dynamite. The ubiquitous Rubberneck, more churlish than ever, noted the destruction with satisfaction. Such a scheme, he was going to be sure, would not be reborn.

It was soon known around the compound that fifteen of the escapers had been captured and returned to the cooler at Stalag Luft III. But what of the others? Surely *all* could not have escaped the Nazi dragnet so soon after the guards had raised the alarm? Perhaps some, whom the Germans might class as the ring leaders of the prison break, had been purged to other prison camps — say, Kolditz Strafelager?

One crisp morning in early April Hauptmann Pieber came into the compound and made his way to the room of Group Captain H.M. Massey, the Senior British Officer of the section. He saluted respectfully and announced that Oberst Braune, the new Kommandant, would like to discuss certain matters — and would

the SBO please bring his official interpreter. Eleven o'clock.
Bitte?

'What is the matter?' Massey asked. 'What have we done *now*?'

Pieber spoke very quietly. 'I cannot say, Group Captain — only
that it is something very terrible.'

A few minutes before 11 o'clock the SBO and his interpreter,
Squadron Leader 'Wank' Murray, were escorted to the
kommandantur and shown into the Kommandant's office. Braune, a
tall man of about 50 with a lined and rather weary face, dispensed
with the usual field and air-rank courtesies of hand-shaking. He
gave his visitors a small, stiff bow and directed them towards the
two chairs in front of his desk.

Standing at attention and speaking German, he said that he had
been directed by higher authority to convey the following report
to the British officer representing the prisoners in the north
compound of Stalag Luft III. That officer was to be informed that,
as a result of the prison break and the subsequent recapture of
many of the escapers, forty-one of those officers had been shot
while vigorously resisting arrest or attempting further escape.

Group Captain Massey listened in disbelief. He said to Murray:
'Ask him to repeat that. How many were shot?'

'Forty-one,' the Kommandant replied, and Murray translated.

There was a long and terrible silence. And then Massey looked
at Murray and said in a strained voice: 'Ask him how many were
wounded.'

Murray put the question. The Kommandant hesitated. He
looked down at the paper lying on his desk. Then he looked out of
the window.

'I cannot say,' he replied. Murray translated the words to
English. 'I am permitted only to read this report to you — which I
have done.'

Massey insisted: 'Ask him *again*. Ask him how many were
wounded.'

A very long pause. And then came Braune's words. Murray
translated: 'I think — no one was wounded.'

Massey's reaction was explosive: 'No one wounded? How can
you say that forty-one men were shot dead while escaping and
that none were wounded?'

'I am required to read you this report. This I have done,' said
Braune. 'I can do no more.'

Massey asked for the names of the officers who had been killed. But Braune said that such information had not yet been sent to him. Only the report that he had just read.

The Group Captain said that he wished to have the names of the dead men as soon as possible. Would the Kommandant get that information with all speed.

'Yes,' Braune replied. 'I will do that.'

Massey said that he required to know what had happened to the bodies. He would have to arrange for the burials and the disposal of personal effects. Then, he demanded that the Protecting Power also be informed of the killings.

This would be done, said Braune. He would let the Senior British Officer have every piece of information just as soon as he received it. Then he concluded the meeting and had the British officers returned to the compound.

Group Captain Massey sent for the senior officers of all the rooms and shocked the meeting in the camp theatre with the news. He described the meeting in the Kommandant's office and said that he would announce the names of the victims as soon as they became available.

Nazi ruthlessness and brutality had come to be understood by the inmates of Stalag Luft III — but mass murder of prisoners was, until then, something new in Hitler's war machinery. Now, horror lay over the camp.

Such were the mutterings and the glowering fury within the compound that the Kommandant, fearing perhaps a revolt, ordered the sentries to be increasingly vigilant and to shoot on the slightest show of disorder. Consequently, any tardiness on the prisoners' part at evening lock-up would be smartened up by a burst of machinegun fire from the nearest goon-box. One afternoon, when the air-raid siren wailed to announce an aerial armada of American Fortress bombers approaching, some of the prisoners were reluctant to enter their huts as ordered. The Germans knew the sights and sounds of Allied air strength kindled great joy in the hearts of their captives; so a furious guard drew his pistol and emptied its magazine at the tardy men.

However, he was not one of the Fatherland's better shots. Some of the bullets hit a wall of a hut — showing that, at least, the fellow *could* hit a barn door — while the others raised sprays of mud and thawed snow from the *appell* ground. No prisoner was hit.

The first list of names of the executed escapers was pinned to the notice-board one evening. The news spread rapidly through the compound and it was discovered that, instead of forty-one names, there were forty-seven. The men's eyes ran down the list. They were grimly quiet, except for a shocked whisper — perhaps a bitter curse — when a close companion's name was found.

It seemed that all British flying services — as well as such freedom fighting countries as Poland, France, Norway, Czechoslovakia, Belgium, Lithuania and Greece — were represented by their dead. Len Trent saw, with a heavy heart, that two New Zealanders were on the roll. They were Flying Officer P. P. J. Pohe and Flying Officer Arnold Christenson.

A day or two later another short list was pinned to the board. It contained but three names. And it brought the full list up to the round figure of fifty murdered men.

A fortnight later the urns containing the ashes of the fifty victims were delivered to Group Captain Wilson, the new SBO of the compound. In the meantime, Group Captain Massey had been repatriated, along with a group of other badly wounded prisoners, to England.

Oberst Braune arranged the supply of some suitable stone and allowed a work party to build a vault for the urns and a fitting headstone in a nearby cemetery. Around that resting place in Silesia lay the graves of other Allied prisoners who had died at Stalag Luft III.

Meanwhile, the tunnellers in the north compound were at it again. The average Kriegie was like a mole. Put him in a cage with an earth floor and he immediately began turning the soil. So, by July 1944, tunnel 'George', which had its beginnings under a seat in the twelfth row of the camp theatre, was already inching out towards the wire on the east side of the compound. 'George' was 'Harry's' successor and the sand was being hidden under the floor and the elevated stage of the theatre.

A new escape organization had been formed and secret lectures and a training schedule had been set up. They all knew now, through information passed on by a 'tame' goon, that all prisoners caught trying to escape again would be shot. They worked all through the summer and by the time the first snow came 'George' had burrowed just beyond the wire. And, at that stage of excavation, it remained as a project for future development — should that be necessary. For surely the Russians or the British or the Americans *must* advance soon and release them?

Len Trent, now fully recovered from his treatment in the solitary cells, had been flexing his muscles with sport and exercise in the Sagan sun and sharpening up his wits with bridge strategies. All the wisdom of Ely Culbertson had been mentally devoured and the members of the bridge school were very, very serious players, matching skill against skill for the most serious of stakes — food points.

Now with the onset of winter, Trent had organized ice-hockey matches in the compound. He and his helpers had, with considerable ingenuity, built three rinks. Flat areas of ground had been chosen and the perimeters had been formed by mounding ridges of sand about 4 or 5 inches high. The floor of the proposed rink and the low perimeter ridges were hosed with the fire-fighting reel from water in the fire pool. The overnight frost would seal the wet earth against sudden seepage as more water was added — which, in turn was frozen, until a sufficient layer of ice had been formed.

The matches were most earnest affairs, with the Canadians showing considerable ability in what was, to them, a national sport. The vigour that invaded the clashes provoked so much enthusiasm throughout the camp that soon up to a dozen or more German officers would invite themselves along and sit in a row of chairs to watch the international contests.

But on Friday 27 January 1945 the camp was rocked by an event that was to see the end of all ice-hockey matches — and most of everything else at Stalag Luft III.

13

THE MARCH

THE WORDS COME WHISPERING out of the grey yesterdays —
hundreds and hundreds of diary notes and tender messages
pencilled more than 40 years ago under the most ghastly
conditions.

Ursula Trent treasures her husband's chronicles of the awful
traverse from Sagan to Trenthorst, near Hamburg — written, in
the beginning, in a small notebook and then, when the pages could
hold no more, continued on scraps of paper. The diary notes spill
over on to the end-papers, the fly-leaf, the title and the bastard-
title pages of an old book that had been ripped apart, its stiff
covers making a binder for the loose scraps of writings. This
poignant bundle with its messages of love and hope — written
with a tremendous spirit and courage and with a cheerfulness
showing through — is held together with a journey-soiled,
military gauze bandage, just as it was lashed together when the
chronicler had pencilled his last diary note.

The story of what has been called the 'death march' has been
told before in press accounts and in books — but never, I suggest,
as vividly as Trent has described his first-hand experiences of the
shocking privations.

I am indebted to Mrs Trent for showing me the diary; and the
story of Len Trent's journey, in company with the entire camp of
10,000 Allied prisoners, can only be told in his own words.

Some of the entries have been condensed and some of the more
personal messages have been withheld:-

February, 1945
Darling, while the events are still fresh in my mind I shall try and
trace for you the history of our forced march from Sagan to
Spremberg, a distance of 110 kilometres, and the train journey across

Germany to a prison camp near Bremen and Hamburg.

I could very well relate the story one winter's evening, but time and a warm room would make a different tale. And, of course, a full stomach! I had almost forgotten there could be such a thing on this earth. Anyway, here I am, perched on a top bunk which I was lucky to cut in a draw, while around me in piles of straw are twenty-eight other officers shivering under two blankets. The room is about 16 by 60 feet, hung with washing which refuses to dry as the two stoves are only supplied with enough wet pine wood to keep them burning for an hour a day — if we are lucky. We have been here 6 days and received one issue.

However, this won't do. My tale of woe is starting at the wrong end; so let me start at Sagan on 27 January, when we could hear the Russian guns in the distance attacking Breslau. We had reached the conclusion that the goons had left it too late to undertake the removal of 10,000 prisoners so we were wondering how risky it was going to be, being overrun by the Ruskies right on a big defence zone, the Oder River.

I had just come in from completing the arrangements for an ice-hockey match between New Zealand and South Africa on the morrow, and had just sat down on the first game of bridge for a month when Charlie Hubbard came crashing in to announce: 'We march in an hour and take what we can carry!' Slamming the door, he left us wondering if it was just a joke in poor taste. But no — in so many seconds the block was in an uproar. Try and imagine the bombshell. There we had been for 2 years, living our unexciting lives practically in the same room. It seemed nothing could move us from Sagan — and yet there it was; we had to be packed and off within an hour.

We had improvized haversacks ready in case, so we packed a few clothes and as much of our small food reserve as possible, fortified our excited stomachs with as much food as they would take, and looked longingly at the small remainder which we had saved at such cost. What a scene! The room was a shambles. Charlie had kicked a tray of ashes over a pile of discarded clothes. Henry Murray was trying to pack all his books, etc. into a huge case, in between cutting himself and using the lavatory. Poor Henry; he was as white as a sheet and shaking with excitement, for he had been in the rut for over 4 years.

In the other 2 square feet of space Terry was hastily knocking together a sledge, using the back of our chair for runners. There was 6 inches of snow outside and a temperature many degrees below. I didn't think the goons would let us use sledges, but there I was wrong. We were all packed in an hour. But it was another hour before the first block moved off and another hour before we lined up for the count and filed out of the gate — that big gate at which we had so often glanced and wondered under what circumstances we would pass through and quit the camp for keeps.

Even under existing conditions it was a funny feeling to say goodbye to Room 10, Block 104. As we left we had a Red Cross parcel thrown to us. I hastily opened mine and packed the contents in my haversack and joined the line of march. By this time it was after 1 a.m. of 28 January and we were filing down past the French hospital and various other compounds on the road to Halbrau, 17 kilometres distant.

Sledges were breaking down and being discarded with quantities of food, which German civilians were pouncing upon. Yes, the first 10 kilometres or so were besprinkled with clothing, blankets and food which tired shoulders could no longer support — and the day's march was only just beginning.

We staggered in to Halbrau just on dawn, the only excitement so far being supplied by the German major who fired three pistol shots over the heads of scavenging civilians and screamed at them to get away home. As far as we could gather, it wounded his pride to see Germans struggling in the wayside ditches for the leavings of prisoners. All the way to Halbrau we had been stopping and starting, never knowing whether the stop was for 5 seconds or 5 minutes, so the people with packs were afforded no rest. We just stood in the road with aching shoulders, for a sit-down meant one hell of a struggle to get up again. I suppose my pack weighed 25 or 30 pounds and I must say I soon admitted my mistake in not making a sledge — for the sledges were running easily over the packed snow and the goons made no objection to the slight straggling.

After a 10 minute rest that froze us to the bone, we left Halbrau for Freiwaldau, about 20 kilometres distant. I can't remember much of the road. Physical fatigue and reaction to excitement made me plod along as in a dream — and the fear that, if you fell out, you would probably be shot, kept one's feet going automatically. So, my darling, I just placed your vision at the far end of each weary stretch of road and plodded doggedly towards it.

As rest periods became more organized I fell on the side of the road and dozed for a few minutes. Yes, I remember I was very sleepy; but thank God my feet and legs were in good shape and I was as fit as any man on the road; so, except for aching shoulders from the unaccustomed weight, I had little to complain of, compared to some unfortunates. Several people — Ian Richmond included — had only come out of hospital the day before, and lots of people with old wounds were feeling the strain far more than I. Charlie's knee began to give him hell and but for Terry's sledge he never would have made the march.

Just after noon we straggled into the big market square of startled Freiwaldau. The guards had had it, too, and an incredible scene ensued. Light snow was falling, as it had done on and off all the way; but tired men threw themselves on the ground and opened kits for food. Much to our surprise, the locals were permitted to mingle with us and soon a roaring trade was being carried out. Hot water for cigarettes! My God, that hot brew saved our lives. The snow ceased and as the food and drink revived us we began to sit up and take notice. It really was an incredible scene, and the spirit with which the Germans received the *Terrorfliegers* no less surprising. Scores of kids and grown-ups threaded their ways between the groups, which added to the 2000 men which packed that square.

The Kriegies were hastily knocking together sledges with timber and nails supplied for a few cigarettes. Most of the guards had disappeared and Kriegies began to roam far and wide through the village. Any number could have escaped — but to where?

The word had gone around that we were to stay the night and were more or less to find our own shelter, over and above the one large hall which was already packed. I promptly attached myself to Gordon Rackman who was a fluent French and German speaker — my erstwhile French instructor. Leaving Terry, Charlie and Henry in charge of our kit, we set out; but we found ourselves forestalled on every turn. People who were prepared to rent a room or barn for irresistible coffee had already been approached, and the more timid citizens gazed fearfully at us from behind bolted doors.

Eventually we gave up and returned to the square where I located a loft - empty because of the gymnastic endeavours required to reach it. However, in spite of it being open at either end, there was a dry wooden floor so I thought, 'This is it' and called the others. A guard saw me and angrily waved me down, hastening my descent by the way he handled his tommy-gun. It appeared the guards had received a 'rocket' for allowing us to stray about, and the powers had decided to move us on. We formed up and left the square in blocks at 3 o'clock in the afternoon. One nasty episode was caused by a huge bully of an *unteroffizier* screaming at us or the guards — or both — and pointing a a quivering tommy-gun in the most threatening manner. Very disturbing!

Charlie Hubbard had gone sick and we haven't heard of him since. I transferred my pack thankfully to Terry's sledge and helped him pull, much to the relief of my shoulders. On leaving the outskirts of the village we passed through the Americans from Stalag Luft III's west compound, who had been resting in the gutters since dawn. They certainly looked a sorry crew. All went well until just before dark, when the steadily falling temperature reached 21 degrees of frost and it began to snow and sleet, driven by a strong wind which cut clean through every layer of clothing. We were faced with a long, straight road with not a vestige of cover or shelter. It was probably a mile long, but we couldn't see the head of the column or any prospect of a roof for the night.

A small village, about the size of Warboys, appeared in the distance but we couldn't imagine 2000 men finding enough shelter in so few barns and sheds. We were weighing the possibilities of surviving such a night in the open when the column was halted and then commenced to move about 10 yards every 5 minutes — so it appeared the boys were bedding down somewhere.

We in the rear were still worrying about a night on that windswept road, for our hands and feet had gone dead at the first pause. We were all exhausted and yet we knew that anyone who lay down in that snow would never see the light of day. So try and imagine us moving forward in 5 and 10 yard shuffles, with the people on the outside crowding forward and blocking the road so that the occasional lorry found it almost impossible to get past. It finally got so bad that one unfortunate fellow had his foot run over. It made me furious to see a lot of officers acting in such a selfish and foolish manner, but it was probably the instinct of self-preservation overcoming all other considerations.

After 3 hours, just on 8 p.m., the final 300 or 400 of us stumbled into what was probably the biggest farmyard of the village. Every loft and stable was crammed, we four finding shelter in a wood-cum-car shed. Probably fifty people piled in and commenced to strike matches and tread on each other, everyone cursing the other and trying to occupy more than his square yard of space.

More people kept piling in and the poor car was weighed down with the load of bodies on the roof, the wings, the bonnet and the seats. It was impossible to even change one's socks, so Gordon and I brushed the odd flake of snow off and both climbed into his sleeping bag and ate a small piece of dry bread and a piece of frozen bully beef which crunched like crystalline ice cream. With that, we called it a day and endeavoured to stretch out, but there wasn't room for such luxury. His back was up against the car wheel, my back or nose, alternatively, was into the remains of a motorbike. Both our heads were on some complaining person's legs and our feet were over the legs of other protesting fellows.

My hip was kept off the cold cement by two or three small blocks of very angular wood; and after my shoulder had gone numb with cold I supported that on a couple of blocks, too. I then slept fitfully until dawn, when we were all rousted out, the lucky ones getting a little hot water for a drink. Gordon borrowed a litre jug, which we still have. We broke our fast on a slice of dry bread and another quarter tin of frozen bully beef each; all this being achieved in the most incredible confusion of packing, repairing sledges and the bellowings of impatient guards.

At last we filed out about 8 o'clock and commenced a fairly uneventful hike for Muskau. Every hour we stopped for 5 or 10 minutes, when the wayside immediately became lined with men just bursting to 'buy a dog'; an act which was performed in full view of hundreds of their comrades and, more embarrassing still, the cartloads of refugees which were continually filtering past us. I wonder what some of the *frauleins* thought!

The Groupie, walking past us to the head of the column, exchanged the time of day with me so I asked him if nothing could be done to prevent the crowding forward of the previous evening. He said, in his usual vague way, that it would be a good thing if it could be prevented, but offered no further suggestions. At about 2 o'clock I noticed the tendency to crowd forward manifesting itself again, so I organized a bodyguard to back me and pretended that the group captain had appointed me as an official traffic controller.

At the next stop I walked back down the line and in an authoritative voice ordered every sledge off the road. I announced that the group captain had ordered controls every 100 yards up to the head of the column. It was all lies, but at the first announcement I received such an ovation that it encouraged me to go on. I went back for probably a kilometre, and at every 100 yards distance made my announcement at the top of my voice and organized a few acquaintances to keep order. Everywhere down the line the announcement was greeted with approval, so I felt I had done something. But I wondered each time what the Groupie would think if he heard me using his name.

The line started off again and I had to set out and make up the kilometre I had lost. It took me half an hour, walking and trotting, to catch up with Terry and Gordon. But it was worth it, for there was no more pressing forward on that or any subsequent day.

We made the outskirts of Muskau just on dark, when once more we had the inevitable halt while the goons tried to find quarters. Once more the civilians gave us hot water and we offered cigarettes. We were highly organized by this time with our litre jug. Gordon got the water while I had the coffee and sugar all ready to dump in when he was successful. After a drink we still had time to look around; and standing near us I saw a woman of probably 30, with two little children about 3 and 4 with the usual matchstick legs that seemed to characterize all the German children I saw along the route.

I could just perceive them in the growing dark and I was overcome by a desire to hear a kiddie's voice. So I strolled over and offered each of them a small cube of my precious chocolate. It was probably the first they had tasted in their lives and I was very amused at their shy little 'Danke'. The woman was very pleased; but when I offered her a piece she accepted it gratefully but asked if I had a little coffee. With the old sign language I assured her I had only a very little left. Most strange, how they hark after a little decent coffee!

We moved on at last and kept going for half an hour, when once more we were left kicking our heels in the cold for an hour. The local people were quite amiable and Gordon spent much time speaking with the odd person who seemed very ill-informed about the military situation and also very apathetic. With one accord they agreed that Germany was *kaputt*. They seemed as anxious as we that the war should end.

Away we went again, out of the town and up a rise to a glass factory which accepted 500 of us in the furnace room, the retort room, the air-raid shelter and various other very odd places. Here we stayed for 3 days in comparative comfort, for we had straw, light and the means of heating food. The owner became furious at the way his

factory began to rapidly disappear before his eyes. A bunch of
Kriegies resembles a swarm of locusts; for crates, chairs, tools and
fittings just vanished into thin air.

We here received half a (Red Cross) parcel each, which helped the
food situation. But we still kept to starvation rations as we could
never be sure of receiving any more. We were packed ready to leave
at any moment, and of course rumour was rife. But it wasn't until
10.15 p.m. on 1 February that we were finally hauled out in thawing
conditions. The roads were impossible in Muskau, but we hoped for
better sledging conditions beyond the town.

At one halt in a narrow street an old fellow gave us a small bottle of
schnapps for a cake of soap and a few cigarettes. The temperature
was just above freezing and a strong wind made us thoroughly
miserable. The sledges were the very devil to pull and people were
casting them away, all along the route. Finally, we discarded ours and
hoisted our packs on our backs and then commenced the most back-
breaking march I could ever imagine.

At each stop I helped Terry and Gordon off with their packs and
then on again. Terry had some special harness fastened across his
chest which, on one occasion, he forgot to untie — so that I wasted
valuable energy before he remembered it. My sense of humour
helped me over that obstacle, but when he pulled the same trick again
an hour later, I had so little strength left that I just cursed him under
my breath and walked to the side of the road and left him to find his
own way out. I was very quickly ashamed of my shortness of temper,
but at the moment I was furious. I was only glad that I had made no
comment.

The march that night seemed never-ending, and how our shoulders
ached! Once more I conjured up your vision and plodded doggedly
towards it. Finally, at about 6.45 p.m. we stumbled into a barn at
Graustein and slept like the dead for 4 hours, when we were 'ousted'
again with scarcely time to snatch a crust. Three hours later we
walked into an army barracks in Spremberg, where we were given a
cup of hot soup each and hot water to make a brew.

After an hour we were on the road again, but for only 20 minutes.
We were entrained in cattle trucks — forty men per truck. Each
truck was only 8 feet wide by 20 feet long and there was not enough
room for everyone to lie down at the one time. Twenty men had to sit
and stand in one third of the space for 6 hours while the other twenty
lay on top of each other and tried to sleep. It really was an impossible

situation. It was a real fight to try and get anything out of a kitbag to eat. We were locked in and the guards would only open the door at occasional stops — which were surprisingly few — and usually of short duration.

To make matters worse, a lot of people were suffering from sickness and 'squitters' (diarrhoea) which they had picked up in Muskau and which they managed to spread among the others by relieving themselves just outside the trucks, so that it was carried inside on careless people's boots. They couldn't really help it because the guards wouldn't let them move more than a yard from the rails.

Every time anyone went outside we inspected his boots on re-entry, but occasionally the train would start with no warning, leaving four or five people with their pants down. Their antics while trying to get aboard were very amusing, for the train was pretty smart off the mark. We were locked in all the first night, but managed to get a slit of a window open, through which we emptied our urinal — an old 'Klim' powdered-milk tin.

It was funny, really. An officer down the end would partly relieve himself, turn off the tap with difficulty, and with the truck rocking like the devil the tin would be passed from hand to hand in pitch blackness and at great risk to sanitation. But the humour began to pall after the first twenty or so people had used the can. Then the goons solved the problem by not giving us any water for the whole 48 hours.

At one of our later stops some people were trying to get some water as the engine refilled, and a nasty piece of a goon fired a couple of shots over their heads. Naturally, there was one hell of a scramble for the trucks again while parched lips uttered curses against the Reich and all who people it.

Eventually, at 5 o'clock in the evening, we de-trained at Tarmstedt and, forming into blocks we shouldered our packs again and walked 3 kilometres to Menlag, arriving just on dark — when a steady rain began to fall, driven by a freezing wind. The bastards kept us out on the open road while they marched us in by groups of twenty to carry out personal searches. My God! That was the last straw! I was fairly lucky, being kept on the road only 4 hours. We got in and were searched just before 10 o'clock, but the last unfortunate didn't make it until 2 o'clock in the morning.

We had a hot drink, which stilled our chattering teeth, then we were ushered into completely bare rooms — except for a bale of wet wood-straw. This we unravelled, took an armful each, and slept like dead men. Why I am not doubled up with rheumatics, I don't know.

On the train I used my ingenuity and long camp-kit blanket and slung a hammock across the truck above the heads of the madding crowd below. And there I rocked and swayed and wondered just when the ropes would wear through. Ivan Allan followed my lead and during the second night one of his ropes gave way, pitching him on to the groaning bodies below. He tied it up again, but about 3 hours later the train stopped or started with a terrific jolt which nearly threw me out. There was just enough light for me to see that Ivan's hammock was empty — and I gathered from the groans and curses below that he had been thrown out. I chuckled to myself as his head appeared on my level and he, with great difficulty and in great danger, struggled back in again.

I had only just escaped a like fate, for when I came to take down *my* hammock I found the ropes almost cut through. And so ended a nightmare of a trip.

From our compound — the British — 57 went sick on the march and our camp strength at the moment is 1918 officers. The Americans left us at Muskau and we hear their proportion of sick was very much higher. There was one case of pneumonia after that first night of waiting on the road. A goon guard had both legs amputated as a result of frostbite. I have just discovered I had a touch of it on the tip of my thumb which has peeled off in a big callous.

The day after we arrived the sickness caught up with me. I was suddenly sick and the next day started a week of the squitters. Over 75 percent of the camp has suffered and altogether we look a sorry crew. A crude story, but amusing, is told of an unfortunate on the train being slung out of the door on ropes to relieve himself. He was no sooner in action, with the door shut for safety of all inside, when the train rumbled through a station — the platform being crowded! What a sight. I bet the inhabitants were somewhat startled. Hardly British — what!

14

DISMAL DAYS

LEN TRENT, HAVING CONDENSED his descriptions of the first
stages of the journey into one account, then continued setting
down his experiences in diary form. Understandably, there are
gaps. The privations of captivity did not allow for day-to-day —
or even regular — recordings on such scraps of paper that he could
find.

14 February 1945
Your birthday, my darling. It seems that we can expect no mail here
and it seems uncertain if we will have the opportunity to write any, so
I propose to keep a form of diary; not so much to record events but as
an excuse to write 'I love you' occasionally. Darling, how I long to be
with you during these dismal days. Cooped up as we are in cold and
damp quarters, with insufficient light to read by, we can only pack up
and sleep as soon as we have had our frugal evening meal.

How time lags. I can only lie on my bed and hope. And being sick
does not help, for I only long for your company and sympathy the
more. The nearer the end appears, the more impatient we become
and the harder it is to bear this perpetual hunger.

We have one thick soup a day, consisting of a little swede, about
three potatoes each and a tin of bully beef between the six of us. A
sweet of six prunes and two spoonfuls of milk leaves one imagining
the days to come when we shall leave the table satisfied. Yes, it
appears that a week of squitters has left me in a sorry frame of mind.
But it is heartbreaking trying to recuperate on the present fare, after
that back breaking journey followed by a disorder which has left me
little more than skin and bone.

22 February 1945
Darling, a week has gone by during which I have completely

recovered from the tummy trouble, but this only leaves me more hungry than ever before. Never have I been dogged with so much hunger and with so little hope of seeing a satisfying meal. G-rumble, g-rumble! I can just hear you say it. But to illustrate the state of affairs and look on the humorous side! Here I am in a room of twenty-eight — and whereas hitherto I had to listen to the fair sex being ravished by poor wits, from morn till night, now their whole conversation is *food*. Not the women they have had, the women they were going to have — and the way they were going to have them — but the wonderful *meals* they have had, the food they are going to have, and the way they are going to cook it.

Silly, isn't it! But an interesting observation.

A very unfortunate incident occurred the other night. At about 7 p.m. I was standing in our room when suddenly there was a prolonged burst of tommy-gun fire, seemingly just outside our hut. It made us duck our heads a bit, as these walls are very thin. About ten shots were fired by the guard in the corner goon-box only 80 yards away. The target was an unfortunate Kriegie who was only 20 yards from the guard — who evidently fully intended to kill.

Most of the guards here are willing to throw food over the wire in return for cigarettes, and evidently Squadron Leader Bryson had been offered eggs by the guard who was patrolling between the boxes. The whole conversation must have been heard by the goon in the box; and yet when the other guard told Bryson to step over the warning wire, the goon in the box said never a word but waited until Bryson was over the warning wire. He then shone his searchlight on him and endeavoured to fill him full of lead.

Unfortunately, one bullet clipped his liver and lodged in his lungs and poor Bryson is now in hospital with very little hope. Of course it has caused quite a stir. The marine guards profess themselves disgusted with the affair and the Swiss Protecting Power has been summoned to investigate.

24 February 1945

My darling, we have been having some excitement. Yesterday the sirens went as usual and as the sound of aircraft approached we all went outside to see what was up. I had no sooner got outside when an aircraft came whistling down practically overhead. At first I thought it was a Junkers-88, but as it turned out I was amazed to see it was a Mosquito. I had no sooner recognized it than I observed two Me-109s come whistling down at a terrific speed, right on its tail.

My heart pounded. The Mosquito was going fairly slowly and turning slightly towards us and I had scarcely time to offer up a prayer before the first 109 closed. Fortunately, the Mossie pilot was awake, and offered a full deflection shot as the air was rent with a crackle-like thunder. The 109 closed too fast and had to pull away after a two-second burst, which evidently missed.

In the twinkling of an eye, the other 109 closed to within a 100 yards and once again came that terrifying clap of thunder. My God! I expected to see the Mossie blow up in mid-air — and it was practically overhead at only 1500 feet.

The goon pilot must have been a rotten shot or the Mossie pretty adept at evasive action. However, the 109 broke away leaving the Mossie apparently unscathed. The Mossie circled our camp at about 1000 feet, but the Messerschmitts didn't appear again. We didn't know whether we were glad or sorry the excitement was over — when, all of a sudden, the Mossie poked his nose right at our camp.

What a scatter! In a second every Kriegie had thrown himself flat in some hole or other. The rubbish pit was crammed, and I had already edged towards the brick latrine. So I stepped smartly inside and adopted a crouching attitude with my fingers crossed.

The Mossie fired sure enough, but at a huge bread lorry outside our camp. The pilot must have gathered that he was over a prison camp and not an army barracks. The lorry driver sustained head injuries through diving too smartly into a deep ditch. His cab was filled with holes and our bread ration has been cut from one-sixth to an eighth per day.

25 February 1945

I am always a day behind with the excitement, as I can't write it up at night. The light is impossible and fails completely most evenings. Yesterday, just after midday a terrific stream of 'Forts' (American Flying Fortress bombers) flew right overhead. Unfortunately, they were obscured by cloud most of the time, but we caught a glimpse of several formations through the gaps here and there. Over Bremen, 17 miles away, we could see hundreds of vapour trails where fighters higher up had been engaged in a scrap. Unfortunately, we hadn't actually seen the combat.

We were listening to the ack-ack guns of Bremen pounding away and the roar of motors overhead, when several light bombs landed on a target just over a rise in the ground and about a couple of miles away. It made us feel a bit shifty, for at the time there was a clear space right above us and two boxes of twelve (bombers) in sight at 15,000 feet, while occasionally a fighter would flash as it turned in the sun higher up.

Of course we were all very excited at such an encouraging sight. There we were, standing around in groups discussing the size of the bombs that had landed over the ridge, when there was a sudden crackling roar and three bombs landed in a small village in full view of the camp and only a couple of thousand yards away.

They were only small bombs, but with one accord all the brave *Terrorfliegers* flattened themselves on the ground. We were just scrambling to our feet when another load landed on something two miles to the southwest. (As I write, six Mustangs have just flown past at 4000 feet, but no excitement.)

Yes, it was a very encouraging afternoon, for the bombers were flying over us for a full half-hour or more.

Excuse the writing — I am propped up in bed with frozen hands and feet. The one thin slice of bread we have for breakfast doesn't help the circulation much. My God, am I hungry!

29 March 1945
My Angel — my diary! It is just over a month since I wrote, but our case has not been so black — for the day after my last entry we went on to full parcels. My God, were our prayers answered! Twenty trucks of (Red Cross) parcels arrived and, verily I believe, saved us from starvation. The goon rations are hardly worth collecting these days. Each man receives four thin slices of bread, a little margarine, sometimes a smear of jam.

In the midday swede soup there is a cube of meat, if you are lucky, one inch square. Once we could depend on spuds and barley in sufficient quantities to keep the wolf from the door, but since our arrival here we get no barley and now only two small spuds per day per man. So even on full parcels we find it hard to make do.

The Red Cross parcels contain nothing to fill up on, the most substantial item being the meat, of which there are two small tins to last a man a week. Even after a week of full parcels, we were still — and still are — scrambling for the swede peelings thrown out by the kitchen. Only now it is more organized. We don't scramble like pigs anymore, but have them brought to each block on a roster system.

One day after a week of full parcels, Flight Lieutenant Stockings — 'The Colonel' — and I were squatting on the rubbish heap outside the kitchen, trying to find a few swede peelings worth re-peeling after most of the camp had trampled them into the mud in the mad scramble that follows tipping. Well, there we were, hopping about like a couple of sparrows, only not so chirpy, when along comes the *lager* officer — the equivalent of major — and a *haupman*. They paused a moment to see what we were doing. I wish they had spoken, for the *haupman* could speak English, and I would have given a lot to know what they thought of the two enemy officers of equivalent rank grovelling in a garbage heap.

I can honestly say that I didn't feel a bit ashamed, but would have told them they were the ones who should have felt ashamed.

Yes, every day we spend an hour or so carefully re-peeling the mud from the kitchen peelings. A man has to be hungry to do that!

I have a few moments more while our cook is sweating over our primitive stove and home-made oven. I have just finished a week as cook. Made the boys a 'Jimmy cake' — I'll make you one for Xmas!

We saw a terrific terror raid the other night. I was awakened from a deep dream of peace, but there were no angel wings making the roar overhead. Flares were lighting up our room and the hut was fairly shaking, so I rubbed the sleep from my eyes, pulled on a coat and went outside to join the others and see what was to-do. Hamburg, Bremen, Bremenhaven and some other unfortunate city, all within our vision, were catching it. What a to-do! The very earth was trembling as it does in a fair-sized earthquake. Searchlights were everywhere, flares, flashes and all manner of strange lights and — above all — the terrific roar of hundreds of engines.

We could see the flak bursting over all four places and even as I walked outside an aircraft burst into flames and fell as a fiery red ball. What an awful spectacle it was. And before the glow of the first had died down another followed. We wondered how many had been lucky and baled out. There was so much happening that we hardly knew where to look, and we were weighing the chances of one falling in our camp when suddenly the sky a few miles to the north of us was streaked with tracer shells from a night fighter.

He was not far away, for we heard his cannon-fire very distinctly. Sure enough, a tell-tail red fire started and hung in the sky for perhaps 20 seconds and we imagined the frantic activity within the doomed machine. The fire increased; and finally, as if some hand had cut a suspended thread, the glowing ball plunged to earth and blew up just over a ridge north of the camp ... Altogether I saw eight aircraft shot down in probably 20 minutes. Shivering with cold and excitement, I took myself back to bed.

Yes, we have seen a raid of every type now. A fortnight ago we saw a terrific force of Americans fly right overhead. They took half an hour to fly past — both 'Forts' and 'Libs' (Liberator bombers). A week ago we saw hundreds on the way to Berlin, but they were well to the north of the camp. A few days ago the roar of approaching aircraft caused the usual rush outside. The weather was fine and there, passing just to the south of us at about 12,000 feet, was a stream of Lancasters. Suddenly they turned north, then west — which caused them to pass right overhead. What a sight! There were about 300 in a big bunch. No formation. Heading straight for Bremen, 17 miles away.

We watched and waited. No goon fighters appeared. But suddenly, there they were, the little black puffs which used to make my mouth so dry. Then the noise of the guns which were responsible for the flak. What a cannonade! And over the noise of the guns we could hear the crash of the very heavy bombs.

No bombers went down, so far as we could see. But there seemed so many little black puffs that they finally united into one black cloud. Probably a slight exaggeration— but only slight! The sirens blow so often here I wonder why they bother. It is just one long air raid, day and night. Fighters and bombers are always passing in ones and twos or in hundreds. What a prospect! What fools they are to fight on! But it must be almost over, for at the moment of writing their armies seem to be routed and we are sitting back listening for the word we have awaited so long.

Oh, to see you and little Christine again!

4 April 1945
Here we are, wondering if the goons are going to move us again. Montgomery seems to be headed this way, and how we hope to be encircled! We have seen several Mustangs throughout the day. Harbingers of the approaching tanks!

Yesterday I went on a stumping party to obtain wood for the kitchen. Two days before I went out to gather brushwood. All our fuel has to be collected — we get no coal here. It makes a pleasant change, just to get outside the wire for an hour or so. On the brushwood party I sneaked off into the woods and rambled about on my own for an hour, looking for rabbit burrows.

We are on parole, so the guards don't object to a little straying about. I had made a poacher's net, but had no luck. It wasn't a rabbitty spot. There were the first spring flowers I had seen since 1943. Cowslips and white sorrel. Reminded me of the times we used to gather primroses in our little MG in the woods near Forsters!

6 April 1945
Big raid on Hamburg last night; very spectacular! Lots of weird lights and terrific flashes and illuminations of all sorts. The heavy night (bomber) boys all have different ideas as to their origin and spent half the night and all the next day sticking to their arguments.

The weather has turned particularly wet, cold and depressing. To the impatient Kriegie, Montgomery comes on *oh, so slowly.*

We are still on full parcels, which is a blessing — a very great blessing! Don't feel quite so persistently hungry these days, but we are still peeling swede peelings from the kitchen.

8 April 1945
Night before last I got hardly any sleep. What a night! There were low-flying fighters patrolling this area all night. I was just dozing off about 11.30 p.m. when one blighter fired his cannons practically overhead. This sort of thing went on all night; and added to this was the noise of excited Kriegies rushing outside to see what was to do.

Flares being dropped all around us, cannon fire, Bofors guns pooping off and, in the distance, the incessant rumbling of heavy guns. Ah, yes — we felt sure the British would arrive by morning!

I settled down ... when suddenly there was one hell of a bang and a roar, such as I never hope to hear again ... We are still in the dark as to what actually caused it, but it appears a huge rocket ... was fired from the other side of the trees about half a mile away. Whatever it was, I sincerely hope they don't make a habit of it. As it is, we are all a bundle of nerves, without a lot of strange and terrifying things we can't account for.

9 April 1945
11 a.m. What a night! Once more I lay in bed and wondered if I would ever behold your face again ... One lot of bombs fairly rocked the hut. Probably one of the many heavies which were pranging Hamburg.

Very trying, very trying!

We are all very much on edge, what with wondering if the goons are going to move us up to Denmark, and expecting the first British or American tanks to appear at any moment. Everyone is snapping at his neighbour and even good friends are having difficulty in maintaining calm — while mortal enemies are at each other's throats day and night.

Nor am I immune from these feelings, for there are people in this room who annoy me intensely. Their faces make me feel sick and their voices make me want to scream! Silly, isn't it!

15

ON THE ROAD AGAIN

ON THE AFTERNOON OF 9 APRIL the prisoners were summoned to *appell* and told by their German gaolers that they had to be ready to move again at 6.30 a.m. the following morning.

To where? The Kriegies did not have a clue. 'Jesus knows,' suggested the camp adjutant, 'but He won't tell!'

However, there was the inevitable delay in starting the march which, to Trent, proved propitious. He spent the time in knocking together a rough but adequate wheel-barrow in which to trundle his few belongings. He bashed the wooden bottom out of a stave-sided bucket and, with a red-hot poker, pierced a hole in the centre of the disc. This gave him a wheel about 9 inches in diameter — and the rest was comparatively easy. His diary continues:

11 April 1945

We spent the night in an open field; very soggy, very boggy! A heavy fog made us miserable and wet. Bombing and gunning all around us during the night ... However, I got quite a bit of sleep.

The same guard who shot Bryson (who died two days ago) last night shot another fellow through the leg, for no reason. The guard has been placed under arrest, thank God.

The sun is shining, the fog has lifted, we have orders to get cracking. No one is doing anything about it. Guns are booming all around about to the south of us. How we hope to be cut off! But we fear [the Germans] are trying to get us to Denmark.

A jester has just made up a silly rhyme which made me laugh:

The spring has sprung, The sun has riz —I wonder where the Armist-ice!

My barrow caused the village children much amusement — and my comrades much envy. It has kept going over the worst cobble roads. I keep looking at all the little girls about Christine's age and wonder how long it will be before I see her. *And sometimes I wonder if I shall ever see her!*

Aircraft are appearing again. Four fighters have just gone over, rather high. No gunning yet; but the day is still just a pup — 11 a.m.

We are moving off again. Must get ready.

12 April 1945
Just as we stopped for the night I saw a sign post across the road that said: 'Hamburg 60km' — but otherwise I am unaware of our position. The day's march yesterday was only about 12 kilometres and as my beautiful barrow is still going, I found it a pleasant walk — except for the Tempests. Our fighters were straffing the road everywhere and had us into the ditches times without number — but only two silly b....s opened fire; not on us, but on the Navy boys, again. Killed a lieutenant-commander and a petty officer. Very unfortunate. The incident was only 500 yards from where I was.

Spent the night in a very wet and boggy field. Mosquitoes around all night with cannons roaring. One dropped a flare half a mile away and made the night into day. And there we were, it seemed, in full view. But he gunned something just the other side of the wood.

Heigh-ho! Must pack my traps. It's a great life if you don't weaken! Rumour has it we go only 8 kilometres today, and then spend 24 hours in an open field.

And it looks like *rain*!

13 April 1945
9 a.m. Well, here we are and so far the rumour has proved correct. Only hope we stay put for the 24 hours. The field we are in is reasonably dry; at least it isn't a bog. Last night I just threw my two blankets down, put my kitbag under my hip, pulled my woollen hat over my eyes and slept soundly all night.

Terry was just going to sleep and remembered it was his wife's birthday. Had a boiled egg for supper and for breakfast. Gordon picked up fifteen eggs for a tin of coffee and twenty cigarettes. On the road I fixed up a Kriegie's cart — or doll's pram — for him and he was so grateful he gave me an egg.

The Tempests again had us in the ditches once or twice yesterday, but they didn't fire at us. We now have some big 'RAF' signals laid out with towels. But God help us if some stupid P/O Prune decides to shoot up this collection, for there are 200 of us packed into this field.

They tell me there were bags of flares and much gunning in the night, but fortunately I was dead to the world. We passed through Harsefeldt yesterday afternoon, just after a train had been gunned in the station. We in the rear thought that people at the head of the column had caught it.

My wonderful barrow is still working. Thank God!

14 April 1945

9 a.m. Prickie Wright has just wished me many happy returns. We had our day's rest and are now sitting on my pack on the side of the road, waiting to move off. It was a very cold night, with a strong wind. I slept a bit but it was too cold to be pleasant.

I hear we are going 10 kilometres today. Eight Me-109s have just whistled low over our field, so I suppose the war is still going on. Heavy air activity during the night and some terrific bombing somewhere.

The boys have taken advantage of the stop to make carts or buy prams. A damn funny incident yesterday. A proud *frau mit kinder* in pram was seen coming down the road. A bright Kriegie intercepted her and we saw lots of sign language and dipping into pockets. Finally, the *frau* was seen to lift the child — aged about two — out of the pram and we could almost hear her say: 'Now walk, you little *basket*, walk!' She probably received a tin of coffee, a cake of soap and a chocolate bar. The Kriegie proudly marched back, pushing a very smart cream-coloured pram.

Our block is moving off!

Lunch time. I am sitting in the sun with my back to a tree, watching the Navy boys pass through us to the head of the column. What a crew they look, and what strange ships they are sailing! The most weird and wonderful collection of prams, billy-carts and wheelbarrows. I am sure there is not a pram left along our route! Gordon has just bought six eggs for two cigarettes each. What-ho for supper! On the way again!

6 p.m.: Here we are in an apple orchard for the night. The blossom is coming and the trees just in leaf. The orchard is about 260 by 40 yards and there are 1000 RAF officers packed in — each little party with its own camp fire of twigs ... Must make up my bed; still a cold wind.

15 April 1945

9 p.m.: It's getting dark as I sit here 100 yards from the Elbe. We have had a hard day, walking 15 kilometres. Passed through Jork and are now at Cranz. Hamburg is a few kilometres upstream and the sirens are going, even as I write. Must make up my bed. Goodnight, my angel.

16 April 1945

10.30 a.m.: Not a cloud in the sky, but I woke to find frost on my coat. Pretty damn cold. Had an egg for breakfast *mit* potatoes *und* fried spam. A shave and a wash, and now things are looking up. The first party have started across the ferry, but we are the last to leave so it will be some time this afternoon. It appears about a mile across the water, where there is rising ground packed with large houses. I think the town is Blankenhauser.

There seems to be next to nothing in the way of traffic on the river. Our fighters are over every hour. They have already sunk one ferry boat a few days ago; hope they don't pick on this one while I am on it.

We passed through acres of cherry trees in blossom yesterday and had our lunch under the trees. Very pleasant.

Well, I had better get packed up now. They tell me I can take my beautiful barrow on the boat. It seems we are headed for Lubeck. How long will this go on, I wonder! Darling, how I long to see you both!

The prisoners crossed the Elbe by ferry and, near Penaberg, rested for 24 hours in a field. They found the local inhabitants very friendly and there was the usual bartering for eggs in exchange for cigarettes and chocolate. Trent's group did pretty well gaining, along with twenty-two hens' eggs, two goose eggs, some onions and a bunch of rhubarb. Trent records:

At one halt there were two dear little girls about 5 years old, playing with their dolls. So I made friends with them by giving each a piece of chocolate.

They thought it was wonderful, so I then tested their reactions to raisins. After a while they plucked up courage and approached me hand in hand, made a little curtsy and asked if I had any more chocolate.

Of course I gave them another piece ... The futility of war!

The British Tempest fighter-bombers continued to harass the German positions near the line-of-march — and a thunderstorm drenched the prisoners so that they had to settle down, saturated, for their night in the open fields.

Trent was enchanted by the little German girls — about the same age as his daughter Christine would now be — and their wistfulness tugged at his heart-strings. As if to lift his spirits and rekindle hopes of an early reunion with his wife and child, he heard a rumour that the British Army was but 8 miles the other side of Hamburg — and Hamburg itself was only 15 miles distant.

But where *were* they going?

Someone had heard that the German officer in charge of the column was taking the prisoners to the concentration camp at Lubeck. But the RAF Senior British Officer — the 'Groupie' — had told the German that, if such a move was contemplated, the advancing British would seize him and have him tried as a war criminal.

This battle of wits was being fought while British Mosquito bombers made the nights hot with blastings close to the bivouacs; while rain chilled the exhausted prisoners.

Shivering from the frequent hailstorms, hungry and terribly footsore from the shocking condition of the roads, Trent was not getting much sleep. In the draughty and dubious shelter of a cart shed, he wrote:

> Now that I am so close to release, I have an extraordinarily strong desire to live, which seems to make a coward of me. They say that 'cowards die a thousand deaths'. I must fix me some supper and then turn in. Damp coat and damp blanket. You will be nursing a rheumaticky old crock — and I hope very soon.

On 23 April the line-of-march left the town of Barnitz, where the men had rested, and Trent said goodbye to his faithful little barrow. It had proved a helpful implement.

Forty-eight hours earlier they had passed Bad Odesloe where, 6 miles distant, a force of 200 Lancaster bombers was bombing the town.

At a village along the route they were able to have a wash, stripping naked in the street and lathering themselves under a public pump while, at nearby windows, feminine faces peeped around the edges of curtains.

The diary entries continue:

25 April 1945

10 a.m.: If my hand is steady enough I shall record how, a few minutes ago, eight Tempests and rocket-firing Typhoons chased me around the brick barn, along the wall of which I was forced to grovel from time to time. They weren't attacking *us*, but the transport on the Goddamn autobahn, which is only 500 yards away ... We were frightened that a RAF pilot, seeing such a bunch of bods in a small village, would mistake us for troops. We have POW signs out, but pilots don't always see those things.

9 p.m.: We have just heard we stay here yet another day. Hamberge is the name of the village. The Groupie has won. We don't go on to Lubeck, but find new quarters in the surrounding country and await the end of the war. Lots of Spits [Spitfires] have just been over. Two of them had a good look at us. Wish we knew what the pilots were thinking. Time for bed. Goodnight, my angel!

28 April 1945

8 p.m.: We left Hamberge this morning and arrived at Trenthorst, 11 kilometres distant, at midday. It is a huge estate with the biggest barns I have ever seen. I am in a loft 25 by 70 yards with 250 other bods. We are on parole now, so can wander within the bounds of the estate. There is a beautiful lake half a mile long, with lovely trees bordering it and paths running in all directions — so it will be most diverting after the barbed wire and sandy circuit.

How I wish I could wander along the walks with you; everything is spoilt and all time wasted unless you are with me to share in any delight.

Darling, the news is good and our hopes are soaring once more.

29 April 1945

10 a.m.: There was a terrific artillery barrage all last night in the direction of Hamburg. An incredible din! I presume our boys intend to cross the lower Elbe. That will make things interesting for us!

8 p.m.: I was right! Our boys *are* over the Elbe, so once more we stand every chance of being released. Berlin is practically mopped up, Mussolini has been executed and Munich entered. Something must eventuate for us in the course of the next week.

The Colonel and I went for a walk during the afternoon and the sounds of trouble appeared much closer. Fortunately, we are now out of the way of straffing aircraft. No railway or main roads anywhere near us, but we can see and hear a lot of aircraft in action. We await the end with quiet impatience!

30 April 1945

11 a.m.: And it's a lousy day. But what the hell, Archie — what the hell! The war is nearly over and I have a roof over my head and it doesn't leak. And another thing in my favour — the rats didn't pick on *my* potatoes last night, and no rat has scrambled over *my* face since I have been here. The rain has stopped, so I had better fix myself some lunch.

8 p.m.: The Colonel and I went to a village and had coffee with an old girl. Tempests were straffing a mile or so away and frightened the woman and made things difficult for us.

Has been a miserable, cold day. I am in bed trying to get warm. Too dark to see, now. I love you, my sweetheart. Goodnight.

1 May 1945

10 a.m.: The news tells us that our boys are driving for Lubeck, so we have only to wait — and that is our speciality. Miserably cold morning again with, so far, a total absence of aircraft and banging noises. Most peculiar! Of course, the hope at the back of my mind is that the cease fire has sounded. But that hope will be dashed — as all others have been dashed. A terrific barrage will commence any minute now. Still, I hope and grasp at any straw.

2 May 1945

10 a.m.: Went for a walk with Bunty Howard last night, as the Colonel has crocked his foot. Bags of activity and we saw our fighters flying through light flack, some of which was only a mile away. In fact this morning there is quite a flap on, as it is very evident that the front is only a mile or so away and seems to be all around us.

Even as I write, there are terrific bangs, seemingly just over the hedge, with every now and then burst after burst of machine-gun fire. I sincerely believe we will be relieved today. We are now confined to the immediate vicinity of our barns, for these troublesome sounds are too close to be comfortable.

However, we can only sit with our fingers crossed and hope they don't try street fighting through Trenthorst.

Must have me a wash and brush-up, ready to greet the Pongo jobs.
1.30 p.m.: Darling, I was right! Imagine my feelings, right this
moment. At 12.45 p.m. there was a mad cheering down the road. I
couldn't join in the rush as I was frying an egg. But there was no need,
for before it was cooked an armoured car, with Bill Jennings perched
on top, came tearing into our village.

What an incredible scene! But I can't sit here quietly to try to
describe that which is going on all about me. I shall never forget it,
and will tell you the whole story one evening very soon now ... Yes, it
is all incredible and I don't mind admitting that I haven't as yet
properly grasped the idea. Darling ... I wish there was some way of
telling you I am O.K. How you must be worrying — but soon I shall
ring Feltwell 213 — and then!

3 May 1945
11 a.m.: Here we are, still in our old barn and filling in reams of
bumph. Sent off a letter to you yesterday afternoon. Lots of
excitement yesterday afternoon. Goon jet jobs trying to bomb our
columns all about us. Tracer and flak bursting all around and
overhead — very shaky. We actually saw a big bomb detach itself
from a jet flying at 150 feet and heading straight towards us. I
estimated it would fall in our midst and flung myself flat, but the
terrific speed at release meant that it over-shot us by 400 yards, to
explode near a British Bofor Gun.

It is interesting to note that 3 May marked the second anniversary
of Len Trent's imprisonment. His rescue by the British Army
came one day before he would have served two years in captivity.
His journal continues:

4 May 1945
1 p.m.: I left it too late to sign off last night. Just on dusk there was a
bit of excitement with some goon aircraft overhead. Lots of very
pretty flak.
7 p.m.: Went for a walk with Hugill. We captured three goons and
marched 'em back — all aged sixteen, poor young devils. Big flap on.
Two hours ago we got orders to pack and now I'm sitting on my kit
bag waiting for the truck. No more weary walking! I feel very
excited, for our journey home is about to begin and it seems real at

last ... I shall be telling you so very much so very, very soon.

7 May 1945
3.30 p.m.: Darling, I am sitting in the sun at Diepholz aerodrome, hoping and praying for an aircraft to take me to England this afternoon.

I may be taken to Brussels, as 300 of the boys went there this morning. Everything appears very disorganised and haphazard. It seems any number of planes from 1 to 50 may turn up at any time of the day and take you to Brussels or England. How I am praying for an English trip!

We have been taken all over Germany in lorries and have had delay after delay. Very disappointing. We left Trenthorst at 10 a.m. and arrived at Luneburg at 5 a.m. on the 5 May. Spent a day there filling in forms, and left the next morning at 10 a.m. in lorries and trucks and arrived here at 9 p.m. last night.

We had been promised aircraft to fly us home yesterday, but here we are still, and faced with the possibility of Brussels. Patience, patience!
9.20 p.m.: Never a dull moment — and I am lucky! Here I am just over the North Sea and this is the only plane of the day direct for Wing aerodrome and England.

I have been flying for 2 hours in a daze and trying to imagine our first telephone conversation.

My God! There's the coast of England! We are going to fly over London. Darling, I shall be speaking to you now in a matter of minutes!

16

HOMECOMING

For winter's rains and ruins are over,
And all the season of snows and sins;
The days dividing lover and lover,
The light that loses, the night that wins;
And time remembered is grief forgotten,
And frosts are slain and flowers begotten,
And in green underwood and cover
Blossom by blossom the spring begins.

Swinburne's haunting, prosodic lines must surely have foretold of spring in Feltwell! If the joys of reunion had indeed come a little after the first shy crocus had peeped through the snow, then the sweetness of the season was the more wonderful for the waiting.

Len Trent had arrived at Wing, near Aylesbury at about 10 p.m. on 7 May 1945 — a significant day. Germany had officially signed its surrender to the Allies. It had been a direct flight from Diepholz aerodrome, and he and his companions had been directed to a huge hangar which had been set up as a reception centre for repatriated prisoners of war.

The place was staffed by women from the Women's Auxiliary Air Force and Voluntary Ambulance Division whose firm convictions of the moment had persuaded them that the men, having come from the haunts of Hitler, must be lousy. They pursued their quest of the imagined lice with great vigour and a determined intent to kill, puffing clouds of the new wonder-pesticide, DDT, up the legs of the ex-prisoners' trousers and through the sleeves of shirts and jackets until each man's every cavity was either plugged or lined with the white dust.

Having ensured that not one Nazi germ could have survived a landing in Britain, the fumigating girls passed the men into the hands of the clerks who collected all possible particulars while the caterers supplied tea and biscuits. And then Len Trent was able to telephone Feltwell 213.

Ursula answered the call. But all she could hear from her long-lost husband, before he was choked with emotion, was: *'I'm back!'*

When, as must, he regained his composure and his words, he was able to assure her that he was well and that he was about to start on his way to Feltwell. When would he get there? God alone knew — for England was in a glorious uproar of VE Day celebrations; and London, the hub of all the hysteria, had to be navigated before Trent could reach Liverpool Street station and entrain for Lakenheath. So Ursula said she would meet every train that was likely to carry her man to her arms.

All means of transport in London — both private and public — were in chaos as the citizens mobbed through streets and squares and crescents. Not a taxi could be found. The buses and underground trains were running infrequently and in confusion. But eventually Len Trent got to the railhead and, in the small hours of the morning, reached Lakenheath station — and a homecoming that was 2 years, 4 days and 9½ hours overdue.

While Len had been absent, Ursula and little Christine had been living with Doctor A. ('Mac') McDonald and his wife in their picturesque home in Feltwell. It was a very happy arrangement, for Ursula and Mrs McDonald shared in the preparations of meals and in general housekeeping affairs. So, when Ursula and Dr McDonald met Len Trent on the Lakenheath platform, it was to the doctor's home that the homecoming warrior was led. Later, they went to the local Oak Hotel — and what a fine old party was awaiting him! All his local friends were there; and after the corks had popped and the welcome-home toasts had been given and taken, the guest of honour, after an hour of revelry — laced with the excitement of reunion — flaked out from sheer fatigue.

Little Christine, who had been an infant of two when her father was shot down in May 1943, lay asleep in her bed when they returned home. Len Trent, peeping into her room, had seen but a small bundle of bedclothes and had kissed a little tousled head on the pillow. So when, by the light of later morning, a little girl of four entered her mother's bedroom, she and her Daddy faced each other as strangers.

'What are you doing in bed with my Mummy?' the bewildered

child demanded.

That, thought Trent, was quite a question.

England, whose magnetic lodestone had first drawn Len Trent northwards from New Zealand 8 years earlier, now enchanted and enslaved him with even more potent witchcraft as he and his wife and small daughter walked the Feltwell fields and wended their ways through the spring-sweet coppices.

Every wooded lane, bedecked with blossom and awakened from winter dormancy by birdsong, drew him closer and closer to the land's abiding security. He was free — free to walk unhindered; to feel the good English grasses yielding beneath his footfalls; and to smell the tang of cottagers' woodsmoke and to know again the musty perfume of leaf mould.

Contentment, like a benison, now lay gently over the small family.

Len Trent had been home about a fortnight when his kindly hosts, Dr and Mrs McDonald, arranged a dinner party to celebrate their warrior's return.

Several of Trent's old and close friends were invited. Dr Johnny Barr was there, along with Oscar Peacock, a notable Feltwell farmer. And so, too, was the redoubtable Dr David Smith, of Stoke Ferry, who had had the audacity to volunteer for the RAF and serve on operations as a rear gunner in a Wellington bomber. When it was discovered that David Smith was a highly-qualified doctor, he had been removed from his turret and re-equipped with his stethoscope before the ink was dry on the Air Ministry order.

The dinner was a glittering occasion, in marked contrast to the privations Trent had so recently suffered as a prisoner of war — the ladies in their jewelled finery and the gentlemen in formal dress. The subdued, flickering light from the silver candelabra was mirrored in the huge polished oak dining table and, wonder of wonders, there was Trent's favourite dish as the main course — plump Norfolk pheasant with all the trimmings.

The sherry and the table wine, so long denied the guest of honour, was probably a bit more potent than he had suspected. At all events, he was the life and soul of the party, entertaining the gathering with his experiences and provoking much merry repartee. But suddenly, as he ate, he became aware of a silence around the table. He looked up and met nine pairs of eyes fixed on him with considerable amusement. To his embarrassment he found that the hungry ghosts of prison life were still haunting him. He had tilted his plate with his left hand and, with the little finger of his right hand, he was scooping the plate and licking up every last vestige of gravy.

The gathering roared with laughter at Trent's confusion.

Trent was allowed two months' leave to relax before the RAF put any demands upon him. He was then required to report to Cosford for a medical check and the filing of his detailed account of the destruction of his aircraft and the circumstances of his imprisonment.

He wrote four pages about the Ramrod 17 raid and his adventures and misadventures in Stalag Luft III.

While waiting in the officers' mess he saw a highly-decorated Air Force officer with New Zealand shoulder flashes on his tunic. Establishing rapport with a fellow countryman, Len Trent found that he was talking with Bill Tacon — a notable pilot later chosen to command the Queen's Flight. Air Commodore E. W. Tacon, CBE, DSO, MVO, DFC, AFC, RAF (Retd) now lives at Howick, Auckland. He and Len Trent still meet and chat on occasions.

Keen to return to flying, Trent requested a posting to RAF Transport Command. The prospect of longer journeys had more appeal than the monotonous grind of circuits-and-bumps with embryo pilots in training schools. Also, should he ever wish or be compelled to leave the Service and get a flying job with a civilian airline, he wanted some experience at the controls of heavy, four-engined aircraft.

It was at the headquarters offices of Transport Command that he ran into Mindy Blake for the first time since their release from German bonds. The large coir mat in Blake's office was but a thinly-disguised practice pad on which the golf-smitten officer sought to perfect his swing.

Also at Transport Command headquarters, who should enter the waiting room but Len Trent's cousin, Ian Richmond! He, too, was seeking a posting to give him the most flying experience in the RAF's peacetime role.

They laughed and agreed it was something like Old Town Week. Trent ... Richmond ... Blake ... if they stuck around the office long enough they would probably meet up with half the pilots who were at Sagan with them.

Well, they were interviewed and then told to report to Leicester East, a training school close to the city of Leicester, where pilots were shown the comparatively simple mysteries of the ubiquitous Dakota — or DC-3, C-47 or 'Gooney Bird' — which was a general purpose machine.

Again, Trent and Richmond met. This time it was in the officers' mess at Leicester East. They had a drink at the bar and contemplated the future.

But they were kept waiting around the flight office for so long, without getting airborne, that Ian Richmond became disenchanted. He stated that he was fed up, left Leicester East and went to see the people at New Zealand House in London. His application to return home was approved, for he had been away from New Zealand since 1936 and had been a prisoner of war for 3½ years. He was embarked on the next ship and, on arrival in the South Island, took up work on his father's sheep farm.

Trent went on to qualify as a Dakota pilot.

Like the Lockheed Ventura, the Douglas Dakota was developed from a civilian passenger aircraft. As the DST (Douglas Sleeper Transport) it first saw service in the summer of 1936, carrying its full loads of fourteen passengers between New York and Chicago. Three months later the Douglas transports or DC-3s (the 'C' denoting 'Commercial') flew the transcontinental coast-to-coast service between New York and Los Angeles.

So the machines in wartime were doing the type of work for which they had been designed. And they did it remarkably well and for a long time. They groaned and rattled and leaked oil. They ran hot and they ran cold and their wings flapped and flexed in the most un-nerving manner. But for all that they were honest, faithful, forgiving and undoubtedly the most successful aircraft ever built.

Len Trent's next posting was to Syerston, about 6 miles south of Newark. It was a training school for paratroopers and for the skills in dropping supplies by parachutes; and Trent was a flight commander.

For some months he was happily employed in rumbling his twittering human cargoes around the skies and pressing the button that would alert their master to send them leaping into space. He was logging plenty of flying hours, there was not a hostile aircraft nor a puff of ack-ack on his pleasant horizon, and life was good.

About this time, Ursula and Christine were living with an aged relative at King's Lynn, as accommodation was unavailable near Leicester East. So Trent was living in the officers' mess. From the body of resident RAF and Army officers — roughly half and half of each service — there were some very keen bridge players, so some serious nightly engagements were fought.

One night, as a change from the usual bridge game, one of the Army officers suggested Trent accompany him to a cinema in Nottingham where a particular film was being shown. It was a late showing and, along with the 20 or 30 mile trip, it was after midnight when they got back to the mess.

As they entered the building the batman keeping his all-night vigil on the telephone told Trent that the station commander had phoned. Would Squadron Leader Trent return the telephone call immediately he came in!

Len Trent looked at the clock. Surely it would be most uncivil to disturb the station commander at such an ungodly hour! He would retire and phone him in the daylight hours.

He was just dozing off when the batman came tapping on his door. The station commander had just phoned — *again.* 'He *insists* that Squadron Leader Trent comes to the phone *right away*, Sir!'

So he rushed to the telephone, full of excuses and explanations, to be stopped in mid-flow by the command: 'Trent — when I say I want to talk to you right away, I mean *right away.* So, don't bother to dress — come to my house *now* — just as you are!'

As the station commander's house was about a mile down the road, Len Trent did not take his master's word too literally. He paused to slip on his shirt, trousers, socks and shoes and, hurrying to his car, he drove to hear what awful disaster had overtaken him. 'What the hell have I done now?' he pondered. 'Am I posted to some god-forsaken pimple pilot-pool on the backside of nowhere? Do I have to leave at daybreak?'

He knocked on the door and the station commander and his wife — both in evening dress, as they had been entertaining some now-departed guests — welcomed their latest arrival most cordially. 'Come in, Len, come in,' said the host. Trent began to breathe easier, comforted by the friendlier attitude.

'What will you have to drink, Len?'

'Er — nothing at this time of the night, thank you, Sir.'

'Well, I think you had better have a drink. I think you will *need* a drink, Len.'

Trent nominated a gin and tonic, wondering and wondering the while his host was mixing the drink: 'What is happening? What have I *done*?'

The station commander worked very, very slowly on that gin and tonic. He then, as deliberately, topped up his wife's glass and then his own. Then he turned to Trent and said: 'Well, Len, it is my unusual and certainly my undoubted great honour to inform you that you have been awarded the Victoria Cross.'

Yes, Len Trent needed that drink. Dazed and not wholly believing the news, he sank back into a wide, deep chair that was fortuitously close and ready for his arrival. Slowly the facts unfolded.

It was then the early hours of 1 March 1946 — about 10 months after the German surrender and close on 3 years after the Amsterdam affair. Gradually the facts of Ramrod 17 had been pieced together by Air Ministry, from both Trent's own report and from German intelligence records.

Sir Basil Embry, Air Officer Commanding 2 Group, had studied the evidence and had recommended that Squadron Leader Leonard Henry Trent, DFC, be awarded the highest British decoration for valour in combat.

That staggering turn of events meant a considerable change in the pattern of Len Trent's service life. Understandably, the first thing he wanted — and indeed was directed to do — was to fly and break the momentous news to his wife at King's Lynn. So the morning light saw him airborne in a Dakota, en route for Sutton Bridge airfield.

Air Ministry quickly organized a trip to London to attend a series of press interviews and suddenly his comparatively carefree life of trundling learner-paratroopers to their dropping zones was ended. On Friday 12 April 1946 he was summoned to Buckingham Palace for the investiture.

Towards the end of the year, on official recommendation that he take leave to visit his homeland and face the music that fame had orchestrated, he and his wife and small daughter travelled by sea to Auckland. They arrived on a golden day in mid-September and, through the good offices of the RNZAF, Len Trent's mother had been brought from Nelson to greet her notable son and meet her new family.

Trent had earlier requested permission to fly around New Zealand and visit the relatives of all aircrew members who had been killed while participating in raids that he had led. This had been granted. But first there were some civic functions to attend and duties to perform.

The Trents were flown from Whenuapai to Nelson in an Air Force Airspeed Oxford. They were met on arrival by the Mayor of Nelson, who asked if the district's illustrious son would be prepared to march, behind the municipal band, up the main street of the town to attend a public reception.

On 16 September he was the distinguished guest of honour at a reception organized by the Nelson City primary school pupils. A day or two later he visited Nelson College, where he was welcomed by the principal, Mr H. V. Searle, and invited to take the salute in a march past by the college cadets.

The interesting coincidences surrounding the three old members of the 'Rattery' was recalled in the college journal, *The Nelsonian*, of September 1946:

> While a boarder at College House ... he (Trent) shared a dormitory with his cousin, I. G. Richmond (Takaka) and M. M. Shand (Wellington). When he was shot down in May 1943 and taken to Stalag Luft III, his two friends were among the first to greet him, and within a few days all were together again in the same hut.

A week or two after his visit to the college Len Trent received a message from the governors — would he kindly consent to having his portrait painted by the notable artist, Mr Archibald Nicoll of Christchurch? Such a work, they said, would complement the portrait of another illustrious Nelsonian old boy that was gracing the walls of the college library, Lord Rutherford of atomic fame.

Trent acknowledged the request with considerable pride and went to Wigram, where he met the artist and sat for the portrait.

17

BACK TO BRITAIN

EARLY IN 1946, and well before his return to New Zealand to spend his accumulated three months' leave, Trent had transferred from the RAF to the RNZAF. The circumstances had arisen from his visit, soon after his repatriation from Germany, to see an old friend at RNZAF Headquarters in London — the late Hon. Frank Gill, then a wing commander and an officer with a distinguished flying record. The two pilots had trained together at Wigram in 1938.

In the course of the conversation Wing Commander Gill had suggested that, as Trent had indicated his wish to continue a service career in peacetime, he would, presumably, also wish to return to New Zealand and settle with his family in his homeland. Therefore, persuaded Gill, he should apply for a transfer — and this would result in better rates of pay, a reasonable gratuity back-dated 5 years, and prospects of a permanent commission and continuing promotions within the RNZAF.

Trent had accepted the advice; and so New Zealand saw their Air Force Victoria Cross winner arrive with shoulder flashes on his tunic that proclaimed him a true Kiwi — no matter that his deed of valour was performed while he was, technically, a member of the RAF.

Towards the end of his official period of leave in New Zealand — and when most of his prime civic and social engagements had been fulfilled, he was invited by the Air Department to become a member of a team of three formed to select candidates with war-flying experience who were prepared to return to service with the RAF.

The service at that time was embarking on a plan to re-build its strength and suitable officers and non-commissioned officers from the dominions were sought to augment British applications.

Headquarters for the South Pacific area had been set up in Melbourne and given the dazzling initials, RAFMANZ — Royal Air Force Mission, Australia and New Zealand. A Wing Commander Beaney came over from Australia to head the workings of the triumvirate in New Zealand. Along with Squadron Leader Trent was Squadron Leader Hill.

The scheme was well advertised in the country's newspapers and the board proceeded through the main centres of New Zealand, interviewing all applicants and making recommendations for the RAF's decisions. After about 2 months of this work, the selection board was disbanded and Trent was left in charge in Wellington to arrange the ship passages of the chosen men and their families, provide them with a month's pay and wish them bon voyage.

Along with the RAF's recruiting drive there had been an attractive shake-up in its rates of pay. Nor was Air Ministry in London unmindful of a very distinguished, young and versatile officer who had somehow stepped out of the RAF's cockpit to revert to some sort of colonial barnstorming. Trent, it was pronounced, should be offered a permanent commission in the RAF.

The tidy packet that the English offices of the Air Force displayed suited the New Zealander. After some further two-way correspondence, he received a cable instructing him to pack his belongings and put himself and his family on the next ship of his choosing that would get him to Britain.

During his stay in his homeland — a visit that had been stretched from the originally planned 3 months to about a year — his family had grown. Young Timothy, his second child, had been born a New Zealander and when Trent got the call to return to the RAF, the babe had not reached his first birthday. The family had settled into a pleasant home at Silverstream, Heretaunga, and the Air Force's demands on Trent's time had not been so urgent as to seriously interfere with his golf. However, in the better interests of the family future, there were to be some moderate upheavals in the Trents' lifestyles.

They left Wellington towards the end of 1947. They could, in truth, say it was an earth-trembling occasion. For on their last evening in New Zealand Ursula experienced her first earthquake and Len, with vivid memories of the Murchison shocks, probably thought at the time that they were doing the right thing in leaving the Shakey Isles. But the 'quake, of distinct, moderate force, soon subsided and the cinema building, in which they were being entertained, remained firm.

The ship's route was by way of Sydney and Cape Town. The Tasman crossing was shockingly rough and young Timothy was the only tough sailor in the family. His demands for nourishment were insistent and the green-gilled parents crawled alternately from their bunks to spoon great globs of Farax, a fine-grained infant cereal, into the ever open mouth of their son. Then, inversely, they would rush to the washbasin to get rid of their own stomach contents.

From Sydney the ship followed the great circle route to Cape Town, skirting the fringes of the Antarctic. But as they steamed into the roads, old Table Mountain stood majestically clear in glorious sunshine and the vessel's small complement of passengers relaxed topsides in the balm of a southern summer.

A young flight lieutenant and his slim wife were standing at the ship's rail when a mischievous breeze came from nowhere and lifted the woman's light dress high around her waist to display everything — but *everything* — of her nether nudity to a most appreciative audience. The distant beauty of Table Mountain was for the meantime ignored.

After a rough haul up through the Bay of Biscay, the ship berthed at Tilbury and the Trents were met by Ursula's parents and taken to their home in Kent. And when Len Trent reported to Air Ministry he was sent to Transport Command Headquarters at Teddington where, again, he ran into Group Captain Mindy Blake — golf clubs not far away and his large coir practice mat conspicuous on his office floor.

After exchanging pleasantries and some reminiscing, the serious matters of Trent's immediate future were discussed. So, on 11 November 1947 he was directed to report as chief ground instructor at Bircham Newton, a technical-instruction conversion unit and an entrance school which served the whole of Transport Command. From there, the trainee pilots selected to fly Dakota aircraft went on to Leicester East, while those who were to master the 'heavies' — the four-engined Yorks and, later, the Hastings, went to Dishforth in Yorkshire.

Trent was at Bircham Newton until 13 September 1948, when he was appointed chief ground instructor at Dishforth. Despite the fact that he had never flown a York he was nevertheless expected, at this heavy conversion unit, to know the theory of four-engine handling. So he quickly absorbed knowledge by listening to the wisdom of his underling specialist lecturers.

Learning to fly the York was, he found, a breeze and he liked the feel of the tremendous surge of power as the four airscrews thrust the aircraft down the runway and lifted it airborne. The assistance of a flight engineer operating the throttles on take-off was something new, too. The power controls of a York were high near the ceiling of the flight deck. And whereas the pilot *could* work both the throttles and the flight controls at the same time, as with orthodox lighter aircraft, it was generally more convenient for the York pilot to call for the required power and have the engineer apply it. It was a practice that the independently-minded pilots found hard, at first, to accept.

The chief flying instructor was Wing Commander John Grinden, a large outgiving man with a colourful turn of phrase frequently salted with bold and often strictly untrue adjectives. His pipe was invariably in his mouth during the hours of daylight, being deftly flicked from side to side to add emphasis to his point of view. His preferred lecture subject, delivered to each new intake of transport trainees, was radio-telephone discipline and the advice, including many 'bloodies' and copulatory terms, edged out of his mouth past his pipe stem and the corners of his lips.

On the station, Wednesday afternoon had long been regarded as a recreational period when the student-aircrew and instructors were expected to disport themselves voluntarily in games of physical exercise. But according to Grinden, the whole of the unit's manpower was growing gross and slothful by shirking the wielding of the willow or the ardent boot to leather.

He called together all his men, from the lowliest aircrew member to the most senior officer, and spoke to them like a Henry on St Crispen's Day — but with far more colour.

'Look, you lazy bastards are dodging your bloody exercise and treating Wednesdays like goddamn picnics.' He accused them of gorging themselves to great weight and girth in the local tearooms and told them that, come next Wednesday, they would all — 'every bloody one' of them — be required to run in a cross-country race of about three and a half miles.

Trent, enjoying a fairly long-standing remission from the agonies of anchylosing spondylitis that had first become manifest during his flying during the Battle of Flanders, was persistently

keeping himself fit for the skiing holiday he and Ursula now
frequently enjoyed on the Continent.

So, unsuspected by John Grinden and his opponents, he went to
the starting line in sound shape. As the field moved off he
established a position among the front runners and was soon in the
lead. And as the furlongs fell behind, so, one by one, did the
runners flag from the bunch led by Trent. One mile, 2 miles, 3
miles — and the 34 year old squadron leader increased his lead
over the predominantly younger competitors. At the finish he was
the clear winner.

It gave him a tremendous feeling of *elan*. As he was later to
remember, it was one of the outstanding events in his Air Force
life. There he was, a man considerably older than all the
protagonists in the race, who had often been crippled by the
recurring illness that racked his spine and his limbs in its attacks.
And he had beaten youth at its own game.

The following morning Grinden rang Trent in his office. 'Len,'
he drawled in some surprise, 'they tell me you won the bloody
race yesterday! Jesus, that was a great effort. How did you do it?'

Len's reply: 'Just a matter of determination, Sir.' But he never
let on that he had been training nightly for months.

But his freedom from the crippling attacks of spondylitis was
ended soon after the pressures of the Berlin Airlift began to
mount. It was one of the busiest times of Trent's Air Force life and
Transport Command's aircraft were flying around the clock
delivering supplies through the air corridor in defiance of Russia's
territorial claims.

By early 1950 the pains and the constraints of the malady
became so severe he could no longer afford to suffer in silence.
With the early onset of aches and stiffness he had hoped that the
illness would be short-lived. If he reported his indisposition, he
feared a medical examination might result in his losing his flying
category and, consequently, his prospects for a worthwhile future
in the service. Instead, he decided to confide his troubles in
Squadron Leader Peter Stewart, the station medical officer, who
was a particularly close friend and an ardent fellow golfer.

Neither the medical officer of 15 Squadron nor any of the five
New Zealand doctors who had examined Trent at various times
had put a finger on the problem. Most had vaguely murmured
about arthritis and fibrositis. And one, in fact, had ordered the
removal of two of the patient's slightly discoloured, but

nevertheless sound, teeth in the opinion that they were causing 'rheumatics'.

Peter Stewart sized up Trent's illness immediately after he had heard the symptoms described. He sent the sufferer to Nocton Hall, a huge RAF medical centre in Lincolnshire, where extensive tests were carried out. He was hospitalized at Doncaster and over a period of three months he was given radiotherapy of the neck and spine.

During his convalescence he strengthened weakened muscles and co-ordinated his movements by hitting a golf ball with a No. 7 iron. After 6 months his doctors, astonished at his rate of recovery and his regained body movement, sent him to London for the decisions of a medical board. An air commodore and two group captains examined charts and records and questioned the apprehensive Trent — who, by this time, was wondering if the RAF had any non-flying vacancies in such departments as accounts or stores and equipment. Then, to his great joy and almost disbelief he heard the air commodore say: 'Well, Trent, as far as we are concerned you are a walking miracle - and a very lucky young man. We are pleased to advise you that we find you have a full-flying category. A1G1.'

Walking on air, Trent returned to Dishforth and immediately made application for a return to flying duties.

With his tour of duty at that station drawing to a close, he elected to put his name forward in response to the service's urgent need of competent flying instructors, albeit he was a senior squadron leader and perhaps a bit far advanced in age and experience for such a position.

He was accepted and sent to a flight refresher school at Finningley on 29 August 1950 where, for a week or two, he flew Harvards and, as usual in his leisure hours, played golf. Leaving a full bucket of practice balls in the mess one afternoon, he was agreeably surprised to find that the diligent old civilian batman had cleaned the balls to a dazzling whiteness. But on closer examination it was found that the helpful fellow had immersed them in boiling water. Every one of those rare and expensive balls — something like fifty in total — had a stretched and bubbled jacket and was completely useless.

His next posting was to an initial leadership school at Digby, the portals to a return to Flying Training Command. He moved in on 24 October 1950 and found that his commanding officer was Wing Commander Hughie Edwards, VC, DSO, DFC. The two had met on several earlier occasions when State parades and social functions had brought Victoria Cross winners together.

On Trent's first evening at Digby he was invited by Hughie Edwards to play squash. Trent, at the time, could always merit a place in a station team. Noting the CO's decided limp, which was a legacy from a pre-war Blenheim crash, the new arrival thought he would notch up another victory in his long line of squash successes. But no. He was soundly thrashed by his senior officer.

Part of the training syllabus, while he was at Digby, was a series of escape and evasion exercises; and for this the members of the course were moved to Chivenor, in Devon. Hughie Edwards was highly amused that Trent, who had been involved so much in prison-escape adventures in Sagan, should be required to participate in such games. The two Victoria Cross winners spent most of the time walking along the beaches.

From Digby, Trent went on to Central Flying School at Little Rissington and entered the Harvard Flight. The date was 23 November 1950. He found accommodation for his family in the rooms of the Red Lion, a comfortable pub in Stow-on-the-Wold. The proprietor was a Mr Burr, a retired parson who still kept his hand in and his soul pure by lay duties in the local church. He had two notable habits. He required all his lodgers to be within his doors by 11 p.m. each night — otherwise they would be bolted out. And he had a culinary passion for jugged hare, a dish that was served at least twice a week.

Soon to turn up as guests at the Red Lion were Hughie Edwards and his wife Pat, and a keen bridge school was soon in full swing.

Also living at Stow-on-the-Wold and flying at Little Risington was James Coward, a fighter pilot who had lost a leg in a flying accident and had been fitted with an artificial limb. Despite his disability he had pursued his passion for skiing and had become quite proficient on the snow, during a tour in Norway as Air Attache. However, all skiers have their tumbles. And on one occasion when Coward went down in a tangle of arms, legs, skis and poles, he managed to deftly snap off his detachable tin leg before he hit the snow. The ski, with boot still attached and a portion of flesh-coloured artificial leg protruding, went slithering down through a group on the lower slopes, one of whom fainted at the grisly sight.

Eventually James Coward graduated from instructional duties on Harvards to become a chief instructor on one Meteor unit at the same time as Trent was chief instructor on another station, flying the same machines.

Len Trent completed his course at Central Flying School on 21 March 1951 and at the behest of an old 15 Squadron associate, John Glenn — now a group captain — he was posted to No. 3 Flying Training School, Feltwell, where Glenn was commanding officer. Life on the station was somewhat different from the days when 487 Squadron was in its formative stages. Instead of the two-engined Venturas, Harvard trainers now rent the Norfolk air with their buzz-saw raspings as they changed to fine pitch, while aerobatics were more the order of the exercise than low-level practice bombing runs.

Trent and a couple of his companions decided to form their own aerobatic team But when on one occasion the leading Harvard fell off the top of a loop and put the other two machines in dangerous disarray, they decided their aircraft were under-powered for attempting tight-formation stunts.

About a year after he had been appointed CO of Feltwell, Group Captain Glenn was replaced by Freddie Rump, a largely-built Rhodesian who had just been promoted to four-ringer rank and was determined, as a new broom, to sweep the station exceedingly clean.

Soon after Rump had settled in at Feltwell, a group of CFS examiners visited the station and Trent, who had been passed with a B2 instructor category when he had left Central Flying School, decided to present himself for a higher grading. So he and a fellow candidate, a Squadron Leader Owen, went before the experts. However, whereas they both qualified for B1 ratings in practical flying, they both missed in the theory tests.

For Trent there was at least some excuse. Judith, his third child, was born on 23 January 1952 and with Ursula's confinement occupying his mind, swotting had come a poor second place in his attentions.

However, Freddie Rump, full of wrath and righteousness, would brook no excuse. He had the two squadron leaders on the mat in front of his desk and gave them such a verbal lashing that the dazed officers quite believed that their boss imagined them to be saboteurs.

'You've got a minimum time to qualify,' he told them. 'And it's 3 months. And if you don't pass then, I'll see that you are off this unit in double-quick time.'

Trent and Owen, dejected but determined, decided to give every waking moment to study. They thrust most of their mundane, paper-work flight duties on to deputies and flew together as much as possible, practising their instructional patters and criticizing each other's drills and techniques. And to what effect? Well, when Trent presented himself for the examiners' investigations his prowess and knowledge were so impressive that he was invited to join the staff of experts at the Central Flying School.

So, in early October 1952 he left Freddie Rump's domain — but certainly not under a cloud. He reported, once again, at Little Rissington and on 20 October he was appointed Squadron Commander, No. 4 Squadron — which was equipped with Harvard and Vampire trainer aircraft.

No matter that he had never flown a jet aircraft before — the little Vampire was to present no difficulties and he quickly absorbed the sufficient skills to guide others in its handling.

Now a staff member of Central Flying School and entrenched on the 'Hallowed Hill', his RAF career was virtually made. He and his family had good living quarters on the station — a home, indeed, befitting air-commodore status — and the next-door neighbours, though well senior in station, were most friendly. On one side was Group Captain Bill Coles and his family. Coles, a member of the RAF bobsleigh team, was also a great squash player and golfer. He was a delightful character and he and Trent quickly gained rapport.

On the other side of the Trents' house lived Air Commodore Mark Selway, an imposing officer and, Len Trent found, a splendid gentleman. Another near neighbour was Major 'Brad' Bradley, an officer of the United States Army Air Force, who was on an exchange appointment and serving with the RAF. He was a genial soul and became a close friend.

So, for the Trents, service life went well. They were in an agreeable neighbourhood and Len's duties were rewarding and not too demanding of his spirit or his physique. The new courses of pupil pilots came and the old courses passed from the immediate care of CFS. As each group finished its course of training, the pilots performed in a display of aerobatics, competing in honours for the Brabham Trophy, a prize donated by a New Zealander who had served on the staff.

The displays were judged by the squadron commanders and on a particular occasion when the trainees, by this time flying Meteor jets, were showing their competitive paces, Trent, Brad Bradley and another officer were on the landing atop the control tower assessing points. The briefing required pilots to approach the performance area (immediately above the airfield) in line with the main runway and climb from that heading to complete their upward charleys, rolls and whatever their teachings and their prowess might permit.

A couple of performances had been judged when in came a Pilot Officer Ward on a cross approach. He put his Meteor into a vertical climb and, in a series of upward rolls, disappeared into a cloud shelf above the officers' quarters and the station sports field.

Immediately Trent saw the pilot's irregular approach he called down the open trapdoor to the controller below: 'Recall Pilot Officer Ward immediately. He is not to continue with the exercise.'

But he had no sooner given the order than, on looking into the sky again, he saw the Meteor spinning down out of control. The machine was hurtling down, seemingly straight above the housing area; and even as Trent yelled to alert the fire and ambulance services, it crashed with a heart-stopping explosion. Dry-mouthed with the horror of the carnage he might expect to find in the debris of metal and masonry, he clattered down the stairway to his car and roared to the scene.

Ward's aircraft had hit the soccer field close to one of the goal ends. It was a Wednesday afternoon and the sportsground was well attended. But, happily, the action of the game had taken the players and spectators to the other end of the field. The housing area was untouched. Pilot Officer Ward died in the crash; the only other casualty was an airman who lost a leg when he was struck by flying metal.

Young Timothy Trent had, just before the crash, been sent by his mother to post a letter and his tracks had taken him to the danger end of the soccer field. He had been given implicit instructions to hurry straight home and, for once, he had not loitered on the return journey. With the shock of the crash, Ursula Trent had rushed to the door and, to her tremendous relief, had seen her son tearing for the refuge of home as fast as his little legs would bear him.

The sequel to the fatal flying accident was, of course, a court of inquiry. Trent, as the senior officer in control of the aerial display, was called to give evidence and warned that, as such, he might be deemed blame-worthy. But his defence was cast iron. Brad Bradley, although of comparable rank, was senior to Trent by length of service as a major. And, although a member of the USAAF, he was serving with the RAF. Brad had carried out the pre-flight briefing correctly and in Trent's hearing. Furthermore, Trent had immediately taken prompt action, when Ward had infringed the rules of flight, in calling for the culprit's removal from the exercise.

The court found that Pilot Officer Ward had apparently lost control when he stall-turned out of his upward charley and had spun in.

The student pilots who came under Trent's supervision while he was at Little Rissington came from many lands. Along with New Zealanders, Australians and Canadians there were Indians, Pakistanis and South-East Asians. All were good flyers although, on occasion, they provided a few nail-biting incidents. As, at that time, there were no dual-control Vampires on the unit, the pupils had to learn jet handling by theory alone before tackling their first solo flight. Language problems did not help the cause. A Burmese student, flying his first circuit in a Vampire, just managed to make the end of the runway before he stalled at about 20 feet, buckling his undercart considerably but living to fly another day.

Icing conditions, omnipresent in winter flying, made for some very unpleasant moments and on one particular exercise, when Trent and a student were practising beam-approach instrument flying through cloud, their Percival Prentice aircraft became so burdened with ice that, despite full throttle, they were barely maintaining height and safe speed as they flopped in over the end of the runway.

On another occasion when flying with a student in a Harvard, the engine stopped dead while they were practising forced landings. Trent took the controls and guided the machine, in a dead-stick, wheels-up approach, into a field of standing wheat. It left a swathe, about 30 or 40 yards long, mown down.

On 22 June 1953 Len Trent was promoted to the rank of wing commander and lifted up the service ladder. He was posted to Oakington to command the Flying Wing.

He took over the position from Wing Commander 'Butch' Jennings, who went off to Valley, a long-established RAF station in Anglesea.

Oakington, 206 Advanced Flying School, was using dual-control T-11 Meteor turbojets and the old single-seat Mark 5s — and whereas Trent had been checked out on Meteors and had indeed crammed in as many flights as possible in the machines while at Little Rissington, he was at that stage relatively inexperienced as a Meteor pilot.

He had been checked out from Central Flying School on 19 June by Wing Commander Frank Dodd — who was later to become Air Marshal Dodd — and assessed as an above-average pilot of A2 category, and given a green instrument rating.

He made his first flight at Oakington on 26 June — 4 days after leaving Central Flying School — and had the temerity, on that exercise, to check two final handling tests; his earnest students being a Pilot Officer Rolf and Pilot Officer Ross. Little did the young officers know how inexperienced in Meteor flying was their instructor and adjudicator.

18

THE FALL OF A METEOR

WING COMMANDER TRENT, Officer Commanding Flying Wing, 206 Advanced Flying School, RAF Oakington, sat in his Gloster Meteor Mark 5 twin turbo-jet aircraft at dispersal point, Little Rissington. It was a Monday — the morning of 10 August 1953 — and he had just completed a weekend with his family, who were still resident in the station quarters from which he, the breadwinner, had been plucked on his appointment to Oakington almost 2 months earlier. When a house became available, Ursula and the children would join him at his new station.

Now, with his regular two-day family reunion ended, he must return to base and continue with his week-day duties.

He set about his comparatively simple cockpit procedures for starting the Rolls-Royce Derwent engines. Throttles closed; high-pressure and low-pressure fuel cocks on; ground/flight switch to 'ground'; low-pressure fuel pump on. He then depressed the starter button for a couple of seconds to initiate the automatic starting cycle.

He got power instantly. A 'wet start' — analogous of a flooded Primus stove — would have meant some messy sponging of the loose fuel from the engine nacelle and a tinkering with the high-pressure cock. And now, while the engines accelerated to idling speed, he kept an eye on the jet pipe temperature to ensure it did not exceed 500⁰ centigrade.

He gave a quick check around the cockpit before waving the chocks away. No warning lights aglow; flaps up; remote-indicating compass on and direction-indicator coordinated with it and uncaged; radio channel selected; altimeter set to airfield height; brake pressue gaining on the gauge; pitot heater on.

Moving away from dispersal, he tested his brakes. And lining up on the runway he went through his final pre-take-off drill.

Elevator and rudder trims neutral; high-pressure and low-pressure fuel cocks on; low-pressure pumps on; flaps one-third down; pneumatic pressure 450 p.s.i.; airbrakes in; hood closed and locked.

His checks were quick but thorough. These new-fangled jets were greedy beasts and there was little time to waste while they guzzled kerosene in prolonged running time on the ground.

Trent moved the machine forward a yard or two to straighten the nose-wheel. Then he applied the brakes and opened the throttles smoothly to take-off of 14,550 revolutions. The Derwents screamed like a pair of tormented banshees. Then he released the restraints and the Meteor surged forward with an exciting acceleration, dead straight down the runway. No swing. No torque.

At about 80 knots he eased the nosewheel off the ground. But, because of a characteristic blanking of the tailplane in the aircraft's nose-up attitude, the Meteor did not unstick cleanly and he had to fly it off positively at about 125 knots and hold it fairly level until speed built up safely to 165 knots.

The undercarriage had been retracted immediately the aircraft had become airborne; and as soon as it was flying comfortably he took up the flaps. By this time the gluttonous Meteor had consumed about 40 gallons of fuel.

Speed continued to build up quickly and at 290 knots Trent raised the nose for a climb to altitude with the throttles open at take-off setting. He reached 10,000 feet and levelled to survey his domain. It was a sight that ever enchanted him. Around and above was the wide sky. Far to eastward stood a huge white-marble island of cumulo-nimbus, towering to lose its anvil-headed crown in vaporous dissolution. Away to the west were some smudges of little clouds, too young and unsubstantial to even cross the face of a sundial. Below, stretching away to the autumn-hazed perimeters of a vast circular map, lay the patchwork fields, the villages and towns of England's heartland.

Now, as Trent looked down, he saw immediately below him the recognizable countryside between St Neots and Cambridge. He was nearing Oakington. With the anniversary of the Battle of Britain only a week or two away — and with an urge to sharpen his skills in preparation for the RAF's forthcoming celebratory aerial displays, he decided to put the Meteor through its paces.

It was a delightful aerobatic performer. Though never recognized as endearing as such gallant machines as the Hurricane or the Spitfire, the Meteor was, nevertheless, a comfortable aircraft to fly. Vibration-free flight, after the noise and clatter of the propeller-thrust machines, was exhilarating and the wide, unsullied field of view from the cockpit was magnificent. No swing or sway on take-off; no fiddling with fine and coarse pitch; no tricky flare-off needed to pull off a delicate landing. Just an enormous appetite for jet fuel — and, as Trent was to learn, a nasty vice that lurked, awaiting the unsuspecting, in the Mark 5 model.

Using 10,000 feet as his datum starting height, he put on full power and when the speed built up to more than 300 knots he pulled the nose into a vertical climb and started a series of upward rolls. He proceeded to count the number of times the aircraft would roll before stalling — when he would step on either right or left rudder and stall-turn out. And as the machine fell out and down, he would recover from each vertical dive with an eye on the altimeter.

He had done four of those manoeuvres quite neatly and so easily that he was almost bored with the simplicity of the movements. He looked beyond his right knee to the fuel gauges and decided that, as he was so close to base, he had time for one more. He began again at 10,000 feet, pulling the Meteor into a vertical climb and going into his upward-charley routine. At the top and at stall point he kicked on left rudder. The nose yawed and the aircraft chopped down. But Trent had been just a little bit off in his timing — as a golfer can, on occasion, be with his golf swing. He failed to correctly apply the touch of aileron necessary to keep the machine within its exact plane relative to the horizon. And as the Meteor nosed downwards it tended to get too far on to its back; and it went into an inverted spin.

It happened relatively slowly and Trent was not perturbed. He was certain that he could correct the aircraft's attitude as easily as he had so often done when flying Harvards. He took the normal procedures of recovery from upside-down yawing — opposite rudder to the direction of the yaw, stick back gently to bring the nose into the vertical position.

But the Meteor went straight from an inverted spin to a normal spin. Trent had over-compensated with the opposite rudder while the machine was in a stalled situation; and now the pilot was sitting in an upright position with his head pointing towards the sky.

No problem at all, now, Trent thought. The aircraft was spinning quite slowly in a normal, right-side-up situation. He put on opposite rudder and pushed the stick hard against the instrument panel to unstall the wings, expecting any moment that the machine would come out of its gyrations. The altimeter still showed a clear 15,000 feet against the needle so there was, seemingly, all the time in the world.

He was still enjoying the heady delights of such tossings. But steadily the nature of the spin wound up tighter and tighter and more and more vicious. In the downward pitching the Meteor's nose would swing beyond the vertical and in the upward fling it would come up almost to the horizon. In the yawing plane, the machine was snatching away in a very nasty manner.

Trent was getting annoyed. By now the Meteor should have been behaving a bit more obediently. He put two hands on the stick and kept it forced against the instrument panel. He strained on full opposite rudder, quite convinced that the stubborn beast would at any moment come out of its spin. But, although he tried almost every known counter, the aircraft went whirling and buffeting downwards.

He glanced at the altimeter. Jesus! It had unwound to show only 5000 feet between him and solid earth. He had to make a fast and a very hard decision. If he couldn't save the great, spiralling hunk of taxpayers' expensive defence equipment, he should at least try and save his own life. He jettisoned the plexiglass cockpit hood, which left the mother craft with an almighty bang. The outside air intruded with a boisterous rush. And when he unclipped his seat straps the next violent pitch thrust him from the cockpit like a stone from a sling.

For the second time in his Air Force career he found himself plummeting in free fall, following his abandoned aircraft at the whims of gravity and the winds of chance. He snatched for the D-ring and tugged the rip-cord hard. The silk rushed from its imprisoning pack and the lines whipped out and straightened in orderly array, checking Trent's descent with a sudden but soul-comforting jolt as the canopy blossomed white above him.

He counted his blessings. The Meteor Mark 5 did not have a

power-operated ejection seat, so abandonment of the cockpit was left to the pilot's prayer-assisted agility. The machine had a high tail assembly and when the aircraft was in a steep nose-down attitude — as in a spin — the chances of flesh meeting metal were extremely high.

So far, so good. But where was that bloody rogue Meteor? Had it piled into a built-up area? Had lives been lost? A quick scan of the countryside showed an ugly crater blemishing a field of ripening crops. Strewn in and around were pieces of crumpled aircraft.

He landed in a field of mangol-wurzels not far from a farmer and his tractor. The man, who had been pulling and loading the beet on to a trailer, walked to meet this stunt pilot who had suddenly flopped in on top of his cattle fodder. 'Do you do this sort of thing very often?' he asked, possibly assuming it was more or less a way of life in the Air Force.

Trent assured him that he did it as infrequently as he could manage. And then he asked if he could use the farmer's telephone to speak with the station commander.

'I've just bailed out, sir,' Trent informed his boss.

'You've *what?*'

Trent, somewhat apprehensive and quite ashamed of his inability to have curbed the wild Meteor, repeated the news.

'Well, I must say you sound bloody *calm*,' said the station commander. And, after hearing a brief description of events, he said he would come to the farm and together they could inspect the remains of the shattered aircraft.

He arrived about half an hour later, grinning widely with the relief that no lives had been lost. They saw the site of the crash, had a friendly cup of tea with the farmer and his wife, and then Trent went back to his office to write a three page report on the accident.

He described in careful detail every cockpit move he made and every reaction or inaction on the part of the aircraft. The station commander read the report and, in turn, sent it off to Group headquarters.

Trent was feeling quite miserable. In his own opinion he believed that a chief flying instructor should, by his knowledge and his position, be able to get any aircraft out of any flying situation. Accordingly he had no doubts that Group would take a pretty dim view of the whole affair. His job at Oakington would be terminated and his Air Force career would be completely buggered.

The first recipient of the report at 25 Group headquarters was the Chief Training Officer — Air One — Wing Commander Willie Davies, Trent's immediate staff officer and also a skiing friend. He also knew a lot about flying Meteors.

Before making his own report and recommendations to the Air Officer Commanding 25 Group, Davies decided he better know something about the practical aspects of inverted spinning in a Meteor. So he went to Workshop, another Advanced Flying School — by now commanded by James Coward of tin-leg fame — and requisitioned a Mark 7 dual-equipped Meteor. Together, Davies and Coward put the machine through all manner of inverted spins and emerged with both themselves and the aircraft intact.

However, as Willie Davies was a very thorough gentleman, he decided that his findings would not be complete until he had himself tried some inverted spinning in the same type of Meteor that Trent had been flying — a Mark 5.

He climbed to 20,000 feet and put the aircraft into an inverted spin. The Meteor took charge and, in a series of spirals and yaws and pitches it spun down and down. As Trent had done, Davies coaxed it into a normal spin. The nose went down and the spin became tighter and rougher and more and more vicious. Somewhere between 7000 and 5000 feet, Davies bailed out.

He returned to his office and immediately wrote an order; on no account should a Mark 5 Meteor be induced into an inverted spin.

For some reason — possibly the tail-plane assembly, which was later modified — the Meteor Mark 5's peculiar aerodynamic behaviours made it impossible to recover from such a manoeuvre.

Len Trent heard no more about the matter and he continued in his CFI appointment.

In December 1953 the Oakington unit was re-equipped with Vampire jets and on 4 January 1954 Trent flew his last exercise in a Meteor. Although he had flown but a modest 50 hours in the Gloster jets, they had such a short endurance that it seemed he was continually in and out of the cockpit, flight after flight. Frequently the instructor and pupil would have to flame-out one engine to conserve fuel and a common call to the tower, on entering the circuit, was: 'Aircraft C-Charley — twenty-twenty!' which was a call for priority — the machine had only 20 gallons of fuel for each engine, enough for one circuit only.

It was a bit mouth-drying at first, but the pilots got used to it.

The new Vampires were, in the main, dual-control T-11s and so that they might handle them, all the senior instructors went to the De Havilland works for a period of schooling. It was there that Len Trent became very friendly with two of the manufacturer's notable test pilots — Dickie Bligh and Johnny Brown.

The aircraft fleet at Oakington built up quickly and soon there were seventy-three shrill-screaming Vampires at the station. And then there was trouble; the natives became restless. At all hours of the day or night there were always aircraft in the circuit and the noise was a constant source of irritation. Trent, the architect of all the din, was constantly hammered by letters of complaint and rude telephone calls.

But the flying exercises had to continue. After the squadron commanders returned from the De Havilland plant they were highly confident that they knew, among other things, just how to tame a Vampire in its spin.

Like the Meteor, the Vampire could get wound up and become headstrong in its downward gyrations.

One of the squadron commanders was Major Dave Campbell, an American Air Force officer serving on exchange duties with the RAF, and an excellent pilot. Soon after Campbell returned from a special spinning course at C.F.S., Trent elected to fly with him in the right-hand instructor's seat.

'Right Dave,' said the CFI, 'let's see what you have learned of the Vampire T-11.'

Campbell, in the left-hand seat, had the controls and Trent was assuming the role of the student. The cloud base was about 2000 feet and visibility, below the eight-eighths cover, was good. They climbed and soon shot through the overcast to emerge into brilliant sunshine above a sea of milk.

They continued upwards as steeply as the Vampire would climb to about 15,000 feet and, hacking back the throttle while the machine was still above stalling speed and climbing, Campbell hauled back on the stick and, at the same time, kicked on full left rudder.

The Vampire went into a series of flick rolls, the nose dropped,

Venturer Courageous

and they were in a spin. Characteristically, the first five turns were gentle enough; and then the nose went vertically down and they were spinning like a top. The cool voice of Dave Campbell, in practised instructional patter, drawled: 'And now we take recovery action. Pushing the stick hard and firmly into the instrument panel and holding it central, we apply full opposite rudder and out she ... comes. Er — out she ... er — out she ...' But the bitchy Vampire kept going down and down.

'Oh Christ!' Trent muttered, 'Here we go — hitting the bloody silk again!' On no account would they spin on through that thick cloud, the tops of which were coming up fast.

Campbell took his hands off the stick to reach for the canopy release. But before he could jettison the cockpit roof the vagrant aircraft flew itself out of the spin, crazily sorting out its own aerodynamics.

Trent looked at the top of the cloud layer, now immediately below them, and thanked God that their spin hadn't taken them into the misty unknown. Campbell recovered from the vertical dive and both pilots were breathing heavily and fast.

Silently, they climbed up to a safe height. They called the tower and got permission to land. And in Trent's office they pondered the vagaries of the Vampire.

It was a critical aircraft when it got into an advanced stage of spinning and it gave many pilots a fright or two when it got really wound up. The watchword, when spinning a Vampire, was to get out of the movement before it had done its first five turns.

Trent had almost qualified for his third award for forced parachute descent. When he had bailed out of his Ventura over Holland in 1943 he was using an Irvin harness and pack; and in recognition of his reliance on the maker's fine product, he became a member of the notable Caterpillar Club — which took its name from the silkworm. The badge is a small gold caterpillar — green-gem eyes for a descent from a 'cold' crippled aircraft, red eyes for a 'flamer'.

When he next bailed out on 10 August 1953 he was wearing a GQ parachute. He was presented by the makers with a certificate of membership to the GQ Club and given his badge, a small gold parachute.

19
VALIANT DAYS

GROUP CAPTAIN RAMSEY RAY, the tall athletic station commander of RAF Oakington — the sympathetic witness to Len Trent's embarrassment after the Meteor bail-out and the keen golfing companion in leisure hours — had received a posting that would move him up the service ladder. In his place had come Group Captain C. R. J. Hawkins.

Whereas Ramsey Ray had not demonstrated any particular patience with the masses of paperwork incumbent upon the boss of an Air Force station — and had conveniently thrown a lot of it on to Trent's desk — Hawkins was a wizard of penmanship and quick to handle the many letters and reports requiring attention.

Len Trent appreciated his release from the tedium of the pen — although the sages claim it to be a more powerful weapon than the sword — and was able to devote more energies to practical flying duties. He was delighted to find, too, that the station's newly-appointed Wing Commander Administration was none other than his old cobber from Wigram training days and Stalag Luft III experiences, Henry Lamond. The two New Zealanders, with so much to talk about in their reunion, spent a lot of time together both in the daily duties of the station and in the hours of relaxation.

With the onset of winter they set about collecting supplies of household firewood and Trent sought and got a police permit to use blasting powder. He and Lamond went to work felling a large elm tree that had been smitten with a blight peculiar to the species. When they had the large bole sawn in suitable lengths, they split the timber asunder with charges of black powder.

After a Sunday morning's fruitful toil they left their piles of split wood and went home for the midday meal. But on returning to their work site they were angered to find that every faggot of firewood had been uplifted. In a fine old fizz, Trent phoned the station commander to pour out his grievances, only to learn that the phantom firewood filcher was Group Captain Hawkins himself. The boss had watched with interest as Trent and Lamond set about dismembering one of the station's elms. As soon as their backs were turned the CO and his batman had taken car and trailer and collected the booty.

Len Trent and his old commanding officer still correspond. And when they meet — as they occasionally do — they laugh as they recall 'the big firewood grab'.

On 30 June 1955 Trent made his last Vampire flight at Oakington before he reported to his new posting at No 6 Flying College Course, Manby. This was the first course to be reduced from the hitherto 12 month duration to one of 6 months.

He entered Manby on 15 July and, along with a concentration of lectures, ground studies and a full navigation course, he found himself again flying Meteors. For added interest and experience, he also progressed to Canberra jets.

His flying instructor was Wing Commander Ivor Broome, who later rose to the rank of Air Vice-Marshal, and Trent was to unwittingly pull a nasty trick on his mentor when, on a particular occasion, they were practising one-engine flying. With the Canberra's port engine 'flamed-out', they were flying at 1,000 feet on the downwind leg in the landing pattern when Broome told Trent to re-light the dead jet.

Inexplicably, Trent made the wrong move and cut power from the live starboard engine, leaving the aircraft, for a few nerve-twitching moments, powerless. Fortunately, the Canberra had the means of re-lighting flame-outs — a facility denied the Vampire — and the aircraft was soon under full power again without too much altitude lost.

The commandant of No 6 Flying College was Air Commodore Gus Walker, a chunky ex-rugby player, who in pre-war days, had gained his international cap as a half-back for England. Affectionately known as the 'One-Armed Bandit', he had lost his right arm at Syerston during the war when a Wellington bomber crashed on take-off. Walker had jumped into his staff car and rushed to the scene. He was trying to drag the crew members clear of the flames when the bomb load exploded, tearing off his arm just above the elbow.

He had overcome this set-back to adapt himself as both a formidable one-armed tennis player and a remarkably good golfer, playing to a 14 handicap. Trent had some strong tussles with him in both fields.

It had been Gus Walker who had passed on the extraordinary news of Len Trent's winning the Victoria Cross, so there was considerable rapport between them. Ever since those days the two officers have kept in touch and when they meet, as they do from time to time on service occasions like the Bomber Command dinners, Gus Walker hails Len Trent as a brother.

As he neared the end of his six-month course at Manby, Trent began to speculate on where his next posting might take him. Having just come from a flying appointment, he fully expected to be sent piloting a desk at Air Ministry. So his delight was enormous when, with but a month of the course to complete, he had a letter from de Havilland test pilot Dickie Bligh. 'Congratulations, Len,' the note said, 'and keep this under your hat. The breeze around the factory is that you are going to get command of the first Comet squadron in the RAF.'

The big De Havilland Comet, of course, was Britain's newest giant jet transporter and to have command of a squadron of such aircraft would be the dream of any ambitious general-duties officer of the time. So, outwardly calm but inwardly bubbling with expectation, Trent went before his CO at the end of the course to hear the assessment of his school work and the announcement of his next appointment

Knowing what he had heard from Dickie Bligh, how was he going to affect pleasurable surprise when Gus Walker told him the good news about his leading the very first Comet squadron?

'Good morning, Len,' said the Air Commodore when Trent entered his office. 'Sit down, sit down.' He went through the student officer's course records and pronounced his considerable satisfaction with the work completed. Then he paused before delivering the big message. 'Well, Len, you'll be delighted to know, I'm sure, that you are going to command the very ... first ... RAF ... *Valiant* ... V-Bomber squadron!'

Trent had no trouble, whatsoever, in looking surprised. What had gone wrong with Dickie Bligh's smoke signals? What about the Comets? But, when the first wave of bewilderment had passed, he grinned his appreciation. Valiants might not have the same aura of glamour as that surrounding the Comets. But heading a squadron of such mighty new four-engined jets was a damned sight better than sitting every day in Air Ministry.

True, a Comet squadron was to be formed. But the nod had gone to Wing Commander 'Shrub' Sellick as CO of the unit. Sellick, an experienced examining officer and long versed in the ways and methods of Transport Command, had a good knowledge of overseas routes along which the Comets would soon travel. Furthermore, he had probably more friends at court when the choice of command was made.

So Trent, with lesser transport experience but nevertheless more jet hours in his log book than Sellick, went off to RAF Gaydon to learn how to handle the big Vickers-Armstrong Valiant bomber before taking command of 214 Squadron, to be formed at Marham.

A small flight of Valiant experts was first established at Wittering. It was a move designed to indoctrinate specialists in the engine-handling and aerodynamics of the new aircraft, but it was a short-lived appointment. And the work moved to Gaydon.

When Trent first walked up to the huge white Valiant on the tarmac at Gaydon he wondered how puny man was ever able to coax such a mass of metal into the air and — of more importance — get it back to earth without breaking anything. But, before he even touched a switch or lever in the actual cockpit of the monster, he was to be saturated in the theory of the Valiant's internal and external movements and coached, until his knowledge, his hand and foot movements and his reflexes were coordinated and tuned to perfection in the ground-based flight simulator.

The simulator, a complex extension of the Link Trainer, was an exact duplication of the Valiant's flight deck to which, through the magic of electronics, hydraulics and pneumatics, were introduced every conceivable manoeuvre or error or mishap of actual flight. The pilot and his co-pilot, in full flying kit, sat at the controls while behind their capsule and out of sight were the three instructors.

The pilots, obeying their pre-plotted flight plan, took off in simulated flight while the instructor operators played roles ranging from common flying controllers all the way through to God. No whim of wind was too perverse for their meddling, no cold front or screaming typhoon or violent drop in barometric pressure too horrendous for their machinations. And their omnipotence gave them over-riding command of the simulator's electric circuits, too.

After about an hour at the controls, holding course against the buffetings of turbulence, the pilot might well believe he was flying a real aircraft.

On his return from one such simulated cross-country flight Trent was, in theory, preparing to drop height before entering the airfield landing pattern. He touched the switch of the trim tab to get a bit of nose-down attitude and the control column moved forward in response to airflow over the elevators. But the stick kept moving forward, resisting his manual efforts to check it. Then the altimeter began to unwind as height fell off. He called on his co-pilot for assistance and together they hauled back on their poles. But they could not bring the beast to heel nor stay its downward driving. The whole tail plane of the Valiant (in this case, its simulator) moved as elevators and the sail surface was expansive.

Trent realized he had a runaway electric motor on the trim tab circuit. From 35,000 feet the rate of descent was building to a shocking speed. The mach reading reached .85 and when it hit .9, the simulator ran into compressability troubles, shaking and shuddering as it approached the sound barrier.

Horrified and helpless, the straining, perspiring pilots watched the altimeter unwind until with a colossal, ear-splitting crash it met simulated earth in a simulated disintegration.

All mechanical noises stopped. The eerie silence was broken only by the heavy gasps of the pilots and the pounding of their heartbeats as they reached 150 per minute.

Then a deep voice intoned through their headphones: 'Well, there you are, you silly bastards! This is St Peter, giving you yet another ticket back to life. Never let that happen again!'

With the trim tabs' electric motor racing out of control, Trent realized too late that he should have immediately hit the trip switch to cut off power from the rogue circuit.

The ground school at Gaydon was a very thorough academy and every nut and bolt, every fuel line and every electrical and hydraulic system of the Valiant had to be studied and implanted in the mind. The aircrews worked in the classrooms from 9 a.m. to 5 p.m. and continued their learning well into the night. Trent, as leader of the squadron, was determined to be among the top group in the final exams. So, when the chief examiner called him to congratulate him on his high-level rating on the course, he added: 'We all thought it very sporting of you to sit the exams, Len. We fully expected that you, in your position, would object and opt out.'

Trent laughed and said he didn't think he had any choice. In any case, the other squadron members wouldn't have had much of an opinion of him if he hadn't sat the tests.

With their minds attuned to meet every emergency situation in Valiant flight and their hands obedient to instinct, the 214 Squadron pilots and their crews arrived at RAF Marham in time to welcome the first Valiant flown from the Vickers factory. The delivery pilot was Brian Trubshaw, who went on to become the chief test pilot of the notable Concord, and he and Len Trent got to know each other very well.

With the squadron taking delivery of its sixteenth Valiant, Vickers hosted a fine celebratory dinner at Dorchester House, London, and in attendance were, besides the Commander-in-Chief of Bomber Command, Sir Harry Broadhurst, various other high staff officers, station and squadron commanders.

The station commander of Marham was Group Captain Bob Hodges, who later retired from the RAF as Air Chief Marshal Sir Lewis Hodges, KCB, CBE, DSO, DFC. He was a distinguished pilot in the Second World War, flying hazardous missions into occupied Europe in Lysanders to drop and collect secret agents. He now lives in Kent, where he is visited, from time to time, by Len Trent.

Soon after 214 Squadron began flying at Marham, Group Captain Hodges phoned Trent's office. He wanted to keep up his flying hours. Could he have a flight in one of the new aircraft and take his trick at the controls? He had completed a course at Gaydon and, to keep his hand in, he would like to be checked out at the Valiant controls by Wing Commander Trent, the officer commanding 214 Squadron.

Fair enough. The station master's wish was his command. They climbed to the flight deck and, with Bob Hodges sitting in the captain's left-hand seat and Trent settled beside him as supervisor, they proceeded to work their way through the pre-flight check list.

Suddenly there was an almighty explosion and the huge circular disc which formed the roof of the cockpit lifted and settled with a mighty clang.

The Valiant was fitted with power-operated ejection seats. But before the ejector charges could be operated by the pilots' pulling down their face blinds, the roof of the cockpit had to be shed. So, encircling that cover at 6 or 8 inch intervals were explosive bolts. To activate those bolts, there was an emergency handle, guarded by a safety flap, on the left side of the captain's seat.

Inexplicably — for the handle had not been lifted — some slight contact had energized a temperamental electrical circuit. Red-faced, they got out; and while the puzzled flight-sergeant and his ground crew tried to fathom the mystery, the two fliers got airborne in another Valiant.

Although this new jet bomber was designed for high-level operations, the new squadron's immediate exercises centred around low-level formation flying. It was obvious that this new piece of armour in Britain's defence plans would have to be demonstrated with pride. And how better than at a modest altitude where its lines would show to advantage.

The two Russians leaders, Bulganin and Krushchev, were due to visit Britain in April 1956, so all through the early part of that month the squadron practised for 'Operation B and K' — and on 23 April, when the two dignitaries from the USSR and their top-brass British hosts visited Marham, the assembled might of 214 Squadron flew past in low-level formation.

Weather, as any experienced pilot will aver, can be a tricky, deadly foe if safety systems fail or are inadequate for the situation.

On 3 June 1956 Wing Commander Trent was detailed to fly a Valiant from Marham to Flesland, Norway. He had Air Vice-Marshall 'Bing' Cross, AOC of No 3 Group, sitting in Ken O'Rourke's customary seat as co-pilot; and Trent's mission was to deliver the AOC safely at the opening ceremony of Flesland, the latest NATO airfield in Norway. There the senior officer would mingle with, among other notables, General Bull of the Norwegian Air Force and the British Air Attache in Norway.

Trent had made a familiarization dummy-run of the field two days earlier, but bad visibility had prevented his landing there. Now, as they approached Flesland, they were again plagued by cloud that hugged the mountainous country and misted down into the valleys in drizzle.

The Valiant, in 1956, had not been fitted with the NBS (navigational bomb sight) system, which would have given the pilot a clear radar picture of the airfield, its buildings and environs. All the aircraft had was the Green Satin Dopler system

— accurate enough though not pictorial — plus the benefits of radio bearings and standard navigational calculations.

O'Rourke, Trent's regular co-pilot, having vacated his right-hand seat in deference to rank, was standing between his captain and the AOC, keeping tabs on the fuel gauges and various knobs and tits. And, importantly, he was adding a third pair of eyes looking out for clouds with hard centres.

Trent started his instrument approach at about 10,000 feet. He picked up the ILS (instrument landing system) and the needles erected as and when expected. The runway was lined up in azimuth and elevation and he started his let-down. The undercarriage was downed and the pre-landing checks began. Down went 40 degrees of flap. They kept their descent on the glide path and Ken O'Rourke called his confirmations and assurances that all, apparently, was well.

They entered cloud at 5000 feet, very conscious of the mountainous country on both sides of their track. And then they were in steady rain, with all instruments showing correct readings. At 900 feet on that glide path they had about 3 miles to run to the threshold; and they were peering for a glimpse of the lead-in lights when, at about 700 feet, Trent flicked up his eyes and, in a break in the misty rain, he saw he was heading towards a huge lump of rock.

He poured on power, lifted the undercarriage and shouted to his assistant in the right-hand seat: 'Flaps up!' But Air Vice-Marshal Cross, who was anticipating the normal command for full flaps, let down all sails.

Trent, throwing away decorum in the urgency of the moment, struck the AOC sharply on the left arm. 'Flaps UP, you silly bastard!' He got instant obedience.

With the flaps coming up and the drag reduced, the Valiant climbed smartly with its four jets screaming. Trent called the -tower. He was not happy with the weather conditions. He was returning to base.

He often wondered what erring soul had calibrated that landing beam. He wondered a little bit, too, how an air vice-marshal feels when his lineage has been put in doubt by a common wing commander.

The Valiant's early days were ... well, they were *valiant* days, to be sure. The Queen Mother and Princess Margaret called at Marham on their way to a royal function and Group Captain Hodges and Wing Commander Trent proudly escorted their visitors around the station and the aircraft. Then on 23 July 1956 the Queen reviewed Bomber Command and 214 Squadron gave a stirring fly-past before Her Majesty. Later, the Queen inspected the aircraft and their crews in the Marham hangars.

The following month Trent flew on a goodwill mission to the United States to visit General Curtis E.le May, Commander-in-Chief of Strategic Air Command, and show him the power and grace of the mighty Valiant. Accompanying him on the flight as

On the occasion of the Queen's Review of Bomber Command at RAF Marham; Wing Commander Trent and his Valiant crew are presented to Her Majesty, 23 July 1956.

Alongside the Vickers-Armstrong Valiant that Wing Commander Trent
flew to SAC Headquarters, Offat, USA in August 1956. *From left*: Air
Vice-Marshal Mark Selway, RAF Air Attache[1], Washington; Colonel
John Hester, USAF; Wing Commander Trent.

the official representative of the RAF was Air Vice-Marshal
Sydney Bufton, Senior Air Staff Officer of Bomber Command.
Having previously attended a Valiant handling course at Gaydon,
he chose to sit in the co-pilot's seat. Again, Ken O'Rourke, Trent's
regular 'second joe', stood between the two seats on take-offs and
landings to double-check cockpit procedures. Throughout the
flight he attended to fuel handling and necessary calibrations.

The aircraft was airborne from Marham in the early hours of 24
August to land at Goose Bay, Canada, before setting course for
Strategic Air Command headquarters at Omaha, Nebraska. The
British flyers were well received by General le May, a man of
tremendous personality and drive, and the prime architect of
Strategic Air Command. During their brief stay at the American
base they were invited to sit in on a special SAC briefing.

The following day, with the special permission of the United States Air Force, they flew to Loring, Maine, where the first squadron of the new and powerful B-52 bombers was passed. General le May had also flown to the Maine airfield and in the course of the Anglo-American swapping of aeronautical secrets, the general asked Trent about the standard of the Valiant's serviceability — to wit, did it function without too much fiddling with spanners, screwdrivers, fuses and the like?

'Certainly, Sir,' said Trent. The aircraft was a pilot's dream. He suggested that in order to appreciate the magic, why didn't the general come along for a ride on a navigational exercise?

'No — but many thanks.' SAC's C-in-C would be pleased to accept the invitation, but pressure of work dictated otherwise. Trent produced the flying Form 700, which was the aircraft's serviceability log, to show his VIP inquisitor that no report of mechanical fault blemished the pages of the document. He signed it with a confident flourish and, with the general close behind, led the way to the flight deck and the crew took their respective posts. They did their pre-flight checks under the interested eyes of the American general — who then left the aircraft — and were soon airborne, heading into the gloom of approaching night — and a heavy thunderstorm.

But all systems were certainly not 'go'. The Dopler Green Satin navigation system, which was designed to give a constant reading of latitude and longitude — along with other electronic navigational aids — had packed up and was useless. One of the VHF (very high frequency) sets was unserviceable. And the poor navigator, with his electronic bombing and navigation systems dead, could get no help from radar map reading. That left him with not much more assistance than elementary dead-reckoning navigation.

But man is not lost. The diligent fellow resorted to the teachings he had absorbed in his first Air Force classroom. He plotted Britain's mighty, sophisticated new bomber back to Loring with the aid of map, parallel rules, protractor and a much chewed pencil.

Whatever General le May might have thought of limey enterprize after that episode (if he ever got to hear about it), he kept to himself. Perhaps, if such a set of circumstances had invaded the nerve centre of a B-52, the forthright general would have sent the 'goddam ship' back to the maker and demanded a refund. No doubt he would have court-martialled both ground crew and aircraft captain, as 'bad luck' had no place in SAC. The general 'couldn't afford' unlucky crews.

Next day, with the ailing electronic systems repaired by the RAF flight-sergeant technician travelling with the aircraft's crew, the Valiant took off and headed out over the Atlantic towards England. Flying aids did not include an automatic pilot so, after an hour or two of steady flight, Trent handed over the controls to Air Vice-Marshal Bufton for a brief spell and watched a brilliant display of the aurora borealis weaving and waving across the heavens. The pale blue illuminations, like strangely bent searchlight beams, gave him a feeling of vertigo and diminishing coordination.

Fuel was being checked constantly and as the Valiant approached Aldergrove, Northern Ireland, Trent calculated that he had enough to get them to Marham. Well, he *did* have sufficient gallons — but only just. In sight of his destination he saw, with considerable concern, that the gauges were indicating very low reserves. He called the tower for landing permission, dropped height quickly to 5000 feet at 10 miles and made a direct approach to the runway. When he cut his engines at dispersal point, all his fuel gauges were showing empty tanks. His Atlantic crossing had taken 6 hours 15 minutes — a flight time that some newspapers of the day claimed as a record.

Why do gremlins, with particular and fiendish delight, plague aircraft in which so much national pride and wealth has been invested? On 15 September 1956 a matter of only 2 weeks after Len Trent's embarrassing experience with navigational faults in America, he was directed to fly to Turnhouse and demonstrate the abilities of the Valiant to the good burghers of Edinburgh at a Battle of Britain anniversary display.

The big four-jet bomber was still comparatively new and its impending arrival at any airfield was always proclaimed in press headlines. So, when the gleaming white monster landed, there was a very large crowd of Scots, agog with expectation, waiting to see it go through its aerial paces.

The engines were stopped and there followed the usual time on the ground while other events occupied the attentions of the spectators. Then it came time for the Valiant to start engines and prepare to amaze the gathering.

Trent got the all-clear message from the control tower. He

pressed the starter button — but nothing happened. The button just popped out again from its socket, indicating a short circuit somewhere in the system. He tried again. Not a kick. No matter how many times the button was pressed or how much the technicians fussed around the wires and fuses, the starter wouldn't start. The exhibition by the Valiant had missed its slot in the programme of events. By now the spectators were agog with indifference.

Later, and far too late to save Trent's embarrassment in front of the public, the flight-sergeant technician discovered that a terminal of one of the starter batteries had been knocked and cracked.

One day in October 1956, while Wing Commander Trent was working on his newly established mushroom cultivations in an unused air-raid shelter on Marham station, he got the call to arms. The Suez Crisis was on the boil and three squadrons of Valiant bombers had been ordered to Luqa, Malta, in readiness for immediate action.

Trent, with his 214 Squadron aircraft and crews arrived at Malta as part of the punitive force. On 1 November the flyers gathered in the huge briefing room at Luqa. Group Captain Bob Hodges, as senior briefing officer, pulled the curtains aside to show that the bombers were to fly to Egypt and attack airfield targets along the west bank of the Suez Canal.

Each aircraft was to carry, besides its full fuel burden, twelve 1000 pound high-explosive bombs. The captains gasped at the news. But, they were assured, the designers of the Valiant were confident their bomber could lift and carry such a load. The boffins had charts to prove it.

The first off the runway in a night take-off to prove that the boffins' weight and endurance calculations were correct was Trent's aircraft. A wind had decided to veer, so that his heavily laden machine had to use the short runway which ended just short of a gully. But distance, slope, temperature and wind vector had been carefully computed. Yes, they *could* get off!

With his four jet engines screaming against the brakes he let go the restraints and roared down the strip. Just before concrete and asphalt gave way to a rocky ravine the Valiant wallowed into the night. And the force was on its way towards Egypt. The boffins were right.

The crews were briefed to fly into the attack at 33,000 feet, which, for the Valiant, was a fairly low bombing height. They were now equipped with NBS, the navigational bombing system which incorporated a pretty clear radar picture of the target, so they should have been able to operate satisfactorily from about 40,000 feet. But the Egyptians' only interceptor aircraft were Meteors. British Intelligence did not think that they could be vectored onto the bombers at 33,000 feet. The Valiants were too fast for them. Well, supposedly, anyhow.

Trent had no trouble in finding his target. He gave his bomb aimer a nice long bombing run, they dropped their load and returned to Malta without hurt or hindrance. The flight had taken 3 hours 30 minutes.

At the debriefing, a crew from 148 Squadron were still a little twittery from their brief encounter with the enemy. They had just dropped their bomb load when the co-pilot happened to glance in the starboard rear-vision mirror and saw a series of winking lights — which could only mean an attack by a fighter.

'Fighter,' yelled the co-pilot. 'Turn right! Turn right!'
The pilot whipped his aircraft to starboard and climbed, foiling the Egyptian's curve of pursuit, and leaving the crew to ponder: So the enemy's Meteors couldn't be vectored on to a Valiant at 33,000 feet?

On their subsequent sorties the pilots decided to put on an extra 2-3000 feet — 'for the wife and kids'.

Before long, the main thrust of the aerial police action ended; 148 Squadron and the third Marham-based Valiant unit, 103 Squadron, returned to England. Trent and his people and aircraft of 214 Squadron remained to hold the fort for a while and enjoy a bit of leisure on Malta. They experienced the entertainments of the George Cross island from top to bottom — the lower levels being contained in, of course, 'The Gut' — Strada Stretta, the Street called Straight.

They were made honorary members of the notable Marsa Club and one day Trent had a call from the manager. Did any member of the squadron play polo? One of the equestrian teams was short of a fourth player.

Surprisingly, Squadron Leader Doug Petrie rode and had indeed played a chukka or two when he was in India. On hearing this, all his companions hooted with laughter and almost wet themselves at the thought of Petrie horseborne. But, mounted on a borrowed pony and swinging a borrowed stick, the good Petrie was up with the play within the first chukka and proved himself a considerable asset to the team.

The squadron was at Malta until December, by which time boredom had set in. So it was with relief that they left for England on 18 December 1956. When Len Trent got home he found that his mushroom venture had produced such a bumper crop that Ursula couldn't cope. In response to her SOS a fancier from King's Lynn arrived and bought the lot on the spot.

'Shag' Reece, then Wing Commander Administration at Marham recently visited Len and Ursula Trent at their home at Mathesons Bay, North Auckland. They spoke of old prisoner of war days in Stalag Luft III — and of the 'Big Mushroom Glut' at Marham in the winter of '56.

On 14 September 1957 the Valiants joined in the pageantry of a Battle of Britain anniversary fly-past at Hendon; and the following month Trent was briefed to take a detachment of aircraft on display to Changi, Singapore.

From Marham they flew by way of El Adam, Bahrain, Karachi and Ngombo. On the last leg of the journey they encountered, for the first time, the thin vapour that can rise above a tropic storm to extraordinary heights. They climbed to 40,000 feet but were still in haze, not knowing whether the visibility was 50 miles or 50 yards. When they reached 49,000 feet there were still cloudheads rising above them out of the mist. So, with no storm-warning radar in the aircraft, they were apprehensive about ploughing into one of those turbulent masses with thunderheads rising to more than 50,000 feet.

As their aircraft were the first Valiants to fly to Singapore, the crews on the inaugural flight were treated royally. They were guests at dinner parties, special functions and sports gatherings. Trent, inspired by the paintings of Air Vice-Marshal Bates' wife, was to later develop his own talents in art.

On a November morning Len Trent and one of his pilots, John Wynn, who had been one of Britain's top diving stars, were detailed to fly their Valiants up to Bangkok, Thailand, where they were to put their aircraft through their paces for the entertainment and enlightenment of the Thai Air Force. The programme had been carefully arranged and the British Air Attache in Bangkok would be there to receive them when they landed.

The two Valiants approached the Bangkok airfield and Trent called the control tower for permission to begin the aerial display. He called repeatedly, but got no reply. So the aircraft landed, to be greeted frostily by the Air Attache: 'What about the flying display?'

Trent explained that he couldn't fling the Valiants around the sky without official permission. That wasn't regular airfield procedure in any language — or lack of language.

Ah, well, sighed the AA, perhaps things would go better in Laos. He had to fly off to Vientiane within the hour and the two Valiants were scheduled to follow and give the Laotians a feast of aeronautical skills to add to the festivities of the five-hundredth birthday of Buddha. 'Don't worry about the noise,' the AA assured Trent. 'The more din your Valiants make, so much the better. It will add to the explosions of fire crackers and help keep evil spirits and devils away. But don't take the tops off the trees, please!'

The British crews got airborne and headed for Vientiane. They climbed high into the clear summer skies above Thailand and were soon at 33,000 feet and making majestic vapour trails against the bright blue ceiling.

As the Thai Air Force were then flying Vampires — and as they did not know how to use oxygen — they rarely flew above 15,000 feet. So the phenomenon was new to the people in 1957; and, it was reported, they were greatly impressed.

At a height of 1000 feet Trent flew over a huge Buddhist monastry in which spacious grounds stood a tightly-packed crowd of saffron-robed monks. They reminded Trent of a big, swaying patch of marigolds. He pulled back speed and flew over with air brakes out, dropping height so that the watchers could get a closer view of the monster aircraft. Then he pulled in the brakes and, turning the Valiant, he made a low, high-speed run over the monastry before hauling back on the stick to put it into a near-vertical climb. The noise, he reckoned, would be tremendous and would scare the daylights out of any devils game enough to haunt a tightly-packed monastry.

He climbed, made rendezvous with John Wynn's aircraft, and the two headed eastwards towards Vietnam and the Gulf of Tonking. As required of them, they photographed every radar scan of every town and port they flew over before reaching the coast and flying back to Singapore.

The next day's flight was not so comfortable. They had been required to liaise with the Royal Australian Air Force in fighter affiliation exercises above Butterworth, at the north of the Malayan (now Malaysian) Peninsula. Trent was flying at 37,000 feet when the aircraft's heating system failed. With all crew members numb with cold and in imminent danger of frost bite, he turned for base and, on landing, he and his shivering companions fell on to the metal hard-standing at dispersal point and hugged the sun-hot steel.

20
HOMELAND SOJOURN

LEN TRENT RETURNED TO MARHAM on 21 November 1957, flying from Changi by way of Karachi, Bahrain and El Adam. Towards the end of March 1958, much to his delight, he was instructed to take a Valiant to Ohakea to take part in the twenty-first anniversary celebrations of the RNZAF.

Wing Commander Trent, C.O. of 214 (Valiant) Squadron, just before he left Marham to fly to New Zealand in March 1958.

He and his crew flew to Changi along the customary route. From Singapore they went by way of Darwin and Edinburgh Field before leaving Australian soil for New Zealand. The weather forecast they received before the Tasman crossing was a promise of summer sun drenching a smiling land, so Trent was filling his English companions' ears with exaggerated descriptions of his climatically perfect homeland. But, after calling Ohakea when approaching from about 150 miles out, he got a dismal weather report. It was raining heavily. There was eight-eighths cloud at 900 feet and four-eighths at 400 feet. The Englishmen chuckled with glee. It was as if *they* were coming home. A situation-normal SNAFU.

Ohakea had no GCA, no ILS, nothing. Visibility was a solid battleship-grey and the rain was hosing down — enough to put the hardiest pilot on the edge of his seat.

But the Valiant, fortunately, now had an NBS radar which, although it could pick up the position and environs of Ohakea from about 180 miles distance, could contribute no aids for accurately lining up the runway in azimuth and elevation to give a good glide path.

Trent let the aircraft down below 900 feet and broke from solid to four-eighths cloud conditions. At 800 feet he turned onto the downwind leg and, simply by timing himself, he turned cross-wind at five miles, after completing landing checks and dropping the undercarriage. He turned on to his final approach at the correct height but by now he couldn't see the runway for the driving rain. His windscreen wipers were slashing away at the wetness. Then he broke into a patch of clear air, lowered full flap and landed, more like a flying boat, in a shower of spray.

And, like a true New Zealander, he was the only one of the crew to have a raincoat handy when they had to leave the aircraft for the waiting van that would take them to station headquarters.

With the RNZAF's twenty-first birthday air display at Ohakea scheduled for 29 March, Trent and his crew got airborne on Thursday 27 March for some local flying and familiarization with the airfield's environs. Later that day they set off on a reasonably low-level aerial tour of some of the southern cities and towns — with, most naturally, particular emphasis on Nelson and its surrounding districts.

They flew over Wellington, crossed Cook Strait to Picton and Blenheim and, while circling his home town Trent called the

Wing Commander Trent flies his Valiant V-Bomber over Nelson in March 1958.

The Vickers-Armstrong Valiant aircraft that Wing Commander Trent
flew to Ohakea in March 1958.

Nelson Airport control tower. He was surprised and delighted to
get an acknowledgement from Ron King who, before he had
taken an appointment as an airfield controller, had been a fellow
prisoner of war with Len Trent in Stalag Luft III.

The Valiant made a low pass over Nelson College but, as the
academy was close to the general hospital, Trent cut power and
relied on glide to take the aircraft beyond the range of noise
disturbance. Then, aware of his childhood vow to storm up the
Takaka Valley in a mighty aeroplane, he brought the Valiant in
from seaward at about 500 feet and headed for the V-shaped cleft
that speared into the hills from Golden Bay.

As a boy he had seen it as a vast fold in the land. But now he was
surprised and a little concerned to find how the geography of
Takaka had closed in on him. The big, fast Valiant seemed to have
no sooner entered the valley than it had arrived at its head. And its
head was very narrow indeed. Hemmed by high country, Trent
found the turning of such a wide-winged, wide-arcing machine
extremely difficult — in fact, impossible. He had to abort his
steep turn, take off bank, give the four jets full throttle and climb
steeply over the mountain tops.

But he had made good a boyhood ambition; and had done it in a
style far grander than he had ever envisaged.

With reduced power and lowered undercarriage he retraced his track down the valley and headed to fly over the farm of his cousin and wartime companion, Ian Richmond. He gave a wing-waggle and a blast of jet power and Richmond, on his front lawn, waved vigorously in answer.

Then, after a flight down the West Coast, he brought the Valiant back to Ohakea.

At the air display he excited the assembled crowd with the Valiant's capabilities, climbing with full power to come out of the near-vertical attitude in a semi-stall turn; and after a brief performance of low-level high-speed runs over the field, he had given the customers their fill.

His next flight was to take the aircraft back to Australia, where he landed at Edinburgh Field prior to setting course, the following day, for Darwin.

The Valiant's northward track took it right over Alice Springs, a radio reporting point. So, with Flight Lieutenant Fisher at the flying controls, Len Trent looked down from 45,000 feet and wondered about the way of life in a town like Alice — a community that had fascinated him ever since he had read Nevil Shute's colourful novel.

'RAF-air 1-2-3-4 reporting,' he called through his microphone. 'Do you read? My course is 355 degrees true, height 45,000 feet, groundspeed 350 knots indicated.'

After an age — all of 10 seconds, but downright sluggardly by Air Force standards — a tired Okka voice drifted up from the khaki outback: 'R-o-j-e-r, RAF-air 1-2-3-4 ...' and the details of flight were acknowledged.

With curiosity, Trent asked: 'What is it like down there? I can't see a sign of a building from this height.'

Another long pause. Trent could picture the fellow sprawled back in his chair with his jodhpur-booted feet on the desk, as back came the answer: 'W-e-l-l, it's not so bad, *r-e-a-l-l-y*. But the b-l-a-r-d-y flies drive ya' flamin' *crazy!*'

At Darwin they were given overnight shelter in the Royal Australian Air Force station officers' mess, where Mac McColl sipping tea discovered to his considerable alarm, a monstrous praying mantis perched on his shoulder. The crew also made the acquaintance of a huge frog 'Fred the Bog Frog'. He lived in one of a line of WCs which was never used but kept as Fred's home, to the consternation of unsuspecting visitors.

After leaving Darwin for Changi, they had to climb the Valiant to incredible heights to clear the summits of the fearsome tropical thunderheads that stood in their track. On landing, Trent left the aircraft in the care of another RAF captain who would be flying the Valiant in exercises with the RAAF. He flew back to England from Singapore in a RAF Comet.

In April 1958 he was directed to hand over the command of 214 Squadron to a very young and serious-minded officer, Wing Commander Mike Beetham who was to rise to great heights in the service after a tour as Wing Commander Air at 3 Group Headquarters.

Leaving 214 Squadron with a tinge of sadness and, probably, a critical backward glance towards his successor, Trent moved on to his new post as Wing Commander Training at 3 Group Headquarters, Mildenhall.

He was the senior officer of that rank and he was under the command of Air Vice-Marshal 'Bing' Cross. His immediate boss was Air Commodore Bill Coles (of Little Rissington days) who was very patient and helpful in guiding Trent in his first tottering steps as a staff officer.

Air Vice-Marshal Cross was an imposing gentleman, stern in manner as befitted the post and, although not a frightening character, he let it be known in the higher decibels of speech that he would not suffer fools gladly.

Trent recalls an early piece of advice handed to him by Bill Coles. 'Look, Len,' he said, 'If the AOC starts to shout at you, just shout back at him, if you are sure of your ground, but perhaps not so loudly.'

Wing Commander Trent was still required to keep up his flying hours and made it a point to get behind the controls at least once a week. A part of his headquarters duties was to ensure that each squadron within 3 Group was adhering to standard operating procedures; so it was his habit to telephone the commander of any one of the squadrons and request the use of an aircraft and crew for his regular flight and unit check-up.

He usually flew an Anson from 3 Group's communications flight when he visited the various airfields. And, as the RAF shared Mildenhall with a large American Air Force unit, there was usually a lot of mixed air traffic around the station.

Returning to base one misty evening, Trent was given landing permission by the tower controller and was approaching the runway from the direction of Wyton. He was at the point of levelling the Anson for a touch-down when, dead ahead and sweeping menacingly towards him out of the gloom was a great B-52 bomber, wheels and flaps down, flaring out for its landing.

Trent stamped on his rudder pedal and swerved the Anson on to the grass at the side of the runway. He watched the B-52 boom past with bewilderment and anger. Another very near miss, another life and another American air traffic controller out of a job.

The incident — a near miss, and therefore a serious matter for investigation — resulted in a court of inquiry. In still-air conditions the airfield controller had, inexplicably, given Trent permission to land in one direction while allowing the B-52, practising beam-approach landings, to come in from the other end of the runway.

The paperwork of the new headquarters job was enormous and Trent's correspondence trays on his desk were seemingly always a foot deep. But life was not all drudgery at Group Headquarters. Both Air Vice-Marshal Cross and Air Commodore Bill Coles were keen and capable golfers and Trent, ever the enthusiast and consistently playing a low single-figure handicap, was frequently invited to match his skills against one or other of the two senior officers — both on a seven mark.

On one golfing occasion Cross invited Trent to make a fourth in a game with Douglas Bader, the notable legless pilot who had, co-incidentally, also been a prisoner of war in Stalag Luft III — but had been removed to Colditz before Trent's arrival at the Sagan prison camp.

Trent, keen to see how Bader approached his low-handicap game on his artificial legs, was soon impressed. 'I will never forget him standing up there on the first tee,' he recalls. 'And, with a good shoulder turn and reasonable semblance of a pivot he swung his arms and hit the ball a tremendous wallop to send it, straight as a die, 250 yards down the fairway.'

The course was Worlington, probably the most famous nine hole course in England. A particularly hard par-five hole had a deep bunker gashing the complete width of the fairway, so placed to challenge the big hitters who would try to carry it with their second shot. From a well-struck tee shot a player would have to get about 190 yards of carry with his fairway wood to clear the trap and go for his birdie.

Bader hit a very good drive; and as he drew a wood from his bag he was, Trent saw, going for 'a big one' to clear the bunker.

On a nearby fairway the club professional was coaching a woman player, while her husband tagged along. They recognized Bader and came closer to watch the shot.

Bader lined up and belted with his four-wood. The ball flew high and far to land safely over the trap. 'Good shot, Douglas,' Trent said.

'You know, Len,' Bader said as he nodded towards the spectators, 'I saw them coming over for a look and I knew the pressure was on. I could just imagine the pro saying: "Let's walk across and see this tin-legged bastard have a go to carry the bunker".'

There is no doubt the two found a close rapport. 'I've heard a lot of unkind things said about Bader,' says Len Trent. 'He was supposed, by some, to be domineering, boastful and self opinionated. But I found him a warm, big-hearted fellow, ever ready to extend sympathy and a helping hand to others — particularly those with disabilities similar to his own.

'When I was living in Perth — some time after my first meeting with Douglas — I again ran into him when he was on one of his aerial trips for Shell. He was spending most of his time in that city visiting hospitals and giving encouragement to other people who had lost their legs.'

Towards the end of 1958 Bing Cross left 3 Group Headquarters to become Commander-in-Chief of Bomber Command and his place was taken by Air Vice-Marshal Micky Dwyer. The following year it was Trent's turn to receive a promotion. He was pleasantly surprised to learn that he had attained group captain rank, albeit he was still serving in a wing commander appointment at group headquarters.

He continued in his staff-officer role for a further 6 months, during which time he conducted a running badinage-and-paper war with Group Captain Johnnie Johnson — a notable fighter pilot of the war years. Johnson was the station commander of RAF Cottesmore and he, along with all his contemporaries within the group — or within the RAF, for that matter — was required to furnish regular returns of all flying, bombing and navigation exercises accomplished by the station.

But Johnnie Johnson seemed to spend a lot of time shooting pheasants as the guest of the Marquis of Exeter and the AOC was constantly nagging Trent for sightings of the non-existent documents. But Johnson, in time, left Cottesmore and went off to the Imperial Defence College for a year's study course; and Trent found some relief in Johnnie's departure.

In April 1960 Group Captain Trent was appointed station commander of RAF Wittering, a mile or two south-east of Stamford. He succeeded Group Captain Alan Boxer, a fellow New Zealander who also, coincidentally, had been at Nelson College with Len Trent. Boxer later rose to heady heights in the RAF and when Trent saw him a few years later he was RAF equerry to Prince Philip at Buckingham Palace.

When, in the mid-1970s, Len Trent was invited to a formal occasion at the palace he was permitted to bring two guests — in this case his wife and his elder daughter, Christine. As the Queen passed around the Throne Room Trent was presented, and in turn

General Curtis E. le May, USAF and Air Commodore C. Kay, Chief of Air Staff, RNZAF, at Ohakea, 1958.

presented his wife and daughter. And when the Prince approached — with Alan Boxer at the rear, smiling a recognition to Trent — formalities began again. After his presentation and a word or two with the Prince, Trent began: 'Sir, may I present my wife ...' He turned, but to his confusion he found his daughter had changed places with her mother. 'Er -- my *daughter*, Mrs Stone ...'

The Prince and his equerry were grinning broadly at Trent's embarrassment. 'Well, make up your mind,' came the royal quip.

Meanwhile, with Trent's transfer to Wittering, Johnnie Johnson's little documentary shortcomings had been forgotten. But one day, when a force of Bomber Command station bosses and a group of Imperial Defence College graduates were gathered at Marham, Trent heard an unmistakable voice behind him in the bar: 'Guess who's going to be your new SASO!' He turned to get the full dazzle of Johnnie's toothy grin right in his eyes.

Johnson, on the point of emerging from his IDC course, had already received his next appointment. He was bound for 3 Group to take over the controls of Bill Coles' desk as an air commodore.

Now it would be Group Captain Trent's turn to ensure *his* station returns were submitted promptly to group headquarters. Johnnie Johnson, he was sure, would see to *that*.

While Trent was at Wittering, the nearby centre of Stamford was celebrating its quincentenary and to mark the auspicious occasion, the Mayor — the Marquis of Exeter Lord Burghley — and his councillors decided to honour the nearby RAF Wittering Station by giving it the freedom of the city. Trent's troops trained diligently and when the big day came they marched through the streets with bayonets fixed and banners unfurled, watched not only by the good burghers but by much of the top brass of Bomber Command and station commanders from miles around.

Group Captain Trent, need it be said, had to deliver a speech and his carefully prepared words were later the subject of high praise from the Marquis of Exeter — himself a nationally renowned public speaker.

'I must confess that I was very nervous,' Trent explained.

'Well, it certainly didn't show,' said the marquis. 'I was watching your hands, which are always give-away signs of nerves, and they didn't tremble or fidget at all.'

That, suggested Trent, was probably the result of a flying instructor's self discipline. If an airborne tutor shows nervousness

Group Captain Trent receiving the Freedom of Stamford on behalf of RAF Wittering from the Marquis of Exeter, Mayor of Stamford. The occasion, in 1960, was the 500th anniversary of Stamford's charter as a city.

The Marquis of Exeter, Mayor of Stamford, reviewing the guard of honour when RAF Wittering was granted the freedom of the city in 1960.

through hand flutterings it usually transmits to the pupil.

On 11 September 1960 Trent flew a Valiant to Goose Bay, Canada,where he had it refuelled before continuing to Offat Air Base in the United States — the purpose being a goodwill mission to observe the Strategic Air Command's annual bombing competitions. After a few days in America he and his crew returned by way of Bermuda, landing at Kinley Airfield on 16 September.

It was the first time the inhabitants of the island had seen a Valiant aircraft and the crew were feted royally. Trent was buttonholed by the Governor, Sir Julian Gascoigne, and asked to read the second lesson at the Sunday morning service in the cathedral. In the afternoon the two played a round at the Mid-ocean Golf Club.

Sir Julian, Trent soon discovered, was a dedicated and accomplished player. As they were walking up the second fairway, the governor pointing to a solitary golfer practising chipping nearby, asked Trent if he had ever met the notable Tommy Armour, then club professional at Mid-ocean.

'No? Well, let me introduce you,' Sir Julian said.

They walked across to where the dour 'Silver Scot' was engrossed with his seven-iron magic. Armour raised his eyes and nodded frostily. The Governor of Bermuda and his overseas guest might have been but a couple of audacious caddies wasting the time of a busy golf god.

After a brief exchange of words and grunts, Armour dismissed the two intruders from his presence and returned to addressing his practice balls.

While he was the station commander at Wittering, Trent did just as much flying as any standard pilot. His own stand-by crew included a co-pilot, navigator, radar operator and an aero-electronics officer — all members of the station's Operations Centre staff.

Wittering, besides being a nuclear bombing station, also housed a busy nuclear training school under the command of a Wing Commander Brown. During Trent's tenure, another huge complex was added to receive the 'Blue Steel' — Britain's guided missile which had just then been developed to replace the already defunct American-designed 'Skybolt' weapon. Although the new bomb had been tested at the Woomera range, it never came into

The Marquis of Exeter, Lord Burghley — Mayor of Stamford — receiving a plaque from Sir John Baldwin, the first station commander of RAF Wittering. Group Captain Trent, the incumbent station commander on that 1961 occasion, observes the ceremony.

operational use.

On 3 July 1961, just after Trent returned to his office after a leisurely lunch, his telephone rang and the AOC of 3 Group, speaking with some urgency, said: 'Len, I want you to collect your crew straight away, get airborne and fly to Cyprus. You will report to the C-in-C as soon as you land.'

'Today, Sir?'

'I mean within the hour. If there is an aircraft about to take off, stop it. Take the aircraft most readily available and get airborne!'

Trent called his Wing Commander Operations, Dick Broadbent, who did actually check a Valiant that was just taxying for take-off. The machine was returned to the tarmac, rechecked and topped up with fuel and, within the hour (as required by the AOC), it was on its way to Cyprus.

Trent and his men arrived on the island at about midnight and were immediately bustled by road transport to Episkopi to meet Air Marshal McDonald, Commander-in-Chief, British Forces. The fizz, Trent learned, was a disturbance that was later to be known as the Kuwait Emergency.

At Middle East Air Headquarters, Episkopi, he was required to work out aircraft routes and endurances with all-up bomb and fuel loads — should the situation call for a force of Valiants for either police or strike duties.

Trent and his crew worked all through the dark and daylight hours of that day. For the following two days they were on stand-by, answering technical questions and awaiting news of action. But nothing of any moment happened and there were permitted to relax.

They did, in fact, relax in the Cyprus sun for close on 3 weeks. Trent re-discovered the pleasures of small-boat sailing and crewed under Group Captain Downey, an airman whose boatsmanship was eclipsed by his misadventures as a submariner. After shedding the skin from his back — the result of Mediterranean sunburn — Trent piloted a 138 Squadron Valiant back to Wittering on 21 July.

He continued his routine flying duties from that station. On 16 April 1962 he flew his final instrument rating test with a Flight Lieutenant Brown, who was the examiner, and his Master Green ticket was renewed. On 8 May he made his last flight in a Valiant and clocked up a total of 920 jet hours.

He had been telephoned, in April, by a senior officer in Air Ministry and asked if he would like to move and reside in the United States as the Bomber Command representative at the British Embassy in Washington. The prospect excited him and, with about an hour to make his decision, he hurried to talk the matter over with Ursula. It did not take them long.

Just as Len Trent was about to leave RAF Wittering for Washington, his appointment as ADC to Her Majesty Queen Elizabeth was announced. He held this appointment for the three years he was in the United States of America and relinquished it on retirement. As the Queen did not visit Washington during his stay, he had no duties to perform, but as Trent says:

The golden Aiguilettes lent some colour to my uniform once a year when the Ambassador gave a garden party with the traditional strawberries and cream on the occasion of the Queen's Birthday.

They sailed for the United States in the *Queen Mary*, arriving in New York in June 1962. They entrained for Washington, where they were met by the retiring RAF representative, Group Captain Freddie Ball.

Some time later the two officers were to meet again at a RAF Staff College ball when Trent was visiting Britain and staying with his son-in-law, Patrick Stone — then a captain in the British Army. Patrick was attending the RAF Staff College at Bracknell — and Air Commodore Mike Beetham was the commandant of the academy. So it was a happy reunion. Ball, Beetham, Stone and Trent had much to talk about. Len Trent recalls:

Soon after that meeting at the ball, Mike Beetham was short-toured as Commandant of the college. He received a very rapid promotion to air vice-marshal rank and sent to take up a NATO appointment. Again he was short-toured and promoted Commander-in-Chief, British Air Forces, Germany. He was to become knighted at this stage of his career.

On a later visit to England to attend the Queen's review of the RAF at Finningly, I had an invitation to travel on the special train from Liverpool Street Station. Hearing a familiar voice behind me on the platform, I looked around and there was Air Marshal Sir Michael Beetham, all dressed up and adorned with gold braid, sword and trimmings.

'Gee Mike,' I said, 'you look absolutely tremendous.' And thinking to be funny — and exercising the impertinence of a retired officer — I added: 'When are you going to become Chief of Air Staff?'

Grinning, he replied: 'Well, actually, on Monday.'

Mike Beetham had one of the most rapid rises in Air Force history and he went on to achieve the honour of becoming the longest-serving Chief of Air Staff in the annals of the service.

Recently, he retired from the post, having guided the RAF through the Falklands Crisis. Promoted ultimately to the rank of Marshal of the Royal Air Force, he is now trying to wind down and play some golf at Norfolk.

21

FINAL TOUR

ON THEIR ARRIVAL in the United States the Trents, on the recommendations of Group Captain Freddy Ball, Len Trent's RAF predecessor, elected to live away from the bustle and officialdom of Washington and so settled for the comparative quietude of a home across the Potomac River at Lake Barcroft, near Falls Church, Virginia.

The RAF's new appointee to the military and political hub of the United States soon found he was the wearer of several service caps. As the Senior Staff Officer he had, reporting to him on various Anglo-American air matters, a small staff which included two or three wing commanders.

Bound for Washington, 1962: Group Captain and Mrs Trent, with daughters Judith (left) and Christine aboard RMS *Queen Mary*.

As the Resident RAF Bomber Command Representative he had direct lines of communication to Strategic Air Command. One of the British exchange officers, working alongside the Americans in SAC Headquarters, was Group Captain Douglas Lowe who, when Trent saw him a year or two later at the Queen's Review of the RAF at Finningly, had risen to the rank of Air Chief Marshal.

Group Captain Trent also served in Washington as the Senior RAF Intelligence Officer. It was a position that did not present many serious problems or exact too onerous a tour of duty — except, perhaps, a requirement that he should find his way through the military labyrinth that his American hosts call the Pentagon. The successful navigation of that giant maze, he recalls, should qualify a pilot for a General Reconnaissance certificate in his log book.

About half way through Trent's tour of duty in Washington the Milne Committee made a close inspection of British Embassy establishments and that economy drive resulted in the closing of some posts. To fill one of the redundancies Trent, as a group captain, became the Assistant Air Attache for the remaining 18 months of his appointment. That meant added responsibilities and a change from an airfield circuit to the cocktail circuit of the world-wide embassies. He and Ursula were required to attend a cocktail party every night of the working week. Len recalls that at first he drank a couple of quick gins to relax in the company of his Russian counterpart, but after a year he drank out of boredom. When he found himself reaching for a couple of quick gins he began to suspect he had one foot in the alcoholics' camp.

His lasting impressions of that country are of the long and, mostly, pleasant journeys to visit, at least once a year, the many RAF office-holders placed throughout the land in various appointments within Bomber, Fighter and Transport Commands. Some of the travel was made by air; and a lot of mileage was covered by car — both on official missions and on vacational breaks.

Len Trent bought himself a Chevrolet convertible, which proved perhaps the best car he had ever owned, and he was quick to appreciate the generally efficient standards of driving and the road courtesies shown by American motorists.

Perhaps he had expected to find them thrusting and aggressive — caricature figures of the much-maligned 'domineering American'. But, in fact, they proved the opposite — generous in

The Queen chatting with Group Captain L.H. Trent, VC DFC RAF
(Retd) at Windsor Castle, 1978. Centre is the celebrated Odette, the
courageous heroine of the French Resistance movement.

yielding road space, highly disciplined and, in the main, calm in
fast and tight traffic situations.

In truth, with the density of traffic in city streets and fast-lane
highways, American motorists soon found they had to conform to
posted speed limits and sensible standards of driving to survive.

Len Trent was caught speeding once in the deserts of Arizona
by a huge bronzed traffic officer on a motorcycle. Where he came
from Trent wonders to this day, but because of his accent, instead
of a ticket, Len received such a lecture on his hazarding the life of
his family, that after three minutes he was cringing on the floor of
his car and could only murmur 'yes officer'. Timothy and Judy,
who occupied the back seat, were more impressed with the size of
the pistol on the officer's belt.

With about 6 months of his long and often exciting RAF career to be served — and with one of his nine lives still remaining — Captain Len Trent had notification from the Careers Department of Air Ministry that his service was to be terminated at the end of his appointment in the United States.

He and Ursula discussed the future and decided that they would move on Len's retirement, to Perth, Western Australia.

So, ending 3 years of very pleasant service in a most hospitable country on a high note, they said farewell to their many American friends and again boarded the *Queen Mary*. They sailed from New York in first-class accommodation with all amenities; homing, like far-wandering British birds to the land that had, inexorably, drawn the fledgling Trent in 1938. But now his flying days, in the service that had been his life, were over.

Group Captain Leonard Henry Trent, VC, DFC, RAF (Retd) now lives in retirement at Matheson's Bay, North Auckland — a delightful corner of New Zealand where, from his home on a headland, he can gaze out on the horizon of the wide South Pacific Ocean.

He still plays golf — seemingly effortlessly on a five handicap — and a week or two before his sixty-eighth birthday he got an 'eagle' on the five-par seventh hole at Warkworth Golf Club, a bit of two-under-par play that any vigorous 20 year old would be happy to emulate.

His life (or should we say 'lives' — for he surely had many) in his chosen career gave a fulfillment to boyhood dreams and aspirations. Man is not lost if he sees his star and sets a course with determination.

APPENDICES

THE VICTORIA CROSS

Seaman **William Odgers**, HMS *Niger*, Waireka; 28 March 1860
Colour/Sgt **John Lucas**, 40th Regt, Huirangi Pa; 18 March 1861
Ensign **Edward McKenna**, 65th Regt, Camerontown; 7 September 1863
Lance/Cpl **John Ryan**, 65th Regt, Camerontown; 7 September 1863
Ensign **John Thornton Down**, 57th Regt, Poutoko; 2 October 1863
Drummer **Dudley Stagpoole**, 57th Regt, Kaipakopako; 2 October 1863
Asst/Surg **William Temple**, RA, Rangiriri; 20 November 1863
Lt Arthur **Frederic Pickard**, RA, Rangiriri; 20 November 1863
Major **Charles Heaphy**, Auck. Militia, Mangapiko; 11 February 1864
Lt/Col **John Carstairs McNeill**, 107th Bengal Inf; 30 March 1864
Asst/Surg **William George Nicholas Manley**, RA, Gate Pa; 29 April 1864
Samuel Mitchell, HMS *Harrier*, Gate Pa; 29 April 1864
Capt Frederic **Augustus Smith**, 43rd Regt, Te Ranga; 21 June 1864
Sgt **John Murray**, 68th Regt, Te Ranga; 21 June 1864
Capt **Hugh Shaw**, 18th Regt, Nukumaru; 24 January 1865
Capt **Henry Cecil Dudgeon D'Arcy**, SAF, Zululand; 3 July 1879
Farrier Maj **William James Hardham**, 4th NZ Cont., Naauwport; 28 January 1901
2nd/Lt **William Barnard Rhodes-Moorhouse**, RFC, France; 26 April 1915
Cpl **Cyril Royston Bassett**, Div Sig Co, Gallipoli; 7 August 1915
Lt/Col **Bernard Cyril Freyberg**, Royal W. Surrey Regt, France; 14 July 1916
Capt **Alfred John Shout**, AIF, Gallipoli; 9 August 1915
Pte **Thomas Cooke**, AIF, Pozieres; 9 September 1916
Sgt **Donald Forrester Brown**, Otago Regt, France; 15 September 1916
Lt/Cmdr **William Edward Sanders**, RNR; May 1917
L/Cpl **Samuel Frickleton**, NZ Rifle Bgde; 2 August 1917
Cpl **Leslie Wilton Andrew**, Wgt Regt, France; 6 September 1917
Pte **Henry James Nicholas**, Cant Regt, France; 11 January 1918
Lt **Percy Valentine Storkey**, 19th Bat AIF, France; 7 April 1918
Sgt **Richard Charles Travis**, Otago Regt, France; 24 July 1918
Sgt **Samuel Forsyth**, NZE, France; 24 Aug 1918
Sgt **Reginald Stanley Judson**, Auck Regt, France; 26 August 1918
Sgt **John Gilroy Grant**, Wgt Regt, France; 1 September 1918
Temp/Cpl **Lawrence Cathage Weathers**, AIF; 2 September 1918
Sgt **Harry John Laurent**, NZ Rifle Bgde, France; 12 September 1918
Pte **James Crichton**, Auck Regt, France; 30 September 1918
Sgt **John Daniel Hinton**, 20th Btn, NZEF, Greece; 28 April 1941
2nd/Lt **Charles Hazlitt Upham**, 2 NZEF, Crete; 13-25 May 1941
Sgt **Alfred Clive Hulme**, Wgt Btn, Crete; 20-28 May 1941
Sgt/Pilot **James Allen Ward**, RNZAF, Germany; 7 July 1941
Capt **Charles H. Upham**, VC, 2 NZEF, Ruweisat Ridge; Bar to VC; 14 July 1942
Sgt **Keith Elliott**, 22nd Btn, Ruweisat Ridge; 15 July 1942

S/Ldr **Leonard Henry Trent**, RNZAF, Amsterdam; 3 May 1943
2nd/Lt **Moananui-a-Kiwa Ngarimu**, 28th (Maori) Btn, Jebel Tebaga; 26 March 1943
F/O **Lloyd A. Trigg**, RNZAF, Nth Atlantic; August 1943

IN MEMORIAM

The fifty Allied officers murdered by the German Gestapo on recapture after the prison break from Stalag Luft III on 24 March 1944:

F/Lt **Henry Birkland**, RCAF
F/Lt **Edward Brettell**, DFC, RAF
F/Lt **Leslie Bull**, DFC, RAF
S/Ldr **Roger Bushell**, RAF
F/Lt **Michael Casey**, RAF
S/Ldr **James Catanach**, DFC, RAAF
F/O **Arnold Christenson**, RNZAF
F/O **Dennis Cochran**, RAF
S/Ldr **Ian Cross**, DFC, RAF
F/O **Haldo Espelid**, RAF (Norway)
F/Lt **Brian Evans**, RAF
F/O **Nils Fugelsang**, RAF (Norway)
Lt **Johannes Gouws**, SAAF
F/Lt **Alastair Gunn**, RAF
F/Lt **William Grisman**, RAF
F/Lt **Charles Hall**, RAF
F/Lt **Albert Hake**, RAAF
F/Lt **Anthony Hayter**, RAF
F/Lt **Edgar Humphries**, RAF
F/Lt **Gordon Kidder**, RCAF
F/O **Reginald Kierath**, RAAF
F/Lt **Anthony Kiewnarski**, RAF (Poland)
S/Ldr **Tom Kirby-Green**, RAF
F/O **W. Kolanowski**, RAF (Poland)
F/O **S.Z. Krol**, RAF (Poland)
F/Lt **Patrick Langford**, RCAF
F/Lt **Tom Leigh**, RAF
F/Lt **J.L. Long**, RAF
Lt **Neville McGarr**, SAAF
F/Lt **George McGill**, RCAF
F/Lt **Romas Marcinkus**, RAF (Lithuania)
F/Lt **Harold Mitford**, RAF
F/O **Jerzy Mondschein**, RAF (Poland)
F/O **K. Pawluk**, RAF (Poland)

F/Lt **Henri Picard**, CG, RAF (Belgium)
F/O **P.P.J. Pohe**, RNZAF
Lt **Bernard Scheidhower** (France)
F/O **S. Skanziklas**, RAF (Greece)
F/Lt **Cyril Swain**, RAF
Lt **Rupert Stevens**, SAAF
F/O **Robert Stewart**, RAF
F/O **Denys Street**, RAF
F/Lt **John Stower**, RAF
F/O **P. Tobolski**, RAF (Poland)
F/Lt **Ernest Valenta**, RAF (Czechoslovakia)
F/Lt **G.W. Walenn**, RAF
F/Lt **James Wernham**, RCAF
F/Lt **George Wiley**, RCAF
S/Ldr **J.E.A. Williams**, RAAF
F/Lt **J.F. Williams**, RAF

INDEX